Parents with Eating Disorc

This groundbreaking volume presents a new conceptual approach to treating adults with eating disorders and their children. By utilizing Parent-Based Prevention, a state-of-the-art intervention program from Stanford University for families who risk raising children in the context of parental eating disorders, *Parents with Eating Disorders* offers a practical, evidence-based manual to working with affected families with the goal of preventing disordered eating from being passed to future generations. Additional resources include intervention planning and self-assessment forms intended for clinicians to use as they implement the program.

Shiri Sadeh-Sharvit, PhD is a clinical psychologist and Visiting Instructor in psychiatry and behavioral sciences at the Eating Disorders Research Program in the Department of Child and Adolescent Psychiatry at Stanford University School of Medicine. Her clinical and research interests include eating disorders throughout the life cycle, family-based interventions, incorporating technology in mental healthcare, and clinical training.

James Lock, MD, PhD is Professor of Child Psychiatry and Pediatrics, and Associate Chair in the Department of Psychiatry and Behavioral Sciences, at Stanford University School of Medicine, where he also serves as Director of the Eating Disorder Program for Children and Adolescents at Lucile Packard Children's Hospital and Clinics. His work is foundational in family-based interventions for eating disorders in youth.

Parents with Eating Disorders

An Intervention Guide

Shiri Sadeh-Sharvit and James Lock

Routledge
Taylor & Francis Group

NEW YORK AND LONDON

First published 2019
by Routledge
52 Vanderbilt Avenue, New York, NY 10017

and by Routledge
2 Park Square, Milton Park, Abingdon, Oxon, OX14 4RN

Routledge is an imprint of the Taylor & Francis Group, an informa business

© 2019 Taylor & Francis

Library of Congress Cataloging-in-Publication Data
Names: Sadeh-Sharvit, Shiri, author. | Lock, James, author.
Title: Parents with eating disorders : an intervention guide / Shiri
    Sadeh-Sharvit and James Lock.
Description: New York, NY : Routledge, 2019. | Includes
    bibliographical references and index.
Identifiers: LCCN 2018037155 (print) | LCCN 2018037486 (ebook)
    | ISBN 9781315229492 (E-book) | ISBN 9781138293489 (hbk)
    | ISBN 9781138293496 (pbk.) | ISBN 9781315229492 (ebk)
Subjects: | MESH: Feeding and Eating Disorders—therapy | Family
    Therapy—methods | Feeding Behavior | Parent-Child Relations
Classification: LCC RC552.E18 (ebook) | LCC RC552.E18 (print) |
    NLM WM 175 | DDC 616.85/26—dc23
LC record available at https://lccn.loc.gov/2018037155

ISBN: 978-1-138-29348-9 (hbk)
ISBN: 978-1-138-29349-6 (pbk)
ISBN: 978-1-315-22949-2 (ebk)

Typeset in Garamond
by Swales & Willis Ltd, Exeter, Devon, UK

Printed and bound by CPI Group (UK) Ltd, Croydon, CR0 4YY

To Gilad, Roni, Adi, & Shakked, whose unwavering love, support, and encouragement have been fundamental to accomplishing all my endeavors. *SSS*

For all the families who've helped me be a better clinician. *JL*

Contents

Acknowledgments

This book is the product of our many years of work with parents with eating disorders through research, clinical practice, and advocacy. This work originated in Dr. Sadeh-Sharvit's dissertation, where she visited the homes of mothers with eating disorder histories, observed their interactions with their children, and interviewed them about their parenting experiences. Parent-Based Prevention was initially developed and studied with Dr. Eynat Zubery and Ms. Esty Mankovski at Hanotrim Eating Disorders Treatment and Research Center at Shalvata Mental Health Center in Israel. We cannot express enough our gratitude for the advice and support we received from the team at Hanotrim. Later, the program was further expanded and studied by Drs. Sadeh-Sharvit and Lock at the Eating Disorders Research Program at Stanford University Department of Psychiatry and Behavioral Sciences. We would have been unable to complete this effort in the absence of the generous research support provided by Stanford University Child Health Research Institute as well as the Hilda and Preston Davis Foundation. Additionally, we were very fortunate to collaborate on this study with the wonderful Drs. Cristin Runfola and Debra Safer, whose contribution in delivering the intervention and providing intellectual feedback was invaluable. We are also very grateful for the superb Clinical Research Coordinators involved in the randomized controlled trial testing the intervention: Ariella Grossman-Giron, Katherine Arnow, Talya Feldman, Molly Vierhile, Hannah Welch, Bianca Davoodian, and Madeline Sacks. Finally, we are deeply indebted to the dozens of parents with eating disorders who have openly shared with us their experiences and allowed us the opportunity to influence their families to healthier life trajectories.

Stanford, California, Spring 2018

1 Introduction

What is the Parent-Based Prevention of Eating Disorders?

Parent-Based Prevention of eating disorders is a manualized preventive intervention program designed to support parents with eating disorder histories so that their children develop healthy eating behaviors. Parent-Based Prevention encourages healthy feeding, eating, and self-regulation patterns in children, effective parental communication, and enhanced parental collaboration in order to promote healthy lifestyles and resilience in their children. The intervention is geared toward improving parental competence and self-efficacy through psychoeducation, coaching about behavioral changes, and differentiation between age-appropriate experiences and the potential adverse effects of parental eating disorders on child outcomes. It is composed of conjoint meetings with both parents, one family meal assessment, and meetings held with the affected parent alone.

Structure of Parent-Based Prevention

Parent-Based Prevention is delivered over the course of sixteen weeks and is composed of three phases:

- Phase One: Setting up joint goals.
- Phase Two: Distinguishing the parental eating disorder from parental functioning.
- Phase Three: Enhancing parental efficacy and family resilience.

The sequence of the meetings in Parent-Based Prevention reflects its nature as a personalized program that integrates the needs of parents with young children, and a focus on the affected parent as well as their partner and children. During Phase One and Phase Three, both parents take part in the meetings, while in most sessions in Phase Two, only the affected parent – that is, the parent with the eating disorder of the history of one – meets with the therapist. In the first two phases (i.e., the first eight meetings), sessions are scheduled on a weekly basis, and they are followed by four sessions in Phase Three that are held fortnightly. Each meeting begins with setting an agenda for the meeting: reviewing any changes at home, insights that the parents have developed, or related topics that they have identified from the time of the last meeting with the therapist. Sessions 3–12 always conclude with the parents deciding on at least one specific behavioral experiment they want to try at home and which will be evaluated in the consecutive session. A "behavioral experiment" is the term to describe specific actions the parents will test at home, that are aimed at reducing problematic behaviors related to feeding their child that the parents feel need to address during the program. These behaviors may be focused on changing behaviors in the parents or the child. Parents are advised to test their attempted change, and to think of it as an experiment rather than an answer. If the attempted change does not result in the desired outcomes, it will be discussed in the following session, and the behavioral experiment will be refined. After the individual sessions with the affected parent, it is expected that the contents of those sessions will be shared with their partners. In the following session, the therapist explores whether they have communicated with their partners, and if so, regarding what topics. An abridged outline appears in Table 6.1 in Chapter 6.

Purpose and Audience of This Manual

Target Patient Population

This Parent-Based Prevention intervention guide describes an empirically supported program for improving feeding practices, child outcomes, and parental empowerment in families in which a parent has been diagnosed with an eating disorder. An "eating disorder" may be anorexia nervosa, bulimia nervosa, binge-eating disorder, or any other eating disorder, Other Specified Feeding or Eating Disorder (OSFED), or Unspecified Feeding or Eating Disorder (UFED), according to the *Diagnostic and Statistical Manual of Mental Disorders* (DSM-5) definition (American Psychiatric Association, 2013). This manual was developed to support the families of any parent who has been diagnosed with an eating disorder at any time in their lives, whether they are recovered or still struggling with symptoms. In regard to the language and terms being used, the people involved in the program are not patients in the usual sense. In this approach the target audience are families where a parent has had a current or past eating disorder, who are experiencing challenges in feeding their young children, and are interested in minimizing the impact of their concerns and habits regarding eating, food, shape, and weight on their children. The children are not best considered to be patients either; rather, their healthy development and wellbeing is at the center of the program. Thus, the aim of the program is to promote resilience and wellbeing rather than being focused on pathology.

Clinician Qualifications

The clinician delivering this preventive intervention should be a trained therapist and is referred to as such. This manual is intended for clinicians who have been trained and gained experience in: (a) psychotherapeutic interventions with patients with eating disorders, and (b) developmental psychology and parental counseling. The therapists that are most suitable to provide the preventive intervention program presented in this manual are those who have worked with patients with eating disorders and who are familiar with how eating disorders behaviors and thoughts impact the affected individual's life. They should also feel confident in their ability to facilitate changes in the family via parental and couple counseling. Therapists intending to utilize this guide should feel comfortable in their ability to deliver Parent-Based Prevention according to the guidelines and instruction given hereafter, and should be willing to broaden their theoretical knowledge by reading additional references when needed. In general, treatment of individuals with eating disorders should be carried out with additional professional supervision and consultation depending on the clinician's experience.

Reference

American Psychiatric Association. (2013). *Diagnostic and statistical manual of mental disorders* (5th ed.). Arlington, VA: American Psychiatric Publishing.

2 Understanding the Risks for the Offspring of Parents with Eating Disorders

Review of the Literature: Parental Eating Disorders

The gender distribution of eating disorders is greatly skewed toward females (Hoek, 2006). Furthermore, although gender roles have changed in the Western world, mothers typically assume greater responsibility for feeding their children in the first months of life, and they tend to spend much more time than their spouses with young children (Blissett, Meyer, & Haycraft, 2006). As a result, research has focused primarily on mothers with eating disorders. However, while there is scant data on fathers, several studies suggest that fathers' eating disorder psychopathology is associated with comparable impacts on their offspring's eating-related cognitions and behaviors (Lydecker & Grilo, 2016). Given the nature of the current literature, this chapter will focus mostly on mothers with eating disorder histories. We will acknowledge throughout this chapter research findings and theoretical conceptualizations that are relevant to parents of all sexes.

Children's development may be compromised by parental mental disorders. The nature and extent of parental symptoms correlate with those of their offspring (Kim-Cohen et al., 2006). Research shows that 5 to 10 percent of women have an eating disorder at some point of their lives (Hoek & van Hoeken, 2003; Hudson, Hiripi, Pope Jr., & Kessler, 2007), and at least 16 percent of these women become mothers (Maxwell et al., 2011). Given an average of 1.5–2 children per family in Europe and the United States, respectively, it is suggested that at least 1.5 million preschool children are raised in the context of a maternal eating disorder (Bloom & Sousa-Poza, 2010; Cherlin, 2010; Howden & Meyer, 2010). The offspring of mothers with eating disorders have greater difficulties in self-regulation of their eating and emotional functioning than the children of mothers who do not have eating disorders (Micali, 2005).

The Feeding Relationship

The offspring of mothers with a history of an eating disorder are at an increased risk for feeding and eating problems, as well as other developmental, behavioral, and emotional difficulties (Agras, Hammer, & McNicholas, 1999; Micali, 2005; Zerwas et al., 2012). In particular, the development of healthy eating habits appears to be significantly compromised in these children. Evidence suggests that certain aspects of the maternal eating disorder play a distinct role in different developmental stages. As early as six months of age, infants of mothers with anorexia nervosa present more feeding problems. By age four, their mothers report greater child emotional eating (de Barse et al., 2015). The infants of mothers with bulimia nervosa are more likely to be overweight for their age and have more difficulties transitioning to solid foods as compared to children of mothers without an eating disorder (Agras et al., 1999). Notably, the more severe the maternal eating disorder symptoms are, the more controlling her feeding practices are (Stein et al., 2001). However, for toddlers and older children, most aspects of feeding and eating do not appear to be related to a specific maternal eating disorder diagnosis. The infants of mothers with lifetime eating disorders exhibit less positive affect with their mothers during feeding interactions (Stein, Woolley, Cooper, & Fairburn, 1994). Elementary-school children whose mothers have lifetime eating disorders are more likely to have "health-conscious" eating habits (Ammaniti, Lucarelli, Cimino, D'Olimpio, & Chatoor, 2012; Easter et al., 2013; Micali, Simonoff, Stahl, & Treasure, 2011), and by age thirteen they report greater disordered eating and emotional eating as compared to children whose mothers do not have histories of eating disorders (Allen, Gibson, McLean, Davis, & Byrne, 2014).

During early childhood, parents are directly responsible for the food that is offered, the amount that is provided, the timing and context of meals, and who is involved in feeding interactions (Danaher, Fredericks, Bryson, Agras, & Ritchie, 2011; Rapoport & Bourdais, 2008). When parents have histories of eating disorders, these feeding-related decisions become more challenging and stressful (Mazzeo, Zucker, Gerke, Mitchell, & Bulik, 2005). For example, parents with eating disorders are more worried about their children's weight (Sadeh-Sharvit et al., 2015). As a result, they tend to report greater controlling behaviors (Blissett & Haycraft, 2011; Hodes, Timimi, & Robinson, 1997; Hoffman et al., 2013). Of note, maternal concerns regarding child nutrition, feeding and weight were reported as more intense in regard to daughters (Sadeh-Sharvit et al., 2015).

Analyses of recorded feeding interactions of mothers with eating disorders and their children generally revealed increased conflicts, stricter control over children's eating, and more maternal negative emotions in comparison to non-symptomatic dyads (Haycraft & Blissett, 2010; Park, Senior, & Stein, 2003). However, these findings were not replicated in all reports (Hoffman et al., 2013). In addition, these mothers use food more frequently than other mothers for non-nutritional purposes, such as soothing or distracting the child (Agras et al., 1999; Evans & Le Grange, 1995). They also reported rarity of family meals (Sadeh-Sharvit et al., 2015). Furthermore, mothers with eating disorders also express concerns about their children's awareness of the maternal eating disorder. Importantly, these parents have many dilemmas about the ways to promote healthy eating patterns in their children and are motivated to receive help themselves. Many of these women said they felt they had no one to consult regarding the aforementioned issues. This manual addresses this gap that has been noted by clients, professionals, and stakeholders alike (Little & Lowkes, 2000).

Children's Cognitive Development

Insufficient feeding, primarily during early childhood, may be related to the delayed developmental functioning found in the young children of mothers with an eating disorder history. As infants, they have lower body weight and head circumference, and lower verbal functioning compared to children of mothers with no eating psychopathology (Koubaa, Hällström, Hagenäs, & Hirschberg, 2013). There is evidence that toddlers of mothers with eating disorder psychopathology show delayed mental and psychomotor development, in comparison to peers with no maternal eating disorder history (Sadeh-Sharvit, Levy-Shiff, & Lock, 2015). Lower global intellectual abilities, motor skills, and social reasoning were found in the toddlers of mothers with anorexia nervosa, which is inherently characterized by restrictive eating (Kothari, Rosinska, Treasure, & Micali, 2014). When evaluated a couple of years later, these children had higher IQ scores and better working memory, but reduced control of attention, as compared to children whose mothers had bulimia nervosa or no eating disorder (Kothari, Solmi, Treasure, & Micali, 2013). It is possible that maternal eating disorder symptoms are more strongly associated with greater feeding and eating problems in younger children (Squires, Lalanne, Murday, Simoglou, & Vaivre-Douret, 2014; Stein, Woolley, & McPherson, 1999). Older children may be less affected because they are exposed to more diverse eating experiences outside of the home milieu. Thus, the maternal eating disorder may play a smaller role in older children's caloric intake, which results in a decrease in the extent of developmental delay over time.

Broader Maternal and Child Wellbeing

Maternal eating disorders are also linked to a wide range of adverse maternal and child behaviors beyond those associated with eating. Mothers with eating disorders rate their children as presenting more volatile temperaments (Zerwas et al., 2012), less positive emotions, and greater behavioral symptoms than children of mothers with no eating psychopathology (Cimino, Cerniglia, Paciello, & Sinesi, 2013; Micali, De Stavola, Ploubidis, Simonoff, & Treasure, 2014). These mothers also report higher parenting-related stress and lower satisfaction of spousal support (Sadeh-Sharvit, Levy-Shiff, Arnow, & Lock, 2016).

Analyses of playtime interactions between mothers with eating disorders and their children found that mothers with current eating disorder symptoms were rated as more controlling of children's behaviors and less happy during mother–child interactions (Cimino et al., 2013; Sadeh-Sharvit et al., 2016; Stein et al., 1994). The children in the maternal eating disorder group had more behavioral problems and were rated as less responsive to their mothers than those in the control group (Sadeh-Sharvit et al., 2016). The two groups of mothers did not differ in their expression of positive emotions (Stein et al., 1994). Mothers who recovered from their eating disorder, however, had the same levels of sensitivity during free play as mothers in a control group (Hoffman et al., 2013).

A growing number of studies suggest that a maternal eating disorder is not only associated with children's feeding and eating problems per se, but also to broader developmental difficulties that may potentiate the development of eating disorders later in life (Sadeh-Sharvit, Levy-Shiff, & Lock, 2015; Stice, Agras, & Hammer, 1999). The next part of this chapter will propose some fundamental mechanisms that underlie these reported difficulties, including mechanisms that should be the targets of preventive interventions in these patients.

Proposed Mechanisms and Targets of Prevention

There are many complications inherent to the onset, maintenance, and aggregation of the developmental adversities of the offspring of parents with eating disorders. These negative factors include increased genetic risk (Scherag, Hebebrand, & Hinney, 2010), obstetric complications (Micali & Treasure, 2009) and parental comorbidities related to eating, anxiety, and depression (Cimino et al., 2013). Conceptually, the difficulties for parents with eating disorders and their children could be explained using three models. The models describe the processes by which the young children of mothers or fathers with eating disorders may be at risk for feeding and eating problems and additional socio-emotional difficulties. They also account for the parenting-related difficulties documented among these parents. These processes may have unique, additive, or synergetic effects on the child, the parent, the couple, and the family.

a. Disrupted Division of Responsibilities in Feeding

The parental prolonged eating disorder often models the feeding interactions with the child. Mothers with eating disorders are often preoccupied with their child's weight, shape, and eating (Agras et al., 1999; Zerwas et al., 2012). These mothers also report a confusing feeding pattern, characterized by abrupt transitions from over- to under-feeding, although providing limited amounts is the more prevalent pattern (Agras et al., 1999). Weight management problems, obesity, and behavioral and emotional problems may be the consequences of insufficient feeding (Micali et al., 2011; Jacka et al., 2013). In addition, mealtime conflicts involving negative comments on children's appetite and eating preferences affect all participants in the feeding situation – the feeding parent, the child, and the other parent, even if they are not present at this meal (Haycraft & Blissett, 2010; Sadeh-Sharvit et al., 2016). When child feeding is based more on the parental experience, and less on the child's recognition of his or her bodily cues, the child may gradually disconnect their eating behaviors from physical states of hunger and satiety; the risk of overweight and obesity increases in these circumstances (Kral & Rauh, 2010). Thus, parents may need assistance in facilitating a healthy feeding relationship that encourages healthy somato-psychological functions, including hunger and satiety.

A seminal part of Parent-Based Prevention is providing psychoeducation regarding the risk factors for eating disorders and the development of adaptive, sustained eating habits. The information provided to parents is partly based on Satter's Division of Responsibility in Feeding Children model (Satter, 1990). According to the Division of Responsibility model, the parents' role is to prepare, provide, and serve food, and maintain a regular schedule of meals and snacks, during which the child serves him- or herself depending on age and skills. The child's responsibilities are to decide *whether* to eat and *how much* to eat. The primary principle is that crossing parent and child boundaries leads to feeding problems. The Division of Responsibility model has been found advantageous for helping parents of children at risk for obesity regularize feeding practices (Agras, Hammer, Huffman, Mascola, Bryson, & Danaher, 2012; Danaher et al., 2011).

This manual uses the terms "feeding" and "eating" alternately in referring to a wide range of eating behaviors. These behaviors exist on a continuum, varying from unilateral parental behaviors that involve nourishing the child, through joint family meals, and ending in autonomous, self-directed consumption of food prepared by the child. When it comes to young children, feeding and eating typically co-occur, and often at the same meal – for instance, the parent can feed the child with soup, encourage the child to choose some food of the variety on the dining table, or give the child his plate with the foods selected by the parent. Different settings, times of the day, developmental stages, and additional diners at a specific meal can influence which feeding and eating patterns are used. Different combinations of these factors can lead to feeding and eating practices that are directed by the parent, or the child's initiative, or conjointly by parent and child. However, since Parent-Based Prevention is designed for children younger than 6 years old, it is assumed that population relies on adults for both feeding and eating.

b. Co-occurring Parental Difficulties That Compromise Parental Functioning

Anxiety and mood disorders are two of the most common comorbidities in individuals with eating disorders. Among mothers in the general population, a link exists between elevated levels of anxiety and reported feeding problems; maternal abandonment fears, feelings of inadequacy, incompetence, and helplessness are associated with difficulties feeding their young girls, and maternal core beliefs of expected emotional deprivation and subjugation connected with feeding difficulties of their young boys (Blissett, Meyer, Farrow, Bryant-Waugh, & Nicholls, 2005). Interactions between mothers with eating disorders and their young children are characterized by more negative emotions and more controlling behaviors during feeding times and in contexts unrelated to food, i.e., during free play (Sadeh-Sharvit et al., 2016; Stein et al., 1994). More severe maternal eating disorders symptoms and higher maternal stress regarding child-rearing competence contribute to mothers' difficulties in feeding their children (Runfola et al., 2013). The comorbid mood symptoms may diminish available mental resources and reduce attunement to the child, particularly when the parent is distracted by their mood problems (Bardone-Cone et al., 2010).

Children's adjustment is impacted by child-rearing practices and familial transactional patterns (Low & Stocker, 2005), which are partly mediated by the cognitive and emotional characteristics associated with adult eating disorders (Cassin & von Ranson, 2005; Segura-García, Chiodo, Sinopoli, & De Fazio, 2013). Similar to the effects of the parental eating disorder, the parental co-occurring symptoms may model this agitated responsiveness to their children. Additionally, parents with eating disorders could be more sensitive to, and triggered by, certain behaviors of their children, and consequently augmenting them unintentionally. An example for this biopsychosocial ecological system (Sameroff, 2010) would be a father with binge-eating disorder who struggles with social anxiety and is concerned about their child having the same problem. To increase the child's resilience, the parent's sensitivity to detect signs of stress in social circumstances may inadvertently aggregate these very behaviors in the child. In a relationship that is already affected by stressful mealtimes, this cumulative stress could be very taxing to all family members (Blissett et al., 2005). These parental concerns influence responsiveness to children, impact the nature of the parent–child relationship and unintentionally reinforce maladaptive behaviors in both parents and their children. Therefore, addressing the impact of comorbidities on parenting practices and parental efficacy should be a crucial component of any preventive intervention that is focused on the children's wellbeing.

c. Problems in Spousal Communication over Child Feeding and Daily Routines

Effective communication between a parent with an eating disorder and his or her partner is essential because it aids the unaffected spouse in understanding the types of emotional and instrumental supports the other parent's needs (Bulik, Baucom, Kirby, & Pisetsky, 2011). Although spousal support can moderate the associations between the parental eating disorder and child outcomes, this is only applicable when parental stress is low (Sadeh-Sharvit, Levy-Shiff, Arnow, & Lock, 2015). Decreased spousal involvement in the child's daily routine, namely feeding, may potentiate these difficulties

(Kluwer, 2010). High-conflict communication between the parents or contentious problem-solving may compromise parents' ability to receive support from their partners in child-rearing dilemmas.

Parent-Based Prevention aims at fostering adaptive communication around parenting, focusing on the wellbeing of the child. Thus, the intervention concentrates on parental discrepancies regarding feeding their child and supporting his or her development. Thanks to improved parental efficacy and communication, additional aspects of the parental collaboration can be identified and modified. Some parents and therapists mistakenly believe that the therapist should attempt to resolve additional individual or systemic problem he identifies. Nonetheless, the heart of this short-term intervention is to minimize any behaviors that could trigger feeding and eating difficulties and additional adverse outcomes among the children. The therapist's interventions should be planned and carried out with this focus in mind.

References

Agras, S., Hammer, L., & McNicholas, F. (1999). A prospective study of the influence of eating-disordered mothers on their children. *International Journal of Eating Disorders*, 25(3), 253–262.

Agras, W. S., Hammer, L. D., Huffman, L. C., Mascola, A., Bryson, S. W., & Danaher, C. (2012). Improving healthy eating in families with a toddler at risk for overweight: A cluster randomized controlled trial. *Journal of Developmental and Behavioral Pediatrics: JDBP*, 33(7), 529.

Allen, K. L., Gibson, L. Y., McLean, N. J., Davis, E. A., & Byrne, S. M. (2014). Maternal and family factors and child eating pathology: Risk and protective relationships. *Journal of Eating Disorders*, 2(1), 11.

Ammaniti, M., Lucarelli, L., Cimino, S., D'Olimpio, F., & Chatoor, I. (2012). Feeding disorders of infancy: A longitudinal study to middle childhood. *International Journal of Eating Disorders*, 45(2), 272–280.

Bardone-Cone, A. M., Harney, M. B., Maldonado, C. R., Lawson, M. A., Robinson, D. P., Smith, R., & Tosh, A. (2010). Defining recovery from an eating disorder: Conceptualization, validation, and examination of psychosocial functioning and psychiatric comorbidity. *Behaviour Research and Therapy*, 48(3), 194–202.

Blissett, J., & Haycraft, E. (2011). Parental eating disorder symptoms and observations of mealtime interactions with children. *Journal of Psychosomatic Research*, 70(4), 368–371.

Blissett, J., Meyer, C., Farrow, C., Bryant-Waugh, R., & Nicholls, D. (2005). Maternal core beliefs and children's feeding problems. *International Journal of Eating Disorders*, 37(2), 127–134.

Blissett, J., Meyer, C., & Haycraft, E. (2006). Maternal and paternal controlling feeding practices with male and female children. *Appetite*, 47(2), 212–219.

Bloom, D. E., & Sousa-Poza, A. (2010). Introduction to Special Issue of the *European Journal of Population*: 'Economic Consequences of Low Fertility in Europe,' 26(2), 127–139.

Bulik, C. M., Baucom, D. H., Kirby, J. S., & Pisetsky, E. (2011). Uniting couples (in the treatment of) anorexia nervosa (UCAN). *International Journal of Eating Disorders, 44*(1), 19–28.

Cassin, S. E., & von Ranson, K. M. (2005). Personality and eating disorders: A decade in review. *Clinical Psychology Review, 25*(7), 895–916.

Cherlin, A. J. (2010). *The marriage-go-round: The state of marriage and the family in America today.* New York, NY: Vintage.

Cimino, S., Cerniglia, L., Paciello, M., & Sinesi, S. (2013). A six-year prospective study on children of mothers with eating disorders: The role of paternal psychological profiles. *European Eating Disorders Review, 21*(3), 238–246.

Danaher, C., Fredericks, D., Bryson, S. W., Agras, W. S., & Ritchie, L. (2011). Early childhood feeding practices improved after short-term pilot intervention with pediatricians and parents. *Childhood Obesity (Formerly Obesity and Weight Management), 7*(6), 480–487.

de Barse, L. M., Tharner, A., Micali, N., Jaddoe, V. V., Hofman, A., Verhulst, F. C., . . . & Jansen, P. W. (2015). Does maternal history of eating disorders predict mothers' feeding practices and preschoolers' emotional eating? *Appetite, 85*, 1–7.

Easter, A., Naumann, U., Northstone, K., Schmidt, U., Treasure, J., & Micali, N. (2013). A longitudinal investigation of nutrition and dietary patterns in children of mothers with eating disorders. *The Journal of Pediatrics, 163*(1), 173–178.

Evans, J., & Grange, D. L. (1995). Body size and parenting in eating disorders: A comparative study of the attitudes of mothers towards their children. *International Journal of Eating Disorders, 18*(1), 39–48.

Haycraft, E., & Blissett, J. (2010). Eating disorder symptoms and parenting styles. *Appetite, 54*(1), 221–224.

Hodes, M., Timimi, S., & Robinson, P. (1997). Children of mothers with eating disorders: A preliminary study. *European Eating Disorders Review, 5*(1), 11–24.

Hoek, H. W. (2006). Incidence, prevalence and mortality of anorexia nervosa and other eating disorders. *Current Opinion in Psychiatry, 19*(4), 389–394.

Hoek, H. W., & van Hoeken, D. (2003). Review of the prevalence and incidence of eating disorders. *International Journal of Eating Disorders, 34*(4), 383–396.

Hoffman, E. R., Hodges, E. A., Propper, C., Zipkin, E. C., Bentley, M. E., Ward, D. S., . . . & Bulik, C. M. (2013). Behavioral and psychophysiological responsiveness during child feeding in mothers with histories of eating disorders: A pilot study. *Journal of Psychopathology and Behavioral Assessment, 35*(4), 578–591.

Howden, L. M., & Meyer, J. A. (2010). Age and sex composition: 2010. 2010 Census Briefs. Suitland, MD: US Department of Commerce, Economics and Statistics Administration, US Census Bureau.

Hudson, J. I., Hiripi, E., Pope, H. G., Jr., & Kessler, R. C. (2007). The prevalence and correlates of eating disorders in the National Comorbidity Survey Replication. *Biological Psychiatry, 61*(3), 348–358. doi:10.1097/01. yco.0000228759.95237.78.

Jacka, F. N., Ystrom, E., Brantsaeter, A. L., Karevold, E., Roth, C., Haugen, M., . . . & Berk, M. (2013). Maternal and early postnatal nutrition and mental health of offspring by age 5 years: A prospective cohort study. *Journal of the American Academy of Child & Adolescent Psychiatry, 52*(10), 1038–1047.

Kim-Cohen, J., Caspi, A., Taylor, A., Williams, B., Newcombe, R., Craig, I. W., & Moffitt, T. E. (2006). MAOA, maltreatment, and gene–environment interaction predicting children's mental health: New evidence and a meta-analysis. *Molecular Psychiatry, 11*(10), 903–913.

Kluwer, E. S. (2010). From partnership to parenthood: A review of marital change across the transition to parenthood. *Journal of Family Theory & Review, 2*(2), 105–125.

Kothari, R., Rosinska, M., Treasure, J., & Micali, N. (2014). The early cognitive development of children at high risk of developing an eating disorder. *European Eating Disorders Review, 22*(2), 152–156.

Kothari, R., Solmi, F., Treasure, J., & Micali, N. (2013). The neuropsychological profile of children at high risk of developing an eating disorder. *Psychological Medicine, 43*(07), 1543–1554.

Koubaa, S., Hällström, T., Hagenäs, L., & Hirschberg, A. L. (2013). Retarded head growth and neurocognitive development in infants of mothers with a history of eating disorders: Longitudinal cohort study. *BJOG: An International Journal of Obstetrics & Gynaecology, 120*(11), 1413–1422.

Kral, T. V., & Rauh, E. M. (2010). Eating behaviors of children in the context of their family environment. *Physiology & Behavior, 100*(5), 567–573.

Little, L., & Lowkes, E. (2000). Critical issues in the care of pregnant women with eating disorders and the impact on their children. *Journal of Midwifery & Women's Health, 45*(4), 301–307.

Low, S. M., & Stocker, C. (2005). Family functioning and children's adjustment: Associations among parents' depressed mood, marital hostility, parent–child hostility, and children's adjustment. *Journal of Family Psychology, 19*(3), 394.

Lydecker, J. A., & Grilo, C. M. (2016). Fathers and mothers with eating-disorder psychopathology: Associations with child eating-disorder behaviors. *Journal of Psychosomatic Research, 86*, 63–69.

Maxwell, M., Thornton, L. M., Root, T. L., Pinheiro, A. P., Strober, M., Brandt, H., . . . & Johnson, C. (2011). Life beyond the eating disorder: Education, relationships, and reproduction. *International Journal of Eating Disorders, 44*(3), 225–232.

Mazzeo, S. E., Zucker, N. L., Gerke, C. K., Mitchell, K. S., & Bulik, C. M. (2005). Parenting concerns of women with histories of eating disorders. *International Journal of Eating Disorders, 37*(S1).

Micali, N. (2005). Childhood risk factors: Longitudinal continuities and eating disorders. *Journal of Mental Health, 14*(6), 567–574.

Micali, N., Ploubidis, G., De Stavola, B., Simonoff, E., & Treasure, J. (2014). Frequency and patterns of eating disorder symptoms in early adolescence. *Journal of Adolescent Health, 54*(5), 574–581.

Micali, N., Simonoff, E., Stahl, D., & Treasure, J. (2011). Maternal eating disorders and infant feeding difficulties: Maternal and child mediators in a longitudinal general population study. *Journal of Child Psychology and Psychiatry*, *52*(7), 800–807.

Micali, N., & Treasure, J. (2009). Biological effects of a maternal ED on pregnancy and foetal development: A review. *European Eating Disorders Review*, *17*(6), 448–454.

Park, R. J., Senior, R., & Stein, A. (2003). The offspring of mothers with eating disorders. *European Child & Adolescent Psychiatry*, *12*(1), i110–i119.

Rapoport, B., & Le Bourdais, C. (2008). Parental time and working schedules. *Journal of Population Economics*, *21*(4), 903–932.

Runfola, C. D., Von Holle, A., Trace, S. E., Brownley, K. A., Hofmeier, S. M., Gagne, D. A., & Bulik, C. M. (2013). Body dissatisfaction in women across the lifespan: Results of the UNC-SELF and gender and body image (GABI) studies. *European Eating Disorders Review*, *21*(1), 52–59.

Sadeh-Sharvit, S., Levy-Shiff, R., Arnow, K. D., & Lock, J. D. (2015). The impact of maternal eating disorders and spousal support on neurodevelopmental trajectories in their toddlers. *Abnormal and Behavioral Psychology*, *1*(1). doi:10.4172/abp.1000102.

Sadeh-Sharvit, S., Levy-Shiff, R., Arnow, K. D., & Lock, J. D. (2016). The interactions of mothers with eating disorders with their toddlers: Identifying broader risk factors. *Attachment & Human Development*, *18*(4), 418–428.

Sadeh-Sharvit, S., Levy-Shiff, R., Feldman, T., Ram, A., Gur, E., Zubery, E., . . . & Lock, J. D. (2015). Child feeding perceptions among mothers with eating disorders. *Appetite*, *95*, 67–73.

Sadeh-Sharvit, S., Levy-Shiff, R., & Lock, J. D. (2015). Maternal eating disorder history and toddlers' neurodevelopmental outcomes: A brief report. *Eating Disorders*, *24*(2), 198–205. doi:10.1080/10640266.2015.1064280.

Sameroff, A. (2010). A unified theory of development: A dialectic integration of nature and nurture. *Child Development*, *81*(1), 6–22.

Satter, E. (1990). The feeding relationship: Problems and interventions. *The Journal of Pediatrics*, *117*(2), S181–S189.

Scherag, S., Hebebrand, J., & Hinney, A. (2010). Eating disorders: The current status of molecular genetic research. *European Child & Adolescent Psychiatry*, *19*(3), 211–226.

Segura-García, C., Chiodo, D., Sinopoli, F., & De Fazio, P. (2013). Temperamental factors predict long-term modifications of eating disorders after treatment. *BMC Psychiatry*, *13*(1), 288.

Squires, C., Lalanne, C., Murday, N., Simoglou, V., & Vaivre-Douret, L. (2014). The influence of eating disorders on mothers' sensitivity and adaptation during feeding: A longitudinal observational study. *BMC Pregnancy and Childbirth*, *14*(1), 274.

Stein, A., Woolley, H., Cooper, S. D., & Fairburn, C. G. (1994). An observational study of mothers with eating disorders and their infants. *Journal of Child Psychology and Psychiatry*, *35*(4), 733–748.

Stein, A., Woolley, H., & McPherson, K. (1999). Conflict between mothers with eating disorders and their infants during mealtimes. *British Journal of Psychiatry*, *175*(5), 455–461.

Stein, A., Woolley, H., Murray, L., Cooper, P., Cooper, S., Noble, F., . . . & Fairburn, C. G. (2001). Influence of psychiatric disorder on the controlling behaviour of mothers with 1-year-old infants. *British Journal of Psychiatry*, *179*(2), 157–162.

Stice, E., Agras, W. S., & Hammer, L. D. (1999). Risk factors for the emergence of childhood eating disturbances: A five-year prospective study. *International Journal of Eating Disorders*, *25*(4), 375–387.

Zerwas, S., Von Holle, A., Torgersen, L., Reichborn-Kjennerud, T., Stoltenberg, C., & Bulik, C. M. (2012). Maternal eating disorders and infant temperament: Findings from the Norwegian mother and child cohort study. *International Journal of Eating Disorders*, *45*(4), 546–555.

3   The Broader Context of the Transition to Parenthood in Adults with Eating Disorders and Their Partners

Shiri Sadeh-Sharvit, Madeline Sacks, and James Lock

A birth of a child is arguably one of the most joyful, and stressful, life events. For parents, it initiates a series of biological, psychological, and interpersonal changes that could be a catalyst for significant individual and family growth. The transition to parenthood is influenced considerably by the parents' expectations, their experience in other relationships and life transitions, psychological difficulties, and contextual factors. In this chapter, we will provide a brief review of common processes in the transition to parenthood and how they may be affected in the presence of a parental eating disorder history. Similarly to the reviews of the literature in other parts of this book, there is currently very little information on fathers with eating disorders, and no data are available on the impact of a paternal eating disorder history on the transition to parenthood and the couple relationships.

Parenthood is a fundamental milestone in adult development. Central psychobiological-sociocultural influences prime the sensibilities and tendencies of new parents so that in the time before and after birth, motherhood becomes the center of identity and the main prism through which mothers – and their environment – evaluate themselves (Brown, 2010; Ruble et al., 1990). Beginning in the prenatal period and persisting in the postnatal period, activated schemas of the parent–child relationship are influenced by the present representations of the origin family, especially the mother's relationship with her own mother (Dayton, Levendosky, Davidson, & Bogat, 2010; Stern, 1995). Often, these schemas also exclude the partner, as they relate to childbearing and developing competencies around new motherhood.

Transition to Motherhood

Even in the absence of mental health issues, pregnancy and first-time motherhood are extremely stressful times for a woman. She experiences intense emotional fluctuations related to hormonal changes, her body increases and then decreases in size, and she assumes the entirely new and challenging role of motherhood. Changes in body shape and weight can be difficult to accept, particularly in Westernized cultures where thinness is idealized (Abraham, 1998). Along with physicality, a woman's self-identity is altered by the presence of the fetus and the birth of her child. On the individual level, she assumes responsibility for the life and wellbeing of her offspring. During the prenatal period, she is the sole caregiver; as such, she typically develops a unique bond with the fetus. Her relationship with the fetus precedes and predicts postnatal maternal attachment and mother–infant interactions (Kluwer, 2010; Slade, Cohen, Sadler, & Miller, 2009). As she cares for and engages with her new infant, motherhood becomes central to her identity. It is natural for a new mother to feel anxiety over her efficacy in this role and to be sensitive to any criticisms or challenges (Biehle & Mickelson, 2011; Ruble et al., 1990).

New mothers are a unique patient population that must be understood in the context of their recent transition and newly acquired role, responsibilities, and relationships. This complex, stressful transition to motherhood is only further complicated and disrupted by the presence of severe maternal psychopathology, namely an eating disorder.

Transition to Fatherhood

The perinatal and postnatal periods are transitional, challenging times for not only new mothers, but also for new fathers and female spouses that are not biological mothers. The process of becoming a father is its own unique process, with difficulties pertaining to the assumption of a parental role that is excluded from the experience of carrying, birthing, and breastfeeding the infant (Steen, Downe, Bamford, & Edozien, 2012; Watson et al., 1995). As the new mother experiences immense physical changes, while simultaneously attempting to bond with the infant, adopt a new role, and gain a sense of maternal efficacy (Abraham, 1998), this difficult transition coincides with one of the most stressful periods for the new father as well. For first-time fathers, pregnancy, rather than the postnatal period, appears to be the most stressful time. The second half of the pregnancy and the first year of the infant's life are often marked with a deterioration in marital and sexual satisfaction, work satisfaction, recreation, and sleep habits (Condon, Boyce, & Corkindale, 2004). Given the range of difficulties experienced by new parents, the competency of the primary caretakers, both male and female, should be a target of early intervention programs and clinical services (Watson et al., 1995; Sadeh-Sharvit, Sacks, Runfola, Bulik, & Lock, submitted).

Transition to Parenthood in Adoptive and Single-Parent Families

Families come in diverse shapes and forms. Models that are suitable to heteronormative families require some adaptations when applied to gay and lesbian families, adoptive families, single-parent families, and families where the parents choose to live in separate households. Data suggest that parents in the said family structures share many similar processes in the transition to parenting with those heterosexual, two-parent families experience. However, some unique characteristics should be considered when trying to understand, support, and intervene with these families. As mentioned above, the transition to parenthood is regarded as a major life event and a stressor that rearranges parents' roles, identities, and responsibilities (Belsky, Lang, & Rovine, 1985). Becoming parents may be inherently a more intricate, prolonged, and possibly expensive, procedure when the two biological parents are not married to one another (Goldberg, 2010). Further, these parents' social network may be not apt to provide sufficient support due to barriers such as stigma, isolation, and legislation that is detrimental to minorities and individuals of lower socioeconomic status. Even when their environment wants to help, it may be often misinformed of their unique challenges. For example, for adoptive parents, their strains and excitement during the waiting period are not culturally acknowledged (Rogers, 2018). Frequently, adoptive parents also cope with inter-racial differences and cross-cultural gaps. Same-sex parents report lower depressive and anxiety symptoms when they receive greater family and workplace support, and when their neighborhood and state are perceived as more gay-friendly (Goldberg & Smith, 2011). Sole-parent-headed families may be more financially disadvantageous and ambivalent about relying on support figures who may contest their choices and life circumstances (Nelson, 2000).

Changes in the Family System

Family roles and relationships shift dramatically during and after pregnancy. During pregnancy, the woman is engaged in a hormonally-driven, unique relationship with the developing fetus that necessarily leaves out her partner (Abraham, 1998). The birth of a new child brings about a reorientation of the prenatal family structure. Initially, the family system includes one reciprocal, interpersonal relationship between partners. During the prenatal period, a second relationship is added, between the woman and the fetus. In the perinatal period, the new father begins to establish a bond with the infant. Ultimately, three reciprocal, interpersonal relationships emerge (Astrachan-Fletcher et al., 2008; Feldman, 2000).

A positive and supportive spousal interactional style is necessary for the development of a healthy family system and effective parenting styles. Better pre-birth relationship quality predicts greater parental engagement for both parents – especially in the infant-to-toddler years (Cowan & Cowan, 2006). Maternal adjustment is positively influenced by increased spousal support and marital satisfaction. However, the association appeared to largely proceed in one direction – from couple relationship quality to parenting (Carlson, Pilkauskas, McLanahan, & Brooks-Gunn, 2011).

The Impact of Mental Disorders on the New Parents

Parental efficacy can be viewed from two different, yet equally important, perspectives: the subjective experience of the parents and the objectively-measured, developmentally-appropriate child emotional, behavioral, and physical indicators. Parental self-assessment and child developmental trajectories are multifaceted components of the transition to parenthood. These processes are further complicated in families where one or both parents has a mental disorder (Stein et al., 2014). Parental mental disorders may complicate emotions, cognitions, and behaviors that are related to parenting. Many parents are also worried that their children will be genetically "programmed" to experience similar difficulties. Indeed, studies suggest that perinatal maternal mental disorders, such as depression, may increase offspring's risk for mental illness in childhood and adolescence. At the same time, having a child is also experienced as a validation of parents' strengths and resilience (Howard et al., 2014; Krumm & Becker, 2006).

A reciprocal relationship is most likely at work between parents' psychological difficulties and decreased spousal sensitivity, marital discord, and future parental involvement, which indicates the role of couple functioning in family adjustment and wellbeing (Cowan & Cowan, 2006). Parental psychopathology has been shown to negatively influence child emotional, behavioral, and physical development (Stein et al., 2014). Mental disorders in fathers are associated with later internalizing and externalizing problems in the children of these individuals (Ramchandani & Psychogiou, 2009). Similarly, studies on mothers indicate that maternal mental disorders contribute to low birth weight and maladaptive childhood behaviors and emotional difficulties (Stein et al., 2014). When psychological disorders are present in both parents, a problematic style of co-parenting may emerge wherein conflict and emotional asynchrony are elevated. In these households, children are at increased risk for emotional and behavioral problems (Cowan & Cowan, 2006). However, the presence of mental disorders in parents is by no means deterministic. Child outcomes are influenced by several factors, including parenting style, social support, and the length and severity of the parental mental health disorder. For instance, paternal mental health and father–infant relationship are correlated with maternal psychopathology, which indirectly may augment the child's risk of developmental abnormalities (Paulson & Bazemore, 2010; Gutierrez-Galve, Stein, Hanington, Heron, & Ramchandani, 2015). As such, parents have both an indirect and direct influence on their children, through spousal support, child interactions, and genetics (Howard et al., 2014). The reciprocally influencing quality of parental mental health underscores the importance and potential benefits of early interventions for families in which one or both parents has a mental disorder, particularly in a time as stressful as the adaptation to a new baby (Stein et. al., 2014).

Maternal Wellbeing in Light of an Eating Disorder

When treating mothers who have eating disorders, it is essential that clinicians understand the unique complexities of their transition to motherhood. The pregnancy period appears to be more stressful and emotionally difficult for mothers with eating disorders, and some may arrive at childbirth with depleted energies, a lower sense of self-efficacy, and more negative emotions (Koubaa, Hallstrom, & Hirschberg, 2008; Lai, Tang, & Tse, 2006; Watson et al., 2014). These mothers have more pregnancy-related complications, including greater nausea and vomiting, poor nutrition, and greater weight gain during the pregnancy in comparison to mothers with no eating disorders (Kimmel, Ferguson, Zerwas, Bulik, & Meltzer-Brody, 2016). Additionally, they need to cope with more attention directed at their bodies, from within as well as by health professionals and the environment (Heslehurst et al., 2015), together with changes in body weight, and limited ability to engage in exercise or other compensatory behaviors – all these may compromise a mother's adjustment to her new role (Abraham, 1998; Easter, Treasure, & Micali, 2011).

Past or present eating disorder symptoms place a woman at higher risk of developing postpartum depression and anxiety than in the absence of such psychopathology (Micali, Simonoff, Stahl, & Treasure, 2011). Additionally, eating disorders have been shown to affect typical maternal-infant bonding (Koubaa et al., 2008; Sadeh-Sharvit et al., 2015). Maternal adjustment is further impaired by decreased enjoyment of motherhood, lowered confidence in one's competency as a new mother, dilemmas about child feeding, early-onset feeding and eating problems, and child weight abnormalities (Blissett, Meyer, & Haycraft, 2006; Bryant-Waugh, Turner, East, & Gamble, 2007; Koubaa et al., 2008). While the transition to motherhood can be a stressful experience, many mothers with eating disorders also find that this is an opportune time for psychological growth; most mothers make a significant effort to eliminate or substantially reduce their symptoms (Sadeh-Sharvit et al., 2016).

Fatherhood in the Context of Maternal Eating Disorders

Similar to the scarcity of research around fathers with eating disorders, there is little research on the male partners of adults with eating disorders. The available data stem from studies on the male spouses of mothers with eating disorders, mostly in heteronormative families, i.e., heterosexual couples in traditional parenting roles. Partners of adult women with eating disorders are often unaware of the severity of their wives' symptoms (Bulik, Baucom, Kirby, & Pisetsky, 2011). They also tend to have a higher incidence of psychopathology and may have their own eating-related issues (Cimino, Cerniglia, Paciello, & Sinesi, 2013).

In addition to their own struggles, partners often report difficulties in understanding the nature and severity of their loved one's eating disorder and are unsure how to help (Bulik et al., 2011; Linville, Cobb, Shen, & Stadelman, 2016). Too often, communication patterns can become ineffective, ranging from complete avoidance of confrontation to heightened criticism and conflict (Huke & Slade, 2006; Linville et al., 2016), and inadvertently aggregate maternal eating psychopathology (Arcelus, Haslam, Farrow, & Meyer, 2013). Further, eating disorder symptoms have been shown to increase in the presence of spousal conflict, even when it is not related with the eating disorder. It has been suggested that this increase is a maladaptive coping mechanism used to distract from marital discord (Lai et al., 2006), impacting the couple's ability to communicate and support one another effectively.

Just as maternal eating disorders may complicate the transition to new motherhood, they are also associated with adverse paternal adjustment. Maternal and paternal psychological functioning, the quality of the couple relationship, and maternal and paternal sensitivity are major determinants of child health and wellbeing. Additionally, the increased anxiety and concern that mothers with eating disorders symptomatology experience in response to, and during, feeding (Squires, Lalanne, Murday, Simoglou, & Vaivre-Douret, 2014) may aggravate normative levels of paternal stress, insensitivity, and feelings of inefficacy. The father may find himself not only excluded from the feeding process, but also unable to remedy a distressing situation for his wife and child. Additionally, the father often feels powerless to actively change this situation, which may contribute to his growing feelings of inefficacy, and ultimately decrease paternal involvement (Park, Senior, & Stein, 2003). This may prove to be detrimental to the overall wellbeing and cohesiveness of the family unit because paternal involvement has been shown to mediate the relationship between maternal psychopathology and child behavioral abnormalities (Cimino, Cerniglia, & Paciello, 2015).

Summary

The interconnectedness between parental eating disorder symptoms, involvement in child-rearing, and self-perceived efficacy highlights the importance of assessing and treating the family system as a whole. Alterations to the family system are stressful and challenging even in the absence of parental psychopathology. As with the transitions to parenthood, the necessary reorganization of the family system is further complicated by the presence of an eating disorder. Clinicians who are aware of the reciprocity between maternal psychopathology and developmental processes involved in parenthood can effectively target adverse cognitions and behaviors, both in individual family members and the system as a whole, in a holistic, proactive, and informed manner.

References

Abraham, S. (1998). Sexuality and reproduction in bulimia nervosa patients over 10 years. *Journal of Psychosomatic Research*, *44*(3–4), 491–502. doi: 10.1016/S0022-3999(97)00272-9.

Arcelus, J., Haslam, M., Farrow, C., & Meyer, C. (2013). The role of interpersonal functioning in the maintenance of eating psychopathology: A systematic review and testable model. *Clinical Psychology Review*, *33*(1), 156–167.

Astrachan-Fletcher, E., Veldhuis, C., Lively, N., Fowler, C., & Marcks, B. (2008). The reciprocal effects of eating disorders and the postpartum period: A review of the literature and recommendations for clinical care. *Journal of Women's Health*, *17*(2), 227–239.

Belsky, J., Lang, M., & Rovine, M. (1985). Stability and change in marriage across the transition to parenthood: A second study. *Journal of Marriage and the Family*, *47*, 855–866.

Biehle, S. N., & Mickelson, K. D. (2011). Personal and co-parent predictors of parenting efficacy across the transition to parenthood. *Journal of Social and Clinical Psychology*, *30*(9), 985–1010.

Blissett, J., Meyer, C., & Haycraft, E. (2006). Maternal and paternal controlling feeding practices with male and female children. *Appetite*, *47*(2), 212–219.

Brown, I. (2010). Ambivalence of the motherhood experience. *Twenty-first-century motherhood: Experience, identity, policy, agency*. New York, NY: Columbia University Press, 121–138.

Bryant-Waugh, R., Turner, H., East, P., & Gamble, C. (2007). Developing a parenting skills-and-support intervention for mothers with eating disorders and pre-school children part 1: Qualitative investigation of issues to include. *European Eating Disorders Review*, *15*(5), 350–356.

Bulik, C. M., Baucom, D. H., Kirby, J. S., & Pisetsky, E. (2011). Uniting couples (in the treatment of) anorexia nervosa (UCAN). *International Journal of Eating Disorders*, *44*(1), 19–28. doi:10.1002/eat.20790.

Carlson, M. J., Pilkauskas, N. V., McLanahan, S. S., & Brooks-Gunn, J. (2011). Couples as partners and parents over children's early years. *Journal of Marriage and Family*, *73*(2), 317–334.

Cimino, S., Cerniglia, L., & Paciello, M. (2015). Mothers with depression, anxiety or eating disorders: Outcomes on their children and the role of paternal psychological profiles. *Child Psychiatry & Human Development*, *46*(2), 228–236. doi:10.1007/s10578-014-0462-6.

Cimino, S., Cerniglia, L., Paciello, M., & Sinesi, S. (2013). A six-year prospective study on children of mothers with eating disorders: The role of paternal psychological profiles. *European Eating Disorders Review*, *21*(3), 238–246. doi:10.1002/erv.2218.

Condon, J. T., Boyce, P., & Corkindale, C. J. (2004). The first-time fathers study: A prospective study of the mental health and wellbeing of men during the transition to parenthood. *Australian and New Zealand Journal of Psychiatry*, *38*(1–2), 56–64.

Cowan, P. A., & Cowan, C. P. (2006). Developmental psychopathology from family systems and family risk factors perspectives: Implications for family research, practice, and policy. *Developmental Psychopathology, 1*, 530–587.

Dayton, C. J., Levendosky, A. A., Davidson, W. S., & Bogat, G. A. (2010). The child as held in the mind of the mother: The influence of prenatal maternal representations on parenting behaviors. *Infant Mental Health Journal, 31*(2), 220–241.

Easter, A., Treasure, J., & Micali, N. (2011). Fertility and prenatal attitudes towards pregnancy in women with eating disorders: Results from the Avon Longitudinal Study of Parents and Children. *BJOG: An International Journal of Obstetrics & Gynaecology, 118*, 1491–1498. doi:10.1111/j.1471-0528.2011.03077.x.

Feldman, M. S. (2000). Organizational routines as a source of continuous change. *Organization Science, 11*(6), 611–629.

Goldberg, A. E. (2010) The transition to adoptive parenthood. In: Miller T. (Ed.) *Handbook of stressful transitions across the lifespan.* New York, NY: Springer, 165–184.

Goldberg, A. E., & Smith, J. Z. (2011). Stigma, social context, and mental health: Lesbian and gay couples across the transition to adoptive parenthood. *Journal of Counseling Psychology, 58*(1), 139. doi: 10.1037/a0021684.

Gutierrez-Galve, L., Stein, A., Hanington, L., Heron, J., & Ramchandani, P. (2015). Paternal depression in the postnatal period and child development: Mediators and moderators. *Pediatrics, 135*(2), e339–e347.

Heslehurst, N., Russell, S., Brandon, H., Johnston, C., Summerbell, C., & Rankin, J. (2015). Women's perspectives are required to inform the development of maternal obesity services: A qualitative study of obese pregnant women's experiences. *Health Expectations, 18*(5), 969–981.

Howard, L. M., Molyneaux, E., Dennis, C.-L., Rochat, T., Stein, A., & Milgrom, J. (2014). Non-psychotic mental disorders in the perinatal period. *The Lancet, 384*(9956), 1775–1788. doi:http://dx.doi.org/10.1016/S0140-6736(14)61276-9.

Huke, K., & Slade, P. (2006). An exploratory investigation of the experiences of partners living with people who have bulimia nervosa. *European Eating Disorders Review, 14*(6), 436–447. doi:10.1002/erv.744.

Kimmel, M. C., Ferguson, E. H., Zerwas, S., Bulik, C. M., & Meltzer-Brody, S. (2016). Obstetric and gynecologic problems associated with eating disorders. *International Journal of Eating Disorders, 49*(3), 260–275. http://doi.org/10.1002/eat.22483.

Kluwer, E. S. (2010). From partnership to parenthood: A review of marital change across the transition to parenthood. *Journal of Family Theory & Review, 2*(2), 105–125.

Koubaa, S., Hallstrom, T., & Hirschberg, A. L. (2008). Early maternal adjustment in women with eating disorders. *International Journal of Eating Disorders, 41*(5), 405–410. doi:10.1002/eat.20521.

Krumm, S., & Becker, T. (2006). Subjective views of motherhood in women with mental illness: A sociological perspective. *Journal of Mental Health, 15*(4), 449–460.

Lai, B. P.-y., Tang, C. S.-k., & Tse, W. K.-l. (2006). A longitudinal study investigating disordered eating during the transition to motherhood among Chinese women in Hong Kong. *International Journal of Eating Disorders*, 39(4), 303–311. doi:10.1002/eat.20266.

Linville, D., Cobb, E., Shen, F., & Stadelman, S. (2016). Reciprocal influence of couple dynamics and eating disorders. *Journal of Marital and Family Therapy*, 42(2), 326–340. doi:10.1111/jmft.12133.

Micali, N., Simonoff, E., Stahl, D., & Treasure, J. (2011). Maternal eating disorders and infant feeding difficulties: Maternal and child mediators in a longitudinal general population study. *Journal of Child Psychology and Psychiatry*, 52(7), 800–807.

Nelson, M. K. (2000). Single mothers and social support: The commitment to, and retreat from, reciprocity. *Qualitative Sociology*, 23(3), 291–317. doi: 1005567910606.

Park, R., Senior, R., & Stein, A. (2003). The offspring of mothers with eating disorders. *European Child & Adolescent Psychiatry*, 12(Suppl 1), i110–i119. doi:10.1007/s00787-003-1114-8.

Paulson, J. F., & Bazemore, S. D. (2010). Prenatal and postpartum depression in fathers and its association with maternal depression: A meta-analysis. *Jama*, 303(19), 1961–1969.

Ramchandani, P., & Psychogiou, L. (2009). Paternal psychiatric disorders and children's psychosocial development. *The Lancet*, 374(9690), 646–653. doi: 10.1016/S0140-6737(09)60238-5.

Rogers, R. (2018). Parents who wait: Acknowledging the support needs and vulnerabilities of approved adopters during their wait to become adoptive parents. *Child & Family Social Work*, 23(2), 289–296. doi: 10.1111/cfs.12417.

Ruble, D. N., Brooks-Gunn, J., Fleming, A. S., Fitzmaurice, G., Stangor, C., & Deutsch, F. (1990). Transition to motherhood and the self: Measurement, stability, and change. *Journal of Personality and Social Psychology*, 58(3), 450–463. doi:10.1037/0022-3514.58.3.450.

Ruble, T. L., & Stout, D. E. (1991). Reliability, classification stability, and response-set bias of alternate forms of the Learning-Style Inventory (LSI-1985). *Educational and Psychological Measurement*, 51(2), 481–489.

Sadeh-Sharvit, S., Levy-Shiff, R., Arnow, K. D., & Lock, J. D. (2016). The interactions of mothers with eating disorders with their toddlers: Identifying broader risk factors. *Attachment & Human Development*, 18(4), 418–428. doi: 10.1080/14616734.2016.1164201.

Sadeh-Sharvit, S., Levy-Shiff, R., Feldman, T., Ram, A., Gur, E., Zubery, E., . . . & Lock, J. D. (2015). Child feeding perceptions among mothers with eating disorders. *Appetite*, 95, 67–73.

Sadeh-Sharvit, S., Levy-Shiff, R., Ram, A., Gur, E., Zubery, E., Steiner, E., & Latzer, Y. (2016). Mothers with eating disorders: The environmental factors affecting eating-related emotional difficulties in their offspring. In Y. Latzer & D. Stein (Eds), *Bio-psycho-social contributions to understanding eating disorders*. Cham: Springer International Publishing, 77–90.

Sadeh-Sharvit, S., Sacks, M. R., Runfola, C., Bulik, C. M., & Lock, J. D. (submitted). *Family-based interventions to empower adult women with eating disorders and their partners around the transition to motherhood*.

Slade, A., Cohen, L. J., Sadler, L. S., & Miller, M. (2009). The psychology and psychopathology of pregnancy: Reorganization and transformation. In C. H. Zeanah (Ed.), *Handbook of infant mental health: Research and clinical applications* (3rd edition). New York, NY: Guilford Press, 22–39.

Squires, C., Lalanne, C., Murday, N., Simoglou, V., & Vaivre-Douret, L. (2014). The influence of eating disorders on mothers' sensitivity and adaptation during feeding: A longitudinal observational study. *BMC Pregnancy and Childbirth*, *14*(1), 274.

Steen, M., Downe, S., Bamford, N., & Edozien, L. (2012). Not-patient and not-visitor: A metasynthesis fathers' encounters with pregnancy, birth and maternity care. *Midwifery*, *28*(4), 422–431.

Stein, A., Pearson, R. M., Goodman, S. H., Rapa, E., Rahman, A., McCallum, M., . . . & Pariante, C. M. (2014). Effects of perinatal mental disorders on the fetus and child. *The Lancet*, *384*(9956), 1800–1819.

Stern, D. N. (1995). *The motherhood constellation: A unified view of parent-infant psychotherapy*. London: Karnac.

Watson, H. J., Torgersen, L., Zerwas, S., Reichborn-Kjennerud, T., Knoph, C., Stoltenberg, C., . . . Bulik, C. M. (2014). Eating disorders, pregnancy, and the postpartum period: Findings from the Norwegian Mother and Child Cohort Study (MoBa). *Norsk epidemiologi (Norwegian journal of epidemiology)*, *24*(1–2), 51–62.

Watson, W. J., Watson, L., Wetzel, W., Bader, E., & Talbot, Y. (1995). Transition to parenthood. What about fathers? *Canadian Family Physician*, *41*, 807–812.

4 The Development of Typical and Atypical Feeding and Eating Processes in Children and Youth

Shiri Sadeh-Sharvit, Madeline Sacks, and James Lock

Parents are bombarded with contradicting messages, expectations, and information about their children's eating. It may take a village to raise a child, but as young parents tend to live further away from their families of origin, many lack the opportunity to capitalize on older family members' wisdom and experience about children's development. In an era where parents are often erroneously blamed for their children's problematic behaviors, attitudes, and functioning, children's eating is another dimension in which parents want to be successful, and they may feel guilt and shame if their child does not demonstrate eating behaviors similar to peers, or if their child is over- or underweight. The presence of a current or past parental eating disorder may exacerbate these concerns and increase uncertainty about how to feed their children well, and when to identify problems and how to effectively tackle them.

The purpose of this chapter is to provide a brief and general account of normal as well as non-adaptive feeding and eating behaviors and attitudes in infants and children. As in other parts of this book (and as explained in Chapter 2), we make a somewhat arbitrary distinction between "feeding" and "eating." In this book, we refer to *feeding* as a behavior that occurs when an adult plans and delivers a child's eating, and decides when to terminate feeding or avoid it altogether. Feeding, therefore, represents the feeder's decision to feed the child, a decision that is contingent on the feeder's beliefs about children's eating in general and the particular child's tendencies. Feeding is also a result of the feeder's perception of the child's hunger and satiety cues as well as food preferences. *Eating*, in this context, is considered as an autonomous behavior in which the individual chooses whether to eat or not, in what way (eating with hands or using silverware, when possible), and how much food is consumed. Eating can represent a behavioral response to an inner body cue or occur in the absence of hunger. Development is directed toward a growth from feeding to eating. However, during the early years, these behaviors tend to overlap – a very tired toddler who typically eats by himself will likely be fed by his parents when he is tired but is still hungry; a 10-month-old infant who shows interest in her parents' food could enjoy a few bites of food that has not been introduced yet.

As discussed in Chapter 2 and throughout this book, the concept of Division of Responsibility (Satter, 2012) helps parents navigate early childhood feeding. According to this scheme, for normally-developing children, parents are responsible for providing access to developmentally appropriate nutrition, namely milk or formula in infancy and then increasingly more complex food groups as children progress through development stages. As contended by the Division of Responsibility model, children are responsible for determining whether and how much they eat. As they grow and develop, both physically and mentally, they become increasingly responsible for determining what and how much they eat. However, feeding roles may be quite different when the children are very young or when they are ill; in these scenarios, the parents' management surpasses the child's decisions.

The transition from feeding to independent eating can be tricky. Often times, providing the parents with information about reasonable expectations of their child's eating can considerably reduce parental concerns and put the child's behavior in the appropriate developmental framework. Conversely, lack of knowledge can aggravate parental concerns and lead to less adaptive responses toward the child. Additionally, this chapter focuses on normal feeding and eating trajectories that are rooted in contemporary Western practices (Ogata & Hayes, 2014); clinicians are advised to explore their clients' feeding- and eating-related familial and cultural traditions and beliefs because these must be integrated into any family intervention.

Development of Feeding and Eating Behaviors in Young Children

A baby's first experiences with feeding and eating are dependent on a combination of innate reflexes and parental guidance. In the absence of any birth complications, babies are born with the reflexes that support head-turning toward a feeding source and sucking from a breast or bottle. Parental feeding practices, such as the decision to breast- or bottle-feed, as well as the frequency and amount of nutrition offered to an infant, are largely informed by cultural norms (Musher-Eizenman, de Lauzon-Guillain, Holub, Leporc, & Charles, 2009). For the first six months of life, babies tend to be sustained on an entirely liquid-based diet of breast milk, formula, or a combination of both. Before and during pregnancy, expectant mothers are commonly expected to breastfeed their child. When breastfeeding does not occur, the parents may be subject to criticism by other family members, friends, and even professionals (Labbok, 2008). In these first several months of life, parents are focused on observing their infants, learning and responding to their sleep and hunger cues, and interacting with their infants by talking, smiling, and expressing love and affection (Feldman, 2012). As babies continue to grow and develop, parents introduce solid foods, which gradually become the lion's share of the child's intake. However, although it is normal for children to still nurse or eat formula more frequently and in larger quantities, cultures vary on recommendations and expectations as for when to stop nursing (Grummer-Strawn, Scanlon, & Fein, 2008).

At around 5–9 months, most parents begin to support their baby's interest in independent eating by introducing soft, pureed foods, composed primarily of fruits and vegetables. This process is associated with infants developing fine motor skills, which include grabbing, squeezing and mashing of food, eating finger-foods, using spoons, and so on, and ultimately these activities strengthen the developing child's self-guided eating practices. Psychologically, this stage is characterized by a growing need for independence and increasing curiosity about the world. Children's autonomy becomes central to their development: they have a desire to complete tasks themselves, including independent feeding and exploration of new foods.

During the second year of life, toddlers progress to participating in family meals and eating the same foods as their family. While the quantity and size of these foods are small, family meals support the development in the child of an interest in trying new foods while supporting general communication skills in toddlers and this, in turn, facilitates mealtime interactions and expression of hunger cues.

In the preschool years, around 3–5 years of age, significant increases in initiative, physical and social skills, and thought processes occur. Imitation of adults is a common and crucial practice at this stage. As such, it is important that parents demonstrate adaptive behaviors within the realms of social interaction and health practices, including around feeding and eating. Exposure to new foods takes place gradually, often requiring between ten to sixteen times before the child fully accepts them. These new foods should be offered in a relaxed, non-coercive manner. Additionally, parents should not be discouraged if some foods are not well accepted by their child; children's intake patterns change over time. Notably, young children likely prefer foods and flavors associated with energy- and fat-rich foods. This is because their developing body, brain, and nervous system need fatty acids and carbohydrates as their building blocks (Innis, 2008; Savage, Fisher, & Birch, 2007).

Around mid to late childhood and early adolescence, there may be a plateau in developing taste preference. This phenomenon also has evolutionary and biological underpinnings, because high-carb, high-fat foods are ideal for supporting the rapid and extensive growth and development typical of the pre-puberty phase of life (Ogata & Hayes, 2014). Therefore, parents should expect that their children will show a strong inclination for foods that may be culturally perceived as "unhealthy" and associated with negative health outcomes in adults. Nonetheless, range and variability of food as well as certain aversions are taken to be developmentally typical and should not be worrisome.

,Children's eating preferences greatly reflect the foods that are readily available and accessible in their school and home. Parental modeling is one of the main vehicles for promoting age-appropriate eating preferences, variety, and quantity. Therefore, the importance of family meals for the development of healthy eating habits cannot be understated. The family meal is an eating opportunity as much as it is a social event, where target behaviors can be modeled, shaped, and rewarded. Preparing family meals requires that the caregivers ensure that the child is hungry and alert enough to participate in the meal, and that the meal balances familiar and unfamiliar foods. However, daily family meals are likely a challenge for many parents nowadays, given dual-career families and parents' work hours as well as the demands of school and after-school activities. Therefore, creating a standard of at least one parent at home for dinner on most weekdays is likely a minimum most families could achieve.

Body Image, Eating Behaviors, and Disordered Eating in Adolescents

Children depend on their environment for food; their habits, attitudes, and responses to food and eating are shaped by a transactional relationship with their primary caretakers. These interactions evolve from feeding that is mostly guided by parents to a more autonomous eating that relies on the child's self-regulation, within the structural boundaries the parents and the environment define and in the context of the knowledge and attitudes they provide (Agras et al., 2012). As children mature, more agents in their surroundings play a role in educating on, modeling, and shaping healthy eating behaviors. Unrealistic media messages distort adolescent and adult views on food consumption, body shape, and body size, by accentuating the value of thinness, athleticism, and "clean" or "healthy eating," e.g., avoidance of certain food groups (Benowitz-Fredericks, Garcia, Massey, Vasagar, & Borzekowski, 2012). Data suggest that during the transition from elementary to middle school, body image dissatisfaction increases in both girls and boys; however, the body image of the former is, on average, more negative than their male counterparts (Bucchianeri, Arikian, Hannan, Eisenberg, & Neumark-Sztainer, 2013).

Parental over-control of eating in their children is associated with unintentional negative dietary and psychosocial outcomes in their offspring (Davison & Deane, 2010). Family "fat talk" and weight-teasing of their children and parent dieting are associated with problematic eating behaviors and attitudes in their children (Neumark-Sztainer et al., 2010). Parental pressure on pre-adolescent and adolescent girls to engage in dieting behaviors and physical activity for weight loss was found regardless of current weight or physical activity status, and is not associated with more exercise on the part of the child (Balantekin, Savage, Marini, & Birch, 2014; Davison & Deane, 2010). The negative effects of all these factors can have long-term consequences. Body image disturbances and eating disorders early in life are associated with significantly greater risk of suffering from them and from co-occurring problems in adulthood (Berkman, Lohr, & Bulik, 2007).

Adolescence is a sensitive period for developing obesity and eating disorders, such as anorexia nervosa, bulimia nervosa, and binge-eating disorder (APA, 2013). Additionally, eating disorders manifest differently even between childhood and adolescent. For instance, purging is a significantly greater problem among adolescents with bulimia nervosa than among younger individuals with the same diagnosis (Peebles, Wilson, & Lock, 2006). Therefore, prevention and early intervention are likely the most effective approach for younger individuals, reducing psychopathological eating habits and unhealthy body weight early on.

Common Challenges in Children's Feeding and Eating

Just as personality and individual interests vary from child to child, so too do appetite, enthusiasm about food, and size, shape, and growth trajectories. Beginning in infancy, babies differ in the frequency and amount of nutrition they consume, as well as their silhouette and physical development. It is also important for parents to realize that size and shape are largely genetically determined; as such, some children are hereditarily predisposed to being larger than average and therefore any attempts to manipulate these traits could result in adverse physical and psychological consequences over the course of development (Satter, 2003). Furthermore, it is normal for babies to rapidly put on weight – in particular, fat – in the first year of life. Excess stores of fat are necessary for supporting the extensive physical and mental development characteristic of infancy and early childhood. Infants and children go through periods of relative variations in their size and figure over the course of development, the former corresponding to growth spurts and the latter to plateaus in growth. There is strong empirical evidence that restricting children's intake or ignoring hunger cues out of fear that one's child is fat can actually lead to overweight later in life (Satter, 2003; Savage, Fisher, & Birch, 2007).

At all stages of development, challenges in feeding and eating can occur. The two predominant concerns parents have about young children's eating involve what appears to be as **rigidity** in eating that leads to eating small amounts or a limited range of foods, or **overeating**, which parents fear may cause overweight. Among the first group, there are children who demonstrate highly selective eating that is often associated with higher anxiety in response to food, many aversions, and hypersensitivity to certain smells, flavors, and textures. Children who demonstrate levels of pickiness that appear to be abnormal by clinical standards may have *food neophobia*, which is a fear of new foods. Food neophobia peaks between the ages of 2 to 6 (Dovey, Staples, Gibson, & Halford, 2008), and appears to be highly inheritable (Cooke, Haworth, & Wardle, 2007). A more severe condition is Avoidant/Restrictive Food Intake Disorder (ARFID), an eating disorder that typically begins in early childhood, characterized by a prolonged failure to achieve age-appropriate nutritional and/or energy needs. ARFID significantly impedes children's growth and psychosocial functioning, and demands treatment (APA, 2013; Fitzpatrick, Forsberg, & Colborn, 2015). If parents observe that their child's growth is faltering, that their child's height and weight do not meet age and sex expectations, or that the child's limited menu hinders their participation in age-appropriate activities, they should explore with the therapist whether their child has indeed an eating disorder warranting specialized treatment.

On the other side of the spectrum are the children and adolescents whose parents are concerned that they will become overweight or obese. These feeding and eating concerns do not necessarily indicate adverse eating patterns that are not age- or developmentally-appropriate but can rather reflect parental concerns that their child overeats, eats in response to emotional stimuli, or is inclined toward high-fat, high-carbohydrates foods. The only way to determine whether one's child is overweight is by having a health professional examine his or her growth chart, which plots weight-for-height ratios for normed, age-adjusted norms. In younger children, percentile is often less important than trajectory – in other words, if a child is smoothly following a particular percentile curve, it likely indicates that he or she is developing naturally *for that child*. Should the parents feel worried, they or their pediatrician could plot their child's height and weight on a growth chart and mark every datapoint, beginning with the child's weight and length at birth. Growth charts are available online at the Centers for Disease Control and Prevention (CDC) website for U.S. norms, the Royal College of Paediatrics and Child Health (RCPCH) website for U.K. norms, etc. Many other countries publish growth charts based on country-specific standards.

Parents should consult with their pediatrician about any general medical problems that may be contributing to weight abnormalities, namely if a child's growth has unexplained, rapid shifts across percentile curves. To help children obtain a natural and healthy height and weight, parents should stick to the Division of Responsibility paradigm explained previously, where they provide access to food, set the times of meals and snacks, and decide where the food will be eaten, while children determine the frequency and quantity of what they eat. Nevertheless, it is important that parents realize that some children are genetically predisposed to having larger appetites and being "larger" by cultural and growth chart standards.

In Parent-Based Prevention, the therapist provides psychoeducation about developmental expectations and the variability immanent within these expectations. Should the parents describe their concerns about problems in the regulation of eating (undereating, overeating, rigidity in eating, emotional eating, etc.) and disclose controlling behaviors stemming from these concerns, the therapist facilitates improved understanding of normal and abnormal eating behaviors in children. As necessary, the therapist also helps the parents set the language and tools they can use with their children in challenging interactions, and help troubleshoot any contingencies.

Summary

This chapter has outlined the development of feeding and eating behaviors in children and adolescents. Overall, feeding, eating, and growth in infancy and childhood tend to follow the predictable trajectories outlined previously. However, due to genetic and cultural variability, these "normal" and "expected" practices and growth patterns are not identical for all children. As such, the Parent-Based Prevention therapist should address parental concerns and questions by providing parents with relevant information and supportive guidance in helping their child eat well and prosper.

References

Agras, W. S., Hammer, L. D., Huffman, L. C., Mascola, A., Bryson, S. W., & Danaher, C. (2012). Improving healthy eating in families with a toddler at risk for overweight: A cluster randomized controlled trial. *Journal of Developmental & Behavioral Pediatrics, 33*(7), 529–534. doi: 10.1097/DBP.0b013e3182618e1f.

American Psychiatric Association (APA). (2013). *Diagnostic and statistical manual of mental disorders* (5th edition). Washington, DC: APA.

Balantekin, K. N., Savage, J. S., Marini, M. E., & Birch, L. L. (2014). Parental encouragement of dieting promotes daughters' early dieting. *Appetite, 80,* 190–196.

Benowitz-Fredericks, C. A., Garcia, K., Massey, M., Vasagar, B., & Borzekowski, D. L. (2012). Body image, eating disorders, and the relationship to adolescent media use. *Pediatric Clinics of North America, 59*(3), 693–704.

Berkman, N. D., Lohr, K. N., & Bulik, C. M. (2007). Outcomes of eating disorders: A systematic review of the literature. *International Journal of Eating Disorders, 40,* 293–309. doi: 10.1002/eat.20369.

Bucchianeri, M. M., Arikian, A. J., Hannan, P. J., Eisenberg, M. E., & Neumark-Sztainer, D. (2013). Body dissatisfaction from adolescence to young adulthood: Findings from a 10-year longitudinal study. *Body Image, 10*(1), 1–7.

Cooke, L. J., Haworth, C., & Wardle, J. (2007). Genetic and environmental influences on children's food neophobia. *American Journal of Clinical Nutrition, 86*(2), 428–433.

Currie, C., Zanotti, C., Morgan, A., Currie, D., de Looze, M., Roberts, C., . . . & Barnekow, V. (2009). Social determinants of health and well-being among young people. Health Behaviour in School-aged Children (HBSC) *study: international report* from the 2009/2010 survey. *Health Policy for Children and Adolescents, No. 6.* World Health Organization report.

Davison, K. K., & Deane, G. D. (2010). The consequence of encouraging girls to be active for weight loss. *Social Science & Medicine, 70*(4), 518–525.

Dovey, T. M., Staples, P. A., Gibson, L., & Halford, J. C. G. (2008). Food neophobia and "picky/fussy" eating in children: A review. *Appetite*, *50*(2–3), 181–193. doi: 10.1016/j.appet.2007.09.009.

Feldman, R. (2012). Parent–infant synchrony: A biobehavioral model of mutual influences in the formation of affiliative bonds. *Monographs of the Society for Research in Child Development*, *77*, 42–51. doi:10.1111/j.1540-5834.2011.00660.x.

Fitzpatrick, K., Forsberg, S. E., & Colborn, D. (2015). Family-based therapy for Avoidant Restrictive Food Intake Disorder: Families facing food neo-phobias. In Loeb, K. L., Le Grange, D., & Lock, J. (Eds). *Family therapy for adolescent eating and weight disorders: New applications*. New York and Abingdon: Routledge.

Grummer-Strawn, L. M., Scanlon, K. S., & Fein, S. B. (2008). Infant feeding and feeding transitions during the first year of life. *Pediatrics*, *122*, S36–42. doi: 10.1542/peds.2008-1315d.

Innis, S. M. (2008). Dietary omega 3 fatty acids and the developing brain. *Brain Research*, *1237*, 35–43.

Labbok, M. (2008). Exploration of guilt among mothers who do not breastfeed: The physician's role. *Journal of Human Lactation*, *24*(1), 80–84.

Musher-Eizenman, D. R., de Lauzon-Guillain, B., Holub, S. C., Leporc, E., & Charles, M. A. (2009). Child and parent characteristics related to parental feeding practices: A cross-cultural examination in the US and France. *Appetite*, *52*(1), 89–95.

Neumark-Sztainer, D., Bauer, K. W., Friend, S., Hannan, P. J., Story, M., & Berge, J. M. (2010). Family weight talk and dieting: How much do they matter for body dissatisfaction and disordered eating behaviors in adolescent girls? *Journal of Adolescent Health*, *47*(3), 270–276.

Ogata, B. N., & Hayes, D. (2014). Position of the Academy of Nutrition and Dietetics: Nutrition guidance for healthy children ages 2 to 11 years. *Journal of the Academy of Nutrition and Dietetics*, *114*(8), 1257–1276.

Peebles, R., Wilson, J. L., & Lock, J. D. (2006). How do children with eating disorders differ from adolescents with eating disorders at initial evaluation? *Journal of Adolescent Health*, *39*(6), 800–805.

Satter, E. (2003). Children, the feeding relationship, and weight. *Maryland Medicine: MM – A Publication of MEDCHI, the Maryland State Medical Society*, *5*(3), 26–28.

Satter, E. (2012). *How to get your kid to eat: But not too much*. Boulder, CO: Bull Publishing Company.

Savage, J. S., Fisher, J. O., & Birch, L. L. (2007). Parental influence on eating behavior: Conception to adolescence. *The Journal of Law, Medicine & Ethics*, *35*(1), 22–34.

Stock, S., Miranda, C., Evans, S., Plessis, S., Ridley, J., Yeh, S., & Chanoine, J. P. (2007). Healthy Buddies: A novel, peer-led health promotion program for the prevention of obesity and eating disorders in children in elementary school. *Pediatrics*, *120*(4), e1059–e1068.

5   Two Families Seeking Help

This chapter, and the accompanying Chapters 17 and 18, outline the course of the Parent-Based Prevention program in two families. In this chapter we will sketch out session 1 with two couples, and in Chapters 17 and 18 we will return to these families to describe how the treatment unfolds.[1] We will begin with a review of the parents' background and their reasons for seeking treatment as well as factors precipitating and maintaining the effects of the parental eating disorder history on their parenting and their relationship with their child.

Family A: Stacey and Rob

Stacey is a 34-year-old woman. She reaches out to the therapist after reading a social media post about parents with eating disorder histories, where Parent-Based Prevention was described. On the initial phone screen, Stacey reports being diagnosed with anorexia nervosa at age 14. She received intermittent outpatient treatment for two years and her condition stabilized, but after her dad died when she was 16, she deteriorated, leading to being hospitalized for two weeks. When she was discharged from the hospital, she remembers deciding to get better: "I was motivated to put anorexia behind me and not cause additional pain to my family." Stacey received individual treatment on and off until age 25 and felt she was doing well, maintaining a healthy body weight. In college, Stacey was diagnosed with obsessive-compulsive disorder, for which she never received treatment. Stacey went to an Ivy League university and has a graduate degree. She currently reports high weight and shape concerns (WSCs), but few eating disorder symptoms: "I always plan what I am going to eat throughout the day. There is not much spontaneity there. I weigh myself every night to make sure I have not gained weight." Rob, 40 years old, and Stacey have been married for seven years. They met in a professional event when they were both in graduate school. Rob works in finance and reports no personal or family mental health history. The elder child of blue-collar working parents, Rob and his younger siblings were mostly raised by their grandparents, who lived around the corner. The couple have two children: Emma is a 5-year-old girl and Aidan is a boy of 18 months. Since Emma was born, Stacey – who by then had reached a high-level position in her firm – has become a full-time mom. To maintain the family's same life quality, Rob changed his workplace and now has a job that requires long hours and much traveling.

Stacey read the social media post about Parent-Based Prevention after a three-day camping trip the family went on. Accompanied by two other families with children in a similar age, Stacey and Rob observed that their children appear to be more argumentative during mealtimes than the other children. The three families cooked together each night, and Rob mentioned that Emma and Aidan appeared to eat larger quantities than the other children. In the last night, one of the other mothers told Stacey that Emma had asked if she "could borrow some snacks my parents don't think I should eat" so she could eat them after the family returned from the trip.

When the therapist met with the parents, she first oriented them to the goals and structure of the Parent-Based Prevention program. She also reminded them what she had explained on the initial phone call: that in this first session, after the joint discussion she will interview each parent separately. When the therapist asked the parents how she could help them, Stacey said that she sought treatment due to the constant conflicts with Emma around eating, especially during dinner. Most of the family's diet consists of beans and lentils, which Emma now refuses to eat. Stacey mentioned that although Emma's height and weight are currently in the 50th percentile,

> If I'll let her eat everything she fancies or the massive amounts she wants, she will definitely become overweight. I remember my siblings eating like this, and they are all obese today. Everyone in my family has diabetes or knee problems, and I just do not want my child to suffer from this type of problems.

Regarding her son, Aidan, Stacey said she is not worried: "He is a very active child, always running around. He sits for maybe two minutes at the dining table and is a light eater."

During the first 15 minutes of session 1, the therapist observed that Rob said very little. When she began interviewing him about his thoughts on why he thought they might need help, Rob replied:

> To tell you the truth, doctor – I better not say anything. Things are very tense over dinner. I tried in the past to be more involved, but when I realized I'm not helping but rather making things worse, I decided to leave feeding to Stacey. What my kids eat is not that important to me, and I know it is very important for Stacey. She reads books and blogs about children's nutrition, goes to classes, and consults with our pediatrician. I think she knows best what to do. When I suggest things like letting them eat what they want or going out for dinner,

it makes Stacey upset. I am so grateful that Stacey takes almost full responsibility of the house and the kids so that I can work.

When the therapist prompted Rob to share any additional thoughts about his involvement in feeding, Rob added:

> I guess it does not help very much that we have this culture at my firm where management meetings are always held in the evening, and two to three times a week we take out-of-town guests to corporate dinners. I don't really make it back home on time to be around at dinner and the kids' bedtime. But also, in all fairness, when I'm home or on weekends I feel like I'm not being very helpful. Feeding is sort of Stacey's territory and I try not to be disruptive.

When asked about the effects of her eating disorder on the children, Stacey said:

> I wish they would not have been affected, but if I'm being honest, they are. I know that I am happy with eating only two or three things for dinner. I have been eating almost the same dinner in the past two years – steamed broccoli, baked tofu, and cooked beans, and the kids cannot stand it by now. They demand other food; they sometimes even refuse coming to the dining table unless I offer them something else. And then I find something last minute, like crackers and cheese, which is not really dinner food. I find the evenings daunting because we argue over eating and food every night. In theory, I know that it is important they eat more varied foods, but I do not feel comfortable serving foods that I do not eat myself. It feels almost as if I am poisoning them. But then when we go to friends they eat like they have been starved – gobble down everything that's on the table, and then ask for seconds and thirds. I feel so embarrassed when this happens, but I also wonder if there is anything I should change. I'd like to let them try more foods and not be picky eaters like I might be, but I am afraid that they will know no limits. And I am also reluctant to cook things I do not feel comfortable with.

The therapist then turned to Rob and asked if he could share his thoughts. Rob said:

> I want my kids just not to think about it at all. They should be able to experiment with different tastes, seasoning, types of foods. I am sure they will not become overweight since they are so physically active. Isn't it normal for kids to like decent food? We have so many friends whose kids' diet is so narrow, and we are lucky to have kids who are kind of "foodies." I want to help make things better, but I do not know how.

I eat out every day, and then I get to eat as much food that I'd like and any kind that I fancy, without making it an issue. But I realize that me not eating dinner with my family leaves Stacey and the kids alone in this. I'm telling you that I do want to help and be more involved, but I do not know exactly how.

Then the therapist asked Rob: "What do you think may make it difficult for Stacey to provide more varied meals to your children?" After a short silent pause, Rob replied: "I understand where she is coming from. She is used to eat her few specific items, and I don't know if she has ideas how to make family meals more varied. I really feel for her."

At the therapist's request, the parents described a typical day in their home: everyone wakes up around 6:30am. Rob plays with the kids a bit before going to work, while Stacey gets ready. When Rob leaves for work, Stacey and Aidan take Emma to school, where she eats her first snack at 9am. At 11:30am Emma eats the food that Stacey has put in her lunch box, and Aidan – who is home-schooled – is fed by Stacey at about that time. Stacey picks up Emma at 2:30pm and, together with Aidan, they go to a playground, a park, or the library. Stacey typically offers the children some sliced fruit during that time. Dinner is served at around 5pm, and as mentioned above consists mostly of beans, tofu, and broccoli. In most cases, Rob is not at home by dinnertime and when he arrived, he has typically eaten elsewhere. Stacey usually eats after the children go to bed. During mealtimes, Emma eats independently but needs much prompting and encouragement, while Stacey feeds the collaborative Aidan. After outlining the feeding routine, Stacey added:

This is more how I think things should look like. What happens in reality is quite different, I must admit. It feels like the kids are in a constant quest to get their hands on food. They constantly ask for snacks, treats, candy, sandwiches, and whatnot. And when I surrender and give them any food before dinner, they keep asking for more. I never know if they are truly hungry or if it is just boredom or if they are in that age when kids like driving their moms crazy, but I feel like a bad parent for either "preventing" them from eating the food their body needs, or for being played with and sort of "maneuvered." And what bothers me lately is that Emma started climbing on the kitchen counter, opening cupboards, and grabbing the food she wants. I plan a nice afternoon and some quality time, but we keep on talking about food all the time.

The therapist said gently:

It sounds that both of you take your parenting very seriously and make many efforts in providing your children a nurturing environment. If

I understand correctly, you are pleased with many things about your family, but that there are some aspects of your family life you guys would like to change but are not sure how. Stacey – if I am reading this well, you want to expand your kids' diet and reduce the impact of food on your relationships. But you do not know how to do that. And Rob, if I understood correctly, you would like to support Stacey in her efforts to expand your kids' diet, but you are not sure how to go about that. Is this a fair description? Does this make sense?

As both parents nodded, the therapist replied, consciously using a confident tone: "Well, if this is the case then you have arrived at the right place. Parent-Based Prevention was designed especially for families struggling with similar dilemmas, and I am sure it can help you too!" After the therapist went on to explain about the family meal in the next session, she met with each parent separately.

When they talked privately, Rob shared with the therapist his frustration with Stacey's daily reports on how challenging feeding was that day, and on the kids' disapproval of the meals she had offered. Raised mostly by his grandparents, who lived close by, Rob and his siblings ate whatever food they were served, and he was never concerned about such issues as his children are. As Rob's father used to work many hours outside the home and on weekends, he sometimes wonders whether he lacks a solid model for being a dad. He also mentioned that he enjoys being married to his wife, hoping that the program will improve the couple's communication skills: "We could use some help with discussing potentially conflictual issues, which I typically avoid."

Stacey appeared slightly tense when she met alone with the therapist, who asked her how she was feeling about doing the program. Stacey responded:

> I am not sure about this program. I mean, I know that we must make some changes. But it freaks me out to think that I will need to change my ways and buy foods that I do not eat. And I also feel like I overcame my eating disorder and don't want to start talking about my past.

The therapist reassured Stacey that once the parents and she identified the areas the intervention will focus on, change would be gradual:

> We will discuss how your current eating habits may impact the interactions you have with your kids around eating. We might also want to discuss whether the OCD you mentioned earlier affects the feeding relationships and maybe other aspects of your role as a parent.

Stacey smiled: "OK, I am relieved that this program is less confrontative than I thought, and more hand-holding that I expected." Next, Stacey

Form no. 1 Session 1, Phase One: The Jones Family

PBP session 1 interventions	Information gathered	Possible targets of PBP
1 Introduce the Parent-Based Prevention program	Stacey, 34 y/o. History of AN, OCD. Currently reporting high WSC. Currently a stay-home mom. Rob, 40 y/o. No mental health history.	Explore how maternal symptoms (AN, OCD) affect parenting-related beliefs, concerns, and practices. Educate Rob about Stacey's symptoms.
2 Engage both parents in the intervention	Both parents are motivated and engaged.	Explore ways to involve Rob more at home, in feeding interactions and family meals.
3 Provide information about the likelihood of feeding and eating problems in children of parents with eating disorders as well as additional potential difficulties	Parents appeared accepting of the concepts described.	See above (item #1).
4 Focus the parental concerns and dilemmas that are pertinent to Parent-Based Prevention	Emma is rejecting foods offered by Mom, asking for greater variety.	Expand diversity of diet. Reassess daily routine and when food is offered throughout the day? Is breakfast eaten too late in the day? (Kids are awake for a few hours before first snack/meal.) Teach the division of responsibility.
5 Identify how the parental eating disorder is currently associated with parenting practices and child behaviors	No family meals though parents express interest in having them. Maternal rigidity in eating might affect children's intake.	Same as above.

Copyright material from Sadeh-Sharvit & Lock (2019), Parents with Eating Disorders, Routledge

#			
6	Separate the parent's eating disorder from other aspects of parental functioning	Stacey appears to be self-critical regarding many aspects, not just her parental functioning.	Nurture a stronger maternal self-esteem, self-efficacy, and spousal support.
7	Focus the parents on the individualized goals of the program	Parents agreed with goals stated above.	Review goals in session 3 in light of the family meal.
8	Ensure that both parents understand their importance in this therapeutic approach	Both parents appear on board, Rob wants to help but does not know how, given his commitments at work and conflict avoidance.	Facilitate more spousal support. Check how Rob can assist the process remotely.
9	Prepare for the family meal	OK. Rob: Wants to help but unsure whether he has skills for greater involvement in family life.	— Practice ways of remaining connected despite the work situation. Explore couple communication patterns in other domains.
10	Collect sensitive information about the family, including individual history and functioning and their likely impact on feeding behaviors and child eating.

(A) Parent 1
(B) Parent 2 | Stacey: High weight and shape concerns, guilt, and shame. Remembers negative experiences in origin family, her dad's death described as "traumatic." | Understand more if and how current parental functioning and schemas about maternal role are affected by past experiences. Explore options for individual treatment, should she be interested in such. |

---

* More information about the forms used in Parent-Based Prevention appears in Chapter 8.

described the events preceding the onset of her eating disorder, and particularly negative past events that shaped her internalization of a thinness ideal and her preference to eat few foods. She was tearful when sharing how her father's illness and death have led her to believe she needs to be vigilant and pessimistic, and how surprised she is when her children act differently or endorse more positive attitudes. Stacey shared her insights about the way that her past experiences affect her parenting, and told the therapist that she is motivated to learn more in the program.

Following the first session, the therapist reviewed her notes, which she recorded on Form no. 1.

Family B: Dave and Gabby

Dave, 31 years old, and his wife, Gabby, 32 years old, contacted the therapist requesting help in developing healthy eating habits in their twin boys, Liam and Mason, aged 8. Dave's cousin completed Parent-Based Prevention a month before, and she had told him about it during a recent phone conversation. Dave and Gabby, who have been concerned about their children's eating habits ever since their pediatrician mentioned Liam's weight, decided to reach out to a Parent-Based Prevention therapist in their area, in hopes of learning how to foster a healthful lifestyle in their family.

The therapist sent the parents links to online surveys to complete prior to the meeting (the assessments recommended for use in Parent-Based Prevention are described in Chapter 17). As he reviewed the surveys, the therapist found that Dave received high scores on the eating disorder assessment, indicating a possible present binge-eating disorder. Gabby reported high WSCs, but she did not endorse any eating psychopathology symptoms nor any compensatory behaviors. Additionally, both parents reported symptoms meeting criteria for moderate anxiety, and Dave replied "yes" to questions inquiring about current suicidal ideation and past suicidal ideation and attempts.

When the parents arrived at the clinic for the first session, which took place at a late evening time, Dave said: "Thank God you have a coffee machine here at the building." The therapist acknowledged how it must be difficult for parents of young children to meet so late in the day, and both parents replied: "Don't get us started!" The therapist introduced himself and his training in both eating disorders treatment and working with parents with eating disorder histories. Then, he asked the parents to introduce themselves. Dave opened, sharing that he has been suffering from binge-eating disorder since high school but was never officially diagnosed. When he started dating Gabby, she suggested that the eating behaviors that caused him such distress are part of a "condition," as he called it; Gabby's older sister has also had binge-eating disorder since her early teenage years. Gabby added at that point: "I was able to convince Dave that BED exists, but I still have not been able to convince him that treatment for BED exists!" and both parents laughed. Dave mentioned he attributes his behaviors to "very low self-esteem and constantly comparing myself to others and second-guessing myself," and that if he had solved these issues, he may not have struggled with food that much. Although Dave studied computer science at an Ivy League university and was offered a position with a tech company while still in school, he described feeling intimidated by his co-workers, whom he perceives as more knowledgeable and confident than he might ever be. But although he has never been in treatment himself, Dave was the one suggesting the intervention to Gabby after speaking with his cousin about her experience in the program. Dave explained his interest in the program as a result of his wondering whether his sons' eating behaviors are healthy: "I recognize the young me in them and I don't think that's a good thing." Gabby described herself as "feeling terrible about my body from whenever I could remember." Growing up in a family where everyone was overweight and constantly on a diet, Gabby said there was no other option for her but to develop "a very negative perception of my body," as she put it:

> I always felt fat, always hoped I would be able to feel satisfied with less food. But in the past few years I eat mostly healthy foods, try to work out, and try to feel OK with the way I look.

Gabby works as a high school teacher and loves her job, where she feels appreciated and respected.

The parents reported the twins were born after many IVF cycles, and that during the pregnancy both parents gained about 40 pounds each. Gabby nursed the children until they were 12 months old, "and when we weaned them, things started going off-balance," said Dave. He described often feeling frustrated when trying to feed their children:

> It is like they are either not hungry when we think it's time to eat, or they always want something else than what we have planned, or that until we finish fixing dinner, they somehow manage to get their hands on some kind of an unhealthy treat and chew on it.

Gabby added: "I am not sure we provide really nutritious meals, and that we have our veggies and protein balanced. And I would love to learn how to get our children to eat less carbohydrates, fat, and sugar."

When the therapist interviewed the parents about their children's routine, he noticed that the parents described a pattern of grazing and snacking along the day: the children wake up at about 6:30am and drink fat-free milk. They eat some cereal before leaving for school, where they receive a morning snack, lunch, and an afternoon snack. Dave is the one typically picking up the kids from school, and finds them mostly hungry, asking for something to eat. Dinner is served at home typically at 6pm, but the kids often refuse the foods offered, ask for something else, or claim they are not hungry. The kids go to bed around 8:30pm, and the parents did not mention any difficulties with initiating and maintaining sleep. After the kids are asleep, the parents eat their own dinner, sometimes together but mostly separately, at different times, sometimes at different rooms in the house – Gabby eats in front of the TV while Dave sits at the kitchen table. After reviewing the family's routine, Gabby added:

> Another thing that is bothering me and I would like to change is that we use food to soothe our kids and distract them when they are tense or bored or when we are on a long drive or running some errands. We also do it at home when we have work to do and need the kids to stay busy for a while. I am always wondering about how many calories they put into their bodies, and I feel very guilty.

Before the joint part of session 1 ended, the therapist summarized the meeting, thanking the parents for openly sharing their experiences and dilemmas. He noted that he realized the parents were interested in establishing strategies to develop healthy eating habits in their children and worrying that some of the practices currently carried out at home might lead to unwanted consequences. The therapist added that while the parents are concerned about calories, he is thinking about the use of food to distract and entertain the children, in a way that may not be in concert with their hunger and satiety cues. Offering food when Liam and Mason are fussy or impatient may also impede the kids' ability to develop self-regulation skills. Both parents nodded and asked if these were issues the therapist would be able to guide them on, and he conceded, assuring them that these goals are achievable in the context of Parent-Based Prevention.

Before concluding the joint part of the session, the therapist asked the parents if he could ask them a few things about the questionnaires they had filled prior to the first meeting. He first turned to Dave: "I noticed that you reported having self-harm thoughts in the past. Can you please tell me more about them?" Dave replied:

> Yes, there were times in my life when I felt hopeless and depressed. I was not sure that I was able to push through another day. My girlfriend in high school broke up with me and I swallowed some pills, but fortunately nothing happened, and I woke up the next morning with a headache. Today I rarely have these thoughts, but I cannot say that they are completely gone.

The therapist thanked Dave for his openness and asked Gabby whether she was aware of these issues. Gabby replied that she was familiar with Dave's thoughts, and that she had tried encouraging him to seek individual treatment. The therapist then asked Dave whether these emotions have ever impacted his parenting behaviors, and Dave responded:

There are times when I'm feeling down and care to see no one, not even my kids and my wife. But I try to cope with these experiences and make every effort [to make sure] they do not ruin my time with the kids. It's not always easy, and sometimes I eat to forget these feelings, which might not be a good thing, I know.

The therapist interjected:

You know, Dave, we are not here to judge you. You found out about this program and you brought your family here. This is a huge effort already, and I applaud you for making it. I see that both of you are devoted parents, and that you both are doing your best to help Liam and Mason live a happy, healthful life. As I mentioned earlier when I outlined the game plan of this program, some of the mental wellness issues we have just discussed might be relevant to review again during the Third Phase, that is sessions nine to twelve.

The therapist then proceeded to orient the parents to the family meal in session 2, and concluded the meeting with an optimistic tone, saying: "I am glad you chose to arrive here, and I am certain you and your children can benefit from this program!"

In the separate interviews the therapist conducted with each parent, Dave said:

I am not sure that in the meeting with Gabby in the room I was completely honest about the way that I've been eating recently. I feel ashamed and guilty for not being able to control it better. But I have been stopping at a fast food restaurant almost every afternoon before picking up the kids. Every morning I begin by promising to myself that I will not do that, but then I find myself again driving to this fast food place again.

When the therapist asked what was preventing Dave from sharing this in the joint part of the session, he replied: "Gabby has known me for years and has always been so supportive. I feel so bad letting her down like that." The therapist asked if Dave was willing to share the information about his recent eating habits with Gabby, and Dave agreed. The therapist suggested that Dave disclose it before the next meeting, and Dave consented to doing so.

In the personal interview with Gabby, she spoke about being unhappy with work for a while and hoping to go back to school for a career change. But Gabby also mentioned that she felt "things at home will not work well if I am not around enough." When the therapist asked what she meant, Gabby expressed her concerns about laying too much of a burden on Dave, whom she sometimes perceives as "psychologically fragile," likely to experience more depressive symptoms when he is swamped with responsibilities

Form no. 1 Session 1, Phase One: The Smiths

PBP session 1 interventions	Information gathered	Possible targets of PBP
1 Introduce the Parent-Based Prevention program	Dave, 31 y/o, history of BED and MDD/ Dysthymia, suicidal ideation/ 1 attempt in his teenage years. Gabby, 32, high WSC. High school teacher. Parents married. Liam & Mason, 8 y/o. Elementary schoolers.	Assess whether parental symptoms affect parenting practices, and how.
2 Engage both parents in the intervention	Both parents interested, no previous history of eating disorder treatment.	Remain mindful whether the barriers for seeking individual treatment will impact treatment engagement in PBP.
3 Provide information about the likelihood of feeding and eating problems in children of parents with eating disorders as well as additional potential difficulties	Both parents on board, understanding the importance of the program.	Add psychoeducation/handouts about related parental mental health issues?
4 Focus the parental concerns and dilemmas that are pertinent to Parent-Based Prevention	Parents' concerns: using food for non-nutritional purposes, reducing % of processed foods, do kids eat nutritious meals?	1) Teach the kids emotion–regulation strategies that do not include food. 2) Reduce grazing, establish an eating routine of 3 meals, 2–3 snacks. 3) Psychoeducation about pediatric nutrition. 4) Discuss fat-talk, the importance of supportive language. 5) Concerns about where eating and how eating. No designated space for meals, therefore children eat in front of the TV, on a small table that seats them only, etc.
5 Identify how the parental eating disorder is currently associated with parenting practices and child behaviors	Both parents have high WSC, would like to minimize shaming comments and conflict during meals. Dad's current binge-eating symptoms might affect feeding practices?	

6 Separate the parent's eating disorder from other aspects of parental functioning

Parental functioning experienced as satisfactory for both parents, otherwise than the ED, feeding-related issues.

7 Focus the parents on the individualized goals of the program

Mostly in agreement with goals #1–3 above.

8 Ensure that both parents understand their importance in this therapeutic approach

Both parents on board.

9 Prepare for the family meal

10 Collect sensitive information about the family, including individual history and functioning and their likely impact on feeding behaviors and child eating.

Rationale and guidelines explained.
Dave: secret daily binges, mostly prior to picking up the kids from school.
* *Said it's OK to share with wife, agreed to have a conversation with her prior to the next session.*

(A) Parent 1
(B) Parent 2

Gabby: wants to make a professional change but fears Dave cannot handle more burden.
* *Asked not to share with husband now, understood this topic might not be within the framework of this program (but need to reassess in Phase Three, given their progress by then).*

6) Discuss possible triggers (work environment? difficulties caring for the kids in the afternoon?). Explore in later sessions.

7) Explore social networks and support systems.

* More information about the forms used in Parent-Based Prevention appears in Chapter 8.

and commitments. The therapist inquired whether Gabby had ever shared with Dave her frustration with work, and she replied she did express exasperation about the school where she was currently working, but always minimized how bad it actually was. The therapist asked Gabby whether this was something she was willing to share with Dave, and she refused, asking the therapist not to mention it in the meetings: "I wanted you to know it so that you have all the background information, but I don't want to add to the drama." The therapist replied:

> Thank you for trusting me with this information. I understand that you do not want to disclose it to your husband and that is perfectly fine. We are here to help you reduce negative health outcomes in your children, and that is the focus of the program. However, if you later feel that in Phase Three you'd like to discuss your career decisions and how they might affect your family, it could be relevant material to work on. Many parents who complete the first and second phases of Parent-Based Prevention feel that their communication patterns have improved, and they use these skills to converse on other dilemmas and concerns they have in other spheres. But I completely respect your request and will not share this information with Dave before you allow me to.

When session 1 with the parents concluded, the therapist reviewed the Parent-Based Prevention Form no. 1 he had completed during the meeting, and spent a few moments thinking about ways to nurture healthier habits in this family.

Note

1 All cases illustrated in this book are an amalgamation of many families and individuals the authors have worked with. All identifying details have been considerably changed such that the original individuals will not be able to recognize themselves in the text.

6 Overview of Parent-Based Prevention

This chapter provides a general outline of the Parent-Based Prevention program. The opening chapters of this book described the unique characteristics, challenges, and needs that individuals with eating disorder histories might experience as they build their own families and raise their children. Chapter 5 portrayed how two couples may present at the initial session, illuminating their strengths and resources as well as their concerns and dilemmas. Chapters 6 to 12 will delineate the intervention session by session, over the course of the three phases of the program.

Parent-Based Prevention is a short-term, semi-structured preventive intervention that focuses on reducing the risk of feeding and eating problems and broad development adversities in the young children of parents with eating disorders. The program is comprised of three phases; each of them aims to achieve unique goals. It involves twelve therapist-led sessions over approximately six months. The participants of these meetings with the therapist vary depending on the topic and focus of the session. Table 6.1 presents the outline of the Parent-Based Prevention program, with respect to the focus of the meetings and their scheduling.

In Phase One, the therapist works with the parents to assess the individualized risk portfolio of the family and define the goals of the intervention. This is carried out through focused interviews with the parents, both together and individually, as well as a family meal attended by all family members.

Meetings in Phase Two concentrate on the family's reciprocal transactions around eating, particularly parental cognitions around shape and weight, and their impact on feeding and eating practices. Most meetings in this phase are individual meetings with the affected parent (i.e., the one with a current eating disorder or a history of one). Usually there is only one couple meeting during this phase. Through a series of guided behavioral experiments, the parents are directed in changing unhealthy patterns in their children's eating habits; the therapist and the parent in attendance identify key challenges to promoting healthy eating behaviors and positive body image in the children. Next, they strategize a behavioral change to

Table 6.1 An outline of the sessions in Parent-Based Prevention

Week	Parent-Based Prevention program	Focus of the phase/session(s)
	Phase One: Setting up joint goals	Evaluating the family's attitudes and practices relating to body image, diet, and eating habits, and planning the intervention goals.
1	Session 1: Gearing up for treatment	Formulating the parental concerns and dilemmas as well as barriers for establishing healthy eating habits among the children.
2	Session 2: The family meal	A family meal meeting held at the therapist's office, providing important observational information about the family behaviors and communications regarding feeding and eating.
3	Session 3: Embracing change	Analyzing the family meal considering previous discussions and creating a blueprint of the behavioral change required for reducing maladaptive cognitions and behaviors.
	Phase Two: Distinguishing the parental eating disorder from parental functioning	Facilitating desired changes in the family's habits, practices, and transactions around feeding, eating, and related communication.
		The sessions in Phase Two focus on planning, assessing, and adjusting the behavioral changes aimed at reducing adverse feeding and eating practices.
		Sessions 4–5 and 7–8 are held with the affected parent alone, while session 6 is a conjoint meeting.
4	Session 4: Individual meeting with the affected parent	
5	Session 5: Individual meeting with the affected parent	
6	Session 6: Conjoint meeting with both parents	
7	Session 7: Individual meeting with the affected parent	
8	Session 8: Individual meeting with the affected parent	
	Phase Three: Enhancing parental efficacy and family resilience	Reinforcing the changes that have been achieved in the intervention thus far, while zooming out from the food, eating, and body sphere to identify and target additional risk factors impacting the family.
9	Session 9: Conjoint meeting	The meetings in Phase Three center on enhancing parental learning from the behavioral experiments, reinforcing their accomplishments in creating a more healthful environment, and harnessing the improved parental and spousal functioning to impact broader key issues.
10	–	
11	Session 10: Conjoint meeting	
12	–	
13	Session 11: Conjoint meeting	The sessions are held with both parents, every other week.
14	–	
15	Session 12: Conjoint meeting and Termination	

be tested at home in the following week. Although the other parent does not participate in the meetings, it is emphasized that the suggested change will be such that includes both parents' involvement in engineering the expected modifications. The adapted behaviors are later evaluated in the following session with the goal of creating a longstanding effect.

In Phase Three, the parents meet for the final four sessions, which are intended to translate the insights achieved in the program up to that point into revisiting additional challenges they have in their parenting, beyond their children's diet, body image, and weight. For instance, parents who had developed strategies for setting appropriate boundaries in the feeding interactions with their children may now want to apply these recently acquired skill sets in responding differently to their child's temper tantrums. Alternatively, parents may be interested in utilizing their improved communication capabilities in engineering a different family organization that will better support a child's learning difficulties. The aim is to improve parental efficacy and co-parenting strategies to broader aspects of the child's life and the parent-child relationship. This is done with respect to the short- and long-term risks and resilience of the child. Whereas meetings in Phases One and Two are scheduled once a week, sessions in Phase Three take place fortnightly.

Although the general structure is predefined, Parent-Based Prevention can help parents work through a range of potential problems in their children's development. Hence, this is a modular treatment, in which the therapist and the parents conjointly prioritize the goals for the intervention and then work through them according to the stage in the program.

The therapist should begin every session with grounding the patients on where they are in the intervention and what the agenda of the meeting is. Each session, the therapist follows a set of prescribed interventions, which appear in forms numbered 1–5. The sequence of these interventions is predetermined, and they are designed to lead the discussions in a focused manner so that the program is optimally efficient. These forms are designed to assist the therapist in tracking progress during the meetings and document the central content that is derived from the discussions with the parents. Throughout this book examples on how these interventions unfold in therapy as well as key metaphors and analogues that are helpful with families are provided.

7 Adapting Parent-Based Prevention to Diverse Family Structures and Backgrounds

This book describes a preventive intervention designed to help parents positively influence the health outcomes of their children. Families have diverse structures: parents married to one another, parents cohabitating but not married, single-parent, divorced, separated, three generations living under the same roof, and so on. Families can also have diverse backgrounds, challenging therapists to expand their knowledge, expectations, and strategies. This chapter provides some ideas and methods for adapting Parent-Based Prevention in the aforementioned situations.

Adapting Parent-Based Prevention to Sole-Parent Families

Many of the cases that are illustrated in this book, but not all of them, describe Parent-Based Prevention in intact families, where two parents collaborate in engineering a healthier lifestyle in their children. As such, many of the procedures utilized by the therapist assume that both parents are available to support one another and that they can convene for family meals, share grocery shopping and food preparation responsibilities, and take over each other's duties when one of the parents needs a timeout. In some situations, there is no available second parent for various reasons, including that this is a single-parent family, or that the other parent resides in a different country for the duration of the program. The main challenge in adapting Parent-Based Prevention to single-parent families is helping parents identify, create, and nurture a support system that can help implement the program and leverage its benefits.

The following case may help demonstrate this adaptation:

> Michelle, a 50-year-old woman, sought treatment in hopes of preventing future eating and weight management problems in her 10-year-old son, Leo. Until five years ago, Michelle and Leo lived with Frank, Michelle's former boyfriend, and his son, Jasper. When Michelle and Frank separated, he moved to another state with his son, and they had not been in contact since. Given that Leo was gestated using a

sperm donation and that Michelle's family lived abroad, as a full-time working parent she was worried about "committing to a program that adds more things for me to work on, when I am already very busy." Dr. Gulati, who was Michelle's therapist, suggested that the intervention would focus on targeting a few maladaptive behaviors that were feasible to revisit within the context of the time-limited intervention. Michelle expressed concerns over a few issues: first, Leo commonly ate in front of the TV while Michelle got ready for work or was doing house chores. Michelle reported intense negative emotions around Leo's eating habits, including feeling guilty, frazzled, inadequate, and out of control. Second, Leo had recently been inquiring more about his biological father, and Michelle was not sure how to respond to his questions. Third, Michelle had concerns about poor modeling behavior; she expressed a desire to improve her own eating so that her son improved his habits but at the same time admitted to feeling overwhelmed by this task. The therapist validated Michelle's motivation, and emphasized she appeared eager to make changes and experiment with new methods. He explored possible barriers to follow through with the behavioral experiments. In response, Michelle expressed her anxiety about doing so due to difficulties tolerating her son's distress. For instance, Michelle was worried that she would have trouble refusing Leo's requests to eat while watching TV. Dr. Gulati discussed with Michelle the importance of setting attainable goals, and recommended they focus on improving her child's eating behavior as an initial target and reserve her other important goals for later sessions or for subsequent parental counseling after she concluded this intervention. Therefore, they collaboratively decided to start addressing family meal times and the location thereof. Given Michelle's immense anxiety related to this task, Dr. Gulati encouraged her to seek help in making this change, at least in the first few weeks. While brainstorming ideas for identifying and enlisting such support, Michelle mentioned Leo's sitter, a college student living nearby. Michelle and Dr. Gulati planned that Michelle would reach out to this woman and ask her to help out preparing for the behavioral experiment, and possibly participating in the first family meals.

Single parents may be more vulnerable to challenges in addressing and intervening in how their eating disorder models their parenting behaviors and interactions with their children (Bakker & Karsten, 2013). Some divorced, separated, or single-parent families may also find it difficult soliciting instrumental and emotional social support. However, when providing Parent-Based Prevention to those families, the therapist should remember that the parents have gained successful parenting experiences; the vast majority of parents arrive to the program when their children are weaned and toilet trained, agree to have their seatbelt fastened or buckle up independently, behave appropriately in social situations, and have largely positive interactions with their parents. The therapist should harness these accomplishments and sense of parental self-efficacy and help parents recognize their capabilities to spearhead changes in their children's behaviors. Capitalizing on already-secured parental skills will help optimize the impact of the program on improving child and parent outcomes (Jones & Prinz, 2005).

Providing Parent-Based Prevention in a Culturally-Sensitive Mindset

Eating disorders span various genders, sexual orientations, cultures, and family structures. Cross-cultural issues may impact the roles parents and children assume within the family, developmental expectations from children, and cultural feeding and meal preparation practices, to name a few key factors addressed in Parent-Based Prevention. The therapist should also be open to the opportunity of different gender roles in parenting and diverse weight and shape concerns. Additionally, when the therapist and patients identify with different social and cultural groups and have undergone different acculturation processes, this shapes the patient–therapist interactions: topics that may be perceived as taboo, the degree of self-reflection with strangers, varying levels of compliance with authority figures such as the therapist, and so on (Maxie, Arnold, & Stephenson, 2006).

Parent-Based Prevention is designed to allow tailoring of the program to the individual parents and their family. As such, the program inherently grants the therapist and the parents the opportunity to find solutions that are mindful to the ecological niche in which the family functions. For instance, when patients appear unforthcoming or reluctant to discuss certain topics, the therapist should consider that speaking about mental health issues should be done in a culturally-appropriate manner. Further, adapting a non-stereotyping mindset, especially about gender roles, is likely effective when discussing parents' beliefs and communications. For example, not all Western mothers identify with cultural eating, shape, and weight norms; not all Western fathers arrive late from work and expect a cooked dinner; and many children will happily stop playing a videogame and engage in more physically-active play should they be encouraged by their parents to do so.

The following vignette reflects the challenges in providing Parent-Based Prevention in a culturally-sensitive manner to parents with eating disorder histories who seek help with their parenting:

> Dr. Rubinfeld was trained in Parent-Based Prevention in his previous workplace, a hospital-based outpatient unit for eating disorders in a large North American city. When he relocated with his family to another country, he was surprised by what his patients told him they served their

children. Dr. Rubinfeld felt he was not familiar enough with the norms of the country in which he now practiced to know whether his patients' description of their family's diet represented uncommon feeding practices or an unhealthy lifestyle. He was also confused when his patients did not understand the metaphors he had used during the session. In his weekly consultation meeting with his colleagues, all of whom had been trained in Parent-Based Prevention and delivered the intervention in their private practices, Dr. Rubinfeld described his struggles with helping the family: "I feel very frustrated by not fully understanding the family dynamics of the clients I see. Some parents are reluctant to speak about their family of origin and deny any past negative eating or body shaming experiences they had as teenagers. Therefore, I feel limited in my ability to help them. With another family, I suggested that the children might express greater interest in the food they are served if they are involved in planning and preparing the meals, but both parents insisted that cooking is the parents' responsibility and that their children are in any case too busy with afterschool activities." The consultation team helped Dr. Rubinfeld explore whether his patients' responses were related to their cultural upbringing and the divergent roles of and expectations from different family members. His peers proposed Dr. Rubinfeld considers a culturally-cognizant explanation for the issues with which his present clients contend.

This chapter provides a brief overview of possible issues therapists providing Parent-Based Prevention may encounter in their practice. While increasing sensitivity to all aspects of the family's life is an important task, we bear in mind that this is a preventive intervention whose fundamental assumption is that parents seeking it may already experience present adversities in their children as well as heightened shame and stress. Thus, empowering parents inevitably involves understanding their perspective and the social microcosm in which they function, their competencies, and unique challenges (Preyde, 2008).

Additional Family Contexts Requiring Unique Considerations

When Both Parents are Struggling with a Mental Disorder

Many individuals in Western society find themselves pondering over the types, quantities, and timing of foods they provide their young children. Together with more common lifestyle and work cultures that impact parents to work longer hours and live in greater geographic distance from their extended families, parents have less social support and time spent with their kids than ever before, and they are more isolated than previous generations. Co-occurrence of mental disorders in both parents puts greater strain on the family and may hinder parental self-efficacy. Some comorbidities, such as substance use disorders, may need to be managed independently while the parents are receiving Parent-Based Prevention, should the clinician think both interventions can be delivered concurrently. Nonetheless, this context invites some preparation prior to beginning treatment. The therapist should review with both parents, conjointly and individually, their views as to the unique and synergetic challenges their mental disorders impose on their parenting practices. For instance, fathers with anxiety disorders may be reluctant to engage in some of the food and eating behaviors exposures that the mothers would like them to be involved in; one parent's mood disorder may amplify the second parent's need of spousal support and intimacy during the program; coexisting personality disorders of both parents may compromise spousal communication over their child-rearing behaviors. However, the therapist and parents should bear in mind the central focus of the Parent-Based Prevention program, which is improving child feeding. During Phase Three of the program, when additional risks for the child's healthy development are recognized, the therapist should help the parents select aspects of their co-parenting that they would like to work on. For these families, future parental counseling that reinforces the achievements already made in the treatment is often advised.

Families with Infants

In the case of families that have infants or toddlers who are not capable of acquiring sufficient autonomy in their eating, only some of the strategies that are core to Parent-Based Prevention may be applicable. However, as Parent-Based Prevention focuses on the transition from parent-oriented feeding to more autonomous eating that relies on the child's age-appropriate initiative, many of the interventions may not be suitable for children who cannot yet self-manage their eating. Therefore, most of the behavioral experiments and discussions will not be relevant for the work with the parents of infants. In the case of parents with infants, it may be best to see such parents as psychologically preparing for the gradual shift in their child toward more independence, although they may not be able to apply the program with their young children.

Families with Adolescents

Prevention and early intervention are considered highly effective at the developmental stage when eating habits are shaped. Older children of parents with eating disorders may have observed the parental symptoms or have developed their own concerns and maladaptive eating behaviors. When parents are trying to make changes in their family's diet and meal routine, adolescents may be perceived by their parents to be less amendable than younger children, as the former typically eat more food not prepared at home (e.g., they buy lunch at the school cafeteria), and their eating habits and preferences are more entrenched. However, supporting healthier body image and eating practices is possible even when parents feel they have less impact on their adolescents compared to younger children. Parents may want to consult with the therapist regarding their dilemmas about their older children. In addition, the change in feeding practices would likely affect the eating habits of older siblings, and the parents will seek the therapist's guidance on how to build healthy habits in children of varying ages. Healthful, balanced eating habits can be formed and modeled at any age; we suggest that the therapist allows the parents to share any questions or difficulties regarding their older children, and use clinical judgment, expertise in eating disorders prevention, and knowledge of developmental processes to provide the parents with guidance in the rearing of their older children.

References

Bakker, W., & Karsten, L. (2013). Balancing paid work, care and leisure in post-separation households: A comparison of single parents with co-parents. *Acta Sociologica*, 56(2), 173–187. doi: 10.1177/0001699312466178.

Jones, T. L., & Prinz, R. J. (2005). Potential roles of parental self-efficacy in parent and child adjustment: A review. *Clinical Psychology Review*, 25(3), 341–363. doi: 10.1016/j.cpr.2004.12.004.

Maxie, A. C., Arnold, D. H., & Stephenson, M. (2006). Do therapists address ethnic and racial differences in cross-cultural psychotherapy? *Psychotherapy: Theory, Research, Practice, Training*, 43(1), 85. doi: 10.1037/0033-3204.43.1.85.

Preyde, M. (2008). Mothers of very preterm infants. *Social Work in Health Care*, 44(4), 65–83. doi: 10.1300/J010v44n04_05.

8 Treatment Planning and Real-Time Evaluation Using Assessment Tools

Changing behaviors, cognitions, emotions, attitudes, relationships and the like by means of a behavioral intervention is a massive undertaking. It involves careful self-observation to gauge undesired qualities in the person's psyche, their family, and environment. But changing one's ways necessitates an ongoing evaluation whether the intervention is effectively facilitating the anticipated change. As such, delivering an intervention likely incorporates the identification of patterns and the contexts in which they arise as well as testing whether and how modifications to those patterns progress patients towards their goal (Darcy & Sadeh-Sharvit, 2017). This practice of establishing clinical care on client information collected throughout the intervention, often referred to as measurement-based care, is becoming widespread in behavioral interventions in clinical practice rather than clinical research only (Scott & Lewis, 2015).

One practical way to portray the patient's condition prior to beginning the program, and the change trajectories throughout the intervention, is by using standardizes assessment tools in several timepoints. Self-report tools are a relatively simple, low-cost (or free), and straightforward method for assessing the patient's condition. They allow better real-time monitoring, namely allowing the individual to record their cognitions, emotions, and behaviors, their triggers, and their consequences. Often times, when parents arrive to the session they cannot accurately recall their mindset during a conflict with their children, or the events preceding the conflict. Sometimes, parents may feel uncomfortable sharing important information in the presence of their partner, so that his or her feelings will not be hurt. Moreover, individuals may have a hard time recalling or summarizing their children's health-related behaviors over the week and recording them using the same uniform survey helps observing patterns beyond parental awareness.

An important consideration in advance of using measurement-based care is identifying the key issues the therapist would like to monitor. Do the individualized goals of the intervention include improving access for more nutritious food? increasing sense of parental self-efficacy? reducing mealtime conflicts between parents and children, or between parents? The answer to this question directs the type, quantity, and recurrence of assessments throughout the program. In Parent-Based Prevention we have recognized several factors therapists may want to consider evaluating. First, parental feeding patterns are likely key to the success of the intervention. Since parental practices such as food monitoring and restriction and pressure to eat (as well as pressure to engage in physical activity) have been found to compromise healthy eating and exercise in children (Clark, Goyder, Bissell, Blank, & Peters, 2007), these behaviors are pertinent to the success of the intervention. Second, collecting information on children's eating habits, physical activity, and screen time is an effective way of assessing whether parental efforts translate into observable behaviors. Asking the parents to sum the number of daily meals and snacks as well as weekly family meals and screen hours, provided a reasonable estimate of therapeutic progress. Third, change over time (or lack thereof) in mechanisms precipitating the success of the program, such as improved parental self-efficacy and spousal communication skills, is information the therapist can utilize within the intervention. Fourth, although they are not directly targeted in Parent-Based Prevention due to the program being short-term, measuring parental eating and co-occurring symptoms provides context for the intervention. Finally, some clinicians are interested in evaluating factors associated with the therapeutic alliance and the credibility and acceptancy of the intervention among their patients.

Incorporating tools for measurement-based care is easier than ever in our (Digital) Information Age. Clinicians delivering Parent-Based Prevention may want to search for tools that have demonstrated good psychometric qualities, such as high reliability and validity. We recommend therapists consider using tools that are available online and at no cost. Typically, the self-report surveys that are featured and made available by prominent health organizations (e.g., the World Health Organization, the National Health Organization, Mental Health America, National Eating Disorder Association) have likely been audited by experts and therefore recommended.

Evaluation of the effects of treatment is not in the least carried out by the therapist alone. Rather, routine assessments should be incorporated in the intervention and inform it. One of the key assumptions of Parent-Based Prevention is that the shared decision-making process empowers parents and helps them better accomplish their goals. When the therapist communicates with the patients about the results of the surveys, asks for clarifications, and facilitates a more open dialogue with them, Parent-Based Prevention is further personalized and made more relevant to parents and their families, thereby improving the care provided to patients in their important role as parents.

References

Clark, H. R., Goyder, E., Bissell, P., Blank, L., & Peters, J. (2007). How do parents' child-feeding behaviours influence child weight? Implications for childhood obesity policy. *Journal of Public Health*, 29(2), 132–141. doi: 10.1093/pubmed/fdm012.

Darcy, A., & Sadeh-Sharvit, S. (2017). Mobile device applications for assessment and treatment of the eating disorders. Invited chapter for Agras, S. W., & Robinson , A. (Eds) *The Oxford handbook of eating disorders* (2nd edition). Oxford: Oxford University Press.

Scott, K., & Lewis, C. C. (2015). Using measurement-based care to enhance any treatment. *Cognitive and Behavioral Practice*, 22(1), 49–59. doi: 10.1016/j.cbpra.2014.01.010.

9 Phase One

Setting Up Joint Goals

In Phase One, the parents and the therapist join forces in evaluating the family's beliefs and behaviors around body image and eating habits and identifying the targets of the intervention. During Phase One, the discussions focus on reevaluating feeding and habits, the family's organization around eating and food, and any additional unique risks that are pertinent to Parent-Based Prevention. To establish a rapport and utilize the sessions effectively, the purpose of the intervention should be clearly explained to the parents. By the end of Phase One, the therapist should be able to: make a case formulation of the family and the targets of treatment; work out with the parents a list of the issues to discuss and possibly change; and make sure that the parents received some psychoeducation on the foundations of healthy eating habits in children and that they are familiar with the Division of Responsibility model.

The goals of Phase One are:

1 Engage both parents in therapy. This is an important overarching target since parental perceptions may not be initially aligned. Gaps in knowledge of eating disorders and family practices important for healthful habits, diverse parental schedules affecting differential time spent feeding the children, and different gender roles all hinder the parents' ability to collaborate as a team in the tasks at hand. Therefore, making sure both parents understand their prominent role in shaping their child's body image, eating habits, and healthy lifestyle is fundamental to the success of the program. We suggest readers bear in mind that in many parts throughout this book, we refer to families headed by two parents, either heterosexual or homosexual, as these constitute the lion's share of patients we have served using the Parent-Based Prevention program. Chapter 16 will outline how this intervention can be adapted to single-parent families and other diverse family structures.

2 Understand together how the parental eating disorder and family members' additional characteristics affect child feeding practices, daily routines, and child-rearing functions of the family. The therapist interviews the parents and learns from them their formulation of how these

factors shape and interact with the family's potential risk profile. For instance, when the parents describe concerns about their child's eating habits, the therapist interviews them to explore whether and to what extent this child's eating habits, his or her genetic predisposition for a certain body type, the parental expectations around food consumption, potential nutritional sensitivities, the parents' cognitions associated with their own shape and weight attitudes, or other factors contribute to the difficulties described.

3   Define tailored goals for Parent-Based Prevention. As this intervention strives to help families live a healthier lifestyle and reduce parental worries associated with their children's eating habits, personalizing the intervention is key to maintain parental engagement, interest, and value from the work done. When participants feel that the program is made relevant to their individual family's history, strengths, and unique challenges, they are more likely to remain motivated and force through difficulties, should such arise in the process.

10 Session 1

Gearing Up

In session 1, the therapist and the parents begin formulating the issues that the family faces in establishing healthy eating habits among their children. This meeting lasts approximately 120 minutes and has two parts: a conjoint meeting with both parents, followed by two short (20-minute) individual interviews with each parent.

There are four main goals for session 1:

A Build the therapeutic alliance with both parents.
B Engage both parents in therapy.
C Identify thoughts and behaviors that are related to the parental eating disorder and both parents' additional characteristics that could affect child feeding practices, daily routines, and parental functioning.
D Collect sensitive information about potential differences in parental perspectives on history, parenting styles, and symptoms.

The interventions the therapist uses in order to achieve these goals are delineated below. They also appear in Form no. 1.

1 Introduce the Parent-Based Prevention program.
2 Engage both parents in the intervention.
3 Provide information about the likelihood of feeding and eating problems in children of parents with eating disorders as well as additional potential difficulties.
4 Focus the parental concerns and dilemmas that are pertinent to Parent-Based Prevention.
5 Identify how the parental eating disorder is currently associated with parenting practices and child behaviors.
6 Separate the parent's eating disorder from other aspects of parental functioning.
7 Focus the parents on the individualized goals of the program.
8 Ensure that both parents understand their importance in this therapeutic approach.

Form no. 1 The therapist interventions in Session 1, Phase One

PBP *session 1 interventions*	*Information gathered*	*Possible targets of PBP*
1 Introduce the Parent-Based Prevention program		
2 Engage both parents in the intervention		
3 Provide information about the likelihood of feeding and eating problems in children of parents with eating disorders as well as additional potential difficulties		
4 Focus the parental concerns and dilemmas that are pertinent to Parent-Based Prevention		
5 Identify how the parental eating disorder is currently associated with parenting practices and child behaviors		
6 Separate the parent's eating disorder from other aspects of parental functioning		
7 Focus the parents on the individualized goals of the program		
8 Ensure that both parents understand their importance in this therapeutic approach		
9 Prepare for the family meal		
10 Collect sensitive information about the family, including individual history and functioning and their likely impact on feeding behaviors and child eating.		
(A) Parent 1		
(B) Parent 2		

Note: the therapist should use Form no. 1 to plan the session, record important data, and note possible targets of the intervention.

9 Prepare for the family meal.

10 (In the 20 minutes of individual conversation with each parent) Collect sensitive information about the family, including: individual history and functioning and their likely impacts on feeding behaviors and child eating.

The therapist's interventions during session 1 are elaborated below.

Goal: Create a Therapeutic Alliance with the Parents

Why?

In order to deliver an intervention that is engaging and effective, in the first session the therapist should make the case that Parent-Based Prevention is an important and timely prevention program, and help the parent feel that they are in the hands of an expert who can confidently navigate their family to a healthier course. Participation in a prevention program may be particularly challenging in the case of parents with eating disorders and their spouses; the parent afflicted with the eating disorder may feel ashamed, embarrassed, or blamed in the context of enrolling in a family prevention program due to their illness. Additionally, their spouse may think that their involvement in the program is redundant because they are not the "affected parent." Many partners are also concerned that the parent with the eating disorder may experience an open conversation about the eating problem as overly critical and patronizing; hence, partners may avoid confrontations and authentic discussions. In addition, scheduling appointments may be exceptionally difficult with parents of young children who need child care arrangements. As a result, although clients in every intervention should feel that they have a lot to gain by partaking in the program, creating a good rapport is particularly important in the case of Parent-Based Prevention. The therapist should lead the conversation in a manner that conveys her expertise, care, and competence. This will allow the therapist to later facilitate change in the areas the parents delineate. The therapist's stance should be professional and knowledgeable, yet empathic. By the end of the first session, the parents should feel that the therapist understands the dilemmas they are struggling with and that she is dedicated to helping them find sustainable solutions.

How?

At first, the therapist invites the parents and greets both by a handshake or clear eye contact and a polite smile. The therapist should be serious and professional, and at the same time warm and empathetic to the parents' beliefs, habits, and dilemmas. In every meeting, the therapist openly sets the agenda for the meeting according to the guide. In the first session, the therapist should present herself and her professional background, as well as the setting in which the intervention will take place. The therapist also explains that Parent-Based Prevention is an empirically supported intervention that has been developed by experts to establish healthy eating habits in children. When appropriate, the therapist could mention her experience in providing relevant interventions to clients with eating disorders, families, and children.

The therapist stresses that the more open, honest, and nonjudgmental both parents are throughout the program, the more effective it will be. We found metaphors – like the one that is delineated in Box no. 1 – particularly helpful in creating such a mindset. This type of affirmation is exceptionally important when working with individuals with eating disorders, some of whom may be sensitive to criticism and negative cues from their environment. Furthermore, the therapist tells the parents that she would want to hear from each of them their perceptions of the family's strengths and challenges, and that she will do her best to facilitate productive discussions and proactive problem solving so that their family benefits from the program as much as possible. For example, the therapist may say something along the following lines:

> If we want this program to be effective, it is essential that we express here our thoughts, dilemmas, and worries as openly as possible. That is why I ask the two of you to leave any guilt or self-blame outside the door of this office and to focus on providing each other constructive feedback.

The therapist should answer openly any questions regarding confidentiality and ethics the parents may have. The therapist should also note that she will work with the parents collaboratively to personalize the intervention

---

Box no. 1   "Judgment and Self-Blame Should Wait Outside"

The therapist uses this metaphor to engage both parents in the intervention in a more businesslike approach that will help them collaborate in the task of developing healthy eating habits in their children, with minimal self- or mutual criticism:

> For our work to be effective, I ask you to leave any judgment, shame, or guilt outside this office. It is only natural that you will feel these negative emotions and perceptions when you are doing a parenting program; naturally, people would like to be the best parents that they can be, and many parents are unconsciously programmed to feeling guilty when they think about what they would like to provide for their kids. However, you both have

already made a huge effort by gathering here for the purpose of working together in Parent-Based Prevention. Therefore, these negative emotions, especially when they are intense, could cloud your thinking and disrupt your ability to make good use of this program. These sentiments are completely disadvantageous here. That is why I ask you to leave all the self-blame, guilt, accusations, and resentment in your car, waiting in the parking lot for you to reconsider them when you are done here.

so that it suits their family's unique style, competencies, and difficulties. By the end of the first session, the therapist should be confident that she has led the meeting in a way that helped the parents feel that she is experienced and prepared and knows what it takes to make changes.

Goal: Engaging Both Parents in the Intervention

Why?

At the outset of the program, parents may be unsure whether and to what extent their family may benefit of Parent-Based Prevention. This may be due to lack of knowledge and understanding of what an eating disorder entails, and how a parental eating disorder may compromise the child's feeding and eating habits. Parents are likely to have little or no awareness of how their personal habits and preferences may be associated with potential eating and developmental difficulties in their children. In addition, parents of young children are typically busy with child-rearing responsibilities and might want to postpone thinking about a potential problem until a future time, perhaps when it becomes a more urgent concern. Even when parents realize the timeliness of the intervention and why it is important to make some adaptations presently, they may still be reluctant to discuss the parental eating disorder openly. The reasons for this may be fear of damage to the family equilibrium, limited couple communication skills, or discomfort around discussing the eating disorder.

In the case of two-parent families, engaging *both parents* in the program and establishing the therapeutic alliance with *both parents* are fundamental steps for ensuring that the child feeding improvements made during Parent-Based Prevention are long-lasting. Hence, it is essential that both parents understand their immanent contribution to the program and that without their active involvement the intervention may not be effective. The emphasis on the active participation of the spouse bolsters more emotional, cognitive, and behavioral participation of both parents, as well as greater accountability. It also helps the parents understand that the intervention may require them to revisit their personal habits, parental behaviors, and communication skills. In Chapter 16, we will discuss ways to overcome this hurdle when working with single-parent families.

How?

The therapist invites each parent to talk about themselves for a few minutes. Often, parents do not understand the type and amount of detail expected of them in this self-introduction. A semi-humorous comment by the therapist, along the lines of "You can start with basic information that appears in your LinkedIn page/your driver's license," helps anchor the parents and reduce their anxiety. If the therapist does not have full information about the family members, she should ask follow-up questions. It is also important to be particularly attuned to the parents' achievements and sources of pride, and to validate these in the conversation.

Once she gathers information about each parent, the therapist focuses the conversation on the reasons the parents arrived at the program at this particular time. A recommended approach is to start interviewing the non-affected parent about why the family enrolled in Parent-Based Prevention, using circular questioning. This type of interviewing could raise the spouse's curiosity about their family, including what both parents could do to develop healthy eating habits in their family. For example, the therapist may ask the spouse: "So why do you think that your wife has brought you here?" It is our experience that the answers to this question vary immensely. Some partners respond that they were actually the ones who pushed the affected parent to enroll in the program; some say they do not know what the purpose of the program is; and some partners share that they are unsure how to speak about their concerns of the long-term effects of the parental eating disorder on their children. Through a series of circular and direct questions, the therapist should facilitate a collaborative discussion in which both parents are actively engaged. The goal is to point out any gaps between the parents' observations and behaviors, and to ask follow-up questions in a supportive and accepting manner.

Goal: Provide Information about the Likelihood of Feeding and Eating Problems in Children of Parents with Eating Disorders, and the Additional Potential Difficulties

Why?

Before embarking in the intervention, the parents should understand the context and scientific background to Parent-Based Prevention. Parents are the most potent factor affecting their children's development, and therefore should be an immanent part of any intervention, predominantly one that is directed at young children. Evidently, by arriving at Parent-Based

Prevention, at least one parent has experienced difficulties and dilemmas in feeding their child. Nevertheless, the parents may not understand the scope of the challenges to come. The therapist should provide a succinct summary of the up-to-date empirical data on the associations between parental eating disorders and children's risk of eating and co-occurring problems, and at the same time attempt to instill hope in the parents that they can positively affect the trajectories of their family. Therefore, the therapist should highlight that this evidence is from observational studies on families who have not participated in any targeted intervention, underscoring that data from such interventions indicate benefits for families who complete them (for review, see Sadeh-Sharvit, Zubery, Mankovski, Steiner, & Lock, 2016). The therapist should also provide context for the potential risks mentioned, emphasizing that these are shared among most families headed by a parent with an eating disorder and that Parent-Based Prevention was developed to address these difficulties.

How?

The therapist should tell the parents that she would like to outline the empirical evidence on which the Parent-Based Prevention program was developed. Then she should talk openly and nonjudgmentally about the risk of feeding and eating problems among the offspring of parents with eating disorder histories. Often times, the parents initiate this discussion by asking the therapist about the known risks to their child. Therapists are invited to use empirical data on parents with an eating disorder history that are found in Chapter 2 of this book. The information is to be presented in a factual manner, and with sensitivity to both parents. The therapist should then emphasize that Parent-Based Prevention is designed to reduce these aforementioned risks and improve the child's eating, self-regulation, and overall functioning. After describing the central evidence, the therapist should pause and ask the parents if they have any questions thus far. She should also inquire about their responses, thoughts, and feelings in regard to the information mentioned. At this point, many parents disclose that they have had similar concerns about the potential effects of the eating disorder on their children. Some parents may speak of their own experiences having grown up with a parent or a sibling with an eating disorder, in a context that had endorsed a thinness ideal, appearance, or athleticism. Additionally, many spouses join the conversation by communicating their own worries of the effects of the parental eating disorder on their family. The therapist should be empathetic to the parents' accounts and validate their concerns and personal histories. She should also note of any gaps in parents' beliefs and understandings and share her observations with the parents when appropriate.

Then the therapist should briefly point out that the information she has described was found in families that did not participate in prevention programs aimed at parents with eating disorders. In order to balance the information provided and to encourage and inspire the parents, the therapist states that interventions for parents with eating disorders can help parents improve how they feed their children, target existing challenges associated with healthy development, and augment parental communication. The therapist should highlight that for this program to be effective, it requires the involvement of both parents.

Next, the therapist should ask the parents whether they have any questions regarding the information they have received and should answer all these questions as openly and sincerely as possible. The therapist should remain mindful of the language used and avoid implications that the parents are directly responsible for any existing feeding problems. The therapist encourages both parents' participation in the discussion, talks with each of them, and ensures that they both understand the risk of a parental eating disorder and why the intervention is important. If the parents seem overwhelmed, anxious, or detached in response to the information the therapist shared, she should ask the parents about their thoughts and concerns. This is an opportunity for a discussion that can ignite change in the parental views of feeding and eating, and in their communication about these issues.

Goal: Focus on the Parental Concerns and Dilemmas That Are Pertinent to Parent-Based Prevention

Why?

Once the therapist has presented the parents the overarching context of Parent-Based Prevention, the areas that this intervention targets, and the empirical background for the program's inception, she should help the parents zoom in on the issues that would be at the center of the intervention. This data collection is active in nature, and the engagement of all the participants in the meeting is encouraged. As the therapist and the parents personalize the goals of the intervention, the parents learn what aspects to prioritize, but also educate the therapist on their unique values, hopes, and challenges. Importantly, differentiating between the topics that could be addressed in Parent-Based Prevention and other problem areas that may be important but are not within the scope of the program, the therapist not only augments the parents' thinking of their family, but also increases parental motivation to engage in this short-term, focused program.

The common dilemmas expressed by parents at this point of the intervention could be broadly categorized into three groups: the first type of dilemmas represents an uncertainness of what comprises healthy, age-appropriate eating in children versus unhealthy patterns. Overwhelmed with conflicting messages that are likely intensified by the parental eating disorder, many parents are genuinely confused as to how to best feed their children. Parents doubt their decisions surrounding the types and amounts of food provided, the introduction of new foods, changing feeding routines, the regulation of hunger and satiety in their children, etc. Additionally, some parents are worried about eating outside their usual routine, i.e., how to manage their child's eating in social situations in which food is part of the tradition (birthday parties, Christmas, Hanukkah, Ramadan, Diwali, and other events involving food). Some of these dilemmas are common to many parents, but it appears that the context of the parental eating disorder makes the parents more unsettled about them. The second type of issues that parents could raise involves coping adequately with a present child's low or high growth percentile, or existing worrisome behaviors, such as overeating, secretive eating, and extreme picky eating. Often, the parents have already received comments from professionals and friends indicating that the child's health could be compromised. The third kind of issues pertains to coping with eating disorder behaviors in the parents, of which the child is – or soon will be – aware. Parents are concerned that undesired behaviors could be modeled to the child, and ask how to best approach this. Notably, parents could also identify other important individuals in the child's life who have eating psychopathology themselves (an aunt, a grandfather, or even the au pair), and request skills for diminishing the potential negative impacts of this relationship, while still including this individual in their child's life.

How?

As the parents listen to the therapist discussing potential developmental and socio-emotional risks for the children of parents with eating disorders (described in the earlier step of session 1), they begin recognizing more possible difficulties in their children's behaviors and attitudes toward food, eating, shape, and weight. The therapist asks for clarifications on the issues raised, verifies that she understands both parents' stance on the matter, and lists the parental concerns in Form no. 1. In this conversation, the therapist uses strategies such as circular questioning to expand the parental insights.

It has been our experience that gaps between parents as well as between their perceptions of their different children likely emerge here. Many times, the parent with the eating disorder is concerned about the child's eating or weight and has been frustrated with the spouse who feels that parent's reactions to the child are exaggerated and all too forceful. The spouse may feel that since the parental eating disorder could be very impactful, they do not know how to help the other parent manage their stress. Both parents usually agree that mealtimes are too stressful and conflictual, and that they would like to develop skills to make meals more conversational and less argumentative.

In the case of significant differences in parents' perspective, visualizing their hopes and dreams for their child may facilitate parental communication of their family individualized goals for Parent-Based Prevention. For example, the therapist may suggest that each parent draws a pie chart or a bar graph of what they think their child needs so that he or she is a healthy, functioning, and happy individual. The therapist then suggests ideas for some key elements to reevaluate, such as having friends, being good at sports, getting high grades, being skinny, keeping a low-calorie diet, etc. This technique may allow some parents to talk more openly about their differences. For instance, a partner may say: "In relative terms, my wife thinks that monitoring what our child eats so that he does gain excessive weight is twice as important than the way I see it."

Goal: Identify How the Parental Eating Disorder Is Currently Associated with Parenting Practices and Child Behaviors

Why?

Understanding what an eating disorder entails and what are its implications on the parent and the family is essential in prompting parental awareness and communication over child feeding, and consequently a reduction in adverse behaviors. The unique manifestations of the parental eating disorder should be clarified to both parents when possible. Although the parent with the eating disorder often knows much about it, it is not uncommon for them to not share much information about their past or current eating disorder with their partner. Some partners of mothers with eating disorders, for example, perceive the maternal eating, shape, and weight concerns as an inevitable part of the Western feminine experience. Therefore, they neither believe it reflects a more fundamental problem that is disheartening to their wife, nor think that there is anything they can do about it. Other partners may think that the maternal eating disorder is minimal or encapsulated and is not related to parental practices. For this purpose, the therapist should educate both parents on how certain symptoms of eating disorders persist throughout adulthood. Additionally, it is important to provide information that child-bearing and rearing responsibilities may precipitate greater eating disorder symptoms.

The likelihood of a chronic course of the parental eating disorder is another important issue that should be addressed. Most eating disorders onset in adolescence and early adulthood, which could be at least a few years before becoming a parent. Although improvement and remission may occur in adulthood, some individuals should be prepared to acknowledge persisting symptoms. In addition, for individuals who have recovered from their eating disorder, some eating-related concerns may be reactivated when they become parents, regardless of their current presentation. Parents with histories of eating disorders often find themselves worried about their child's eating, surprised when their child asks for bigger portions of food than they have anticipated, and unsure how to respond when their child requests a second or third helping of high-fat, high-carb, or calorie-dense food.

How?

Exploring and explaining the nature of the maternal eating disorder should be personalized for each couple. Partners vary in the degree of their awareness of the other parent's difficulties; some couples avoid mentioning it, while in other families significant symptoms may be more openly discussed. Therefore, the therapist tries to tactfully identify through a process of focused interviewing and circular questioning how the parental eating disorder currently affects parenting practices and the child.

After both parents share their views on eating disorders and their effects, the therapist provides additional information on eating disorders in adulthood, and phrases it as general evidence on many parents with eating disorders. The therapist should diplomatically introduce the possibility that some of the parent's eating disorder symptoms may be enduring. An analogy to conditions that are commonly viewed as lifetime problems, have biological causes, and require lifestyle management may be helpful for many parents:

> Your spouse's eating disorder can be compared to high cholesterol. There are many reasons why people develop this condition and it varies for every individual. People also respond differently to certain treatments. However, once a person is diagnosed with high cholesterol, it means that there will always remain some sensitivity or vulnerability for relapse. People with high cholesterol should bear in their minds the possibility of deterioration in their condition, and they manage their lifestyle and behaviors accordingly. It would be helpful to think of the eating disorder as somewhat like high cholesterol, as there could be remission or relapse, and it is a lifetime struggle. However, if you had known that you have high cholesterol, you would probably be interested to learn how to safeguard your children from developing it as well. And that is exactly what we do here.

The therapist should express her belief that there is no reason that the parents will not prevent eating problems in their children.

The parental eating disorder creates stressful interactions in many couples. Common strategies parents use are avoidance ("he learned the hard way that he'd better arrive home after dinner and avoid being in the line of fire"), minimization of the problem ("I do not think our daughter is aware of my purging"), hypervigilant responses when the eating disorder is mentioned ("whenever he mentions my eating habits, I start calling him names and shame him for his bad behaviors"), and a fear of their partner's criticism or misinterpretation of their symptoms ("I tried explaining it once; when he said that once I get a job I would feel better and start eating normally, I realized there's no partner here"). Spouses' reactions could range from lack of knowledge of their spouse's eating disorder symptoms, awareness of the symptoms but denial of how mentally tasking they may be or that they could be the product of severe psychological distress, or insistence that the eating disorder is an intra-psychic phenomenon that does not affect parenting. For example, partners could disclose that they have purchased large amounts of low-caloric food, laxatives, or diuretics at their spouse's request, but never conversed with them about why they use them; or partners would avoid being home during mealtimes, so that they would not be caught up in the parent–child conflicts over food. To understand more the family's transactional patterns in communicating about the parental eating disorder, the therapist first explores the nature and frequency of conversations between parents through circular questioning:

> How do you think that your partner would explain what an eating disorder is? What do you know of the implications of your partner's eating disorder on him/her, and on the ways in which he/she feeds your children and her interactions with your child?

These questions raise both parents' curiosity about the extent of the current parental symptoms, consequently inviting further communication between parents beyond the therapist's office.

After the more general prompt, the therapist reviews the dilemmas and concerns mentioned by the parents earlier and invites them to revisit these through the lens of the parental eating disorder. For example, the therapist explores with the parents how much of the feeding problems or mealtime difficulties are associated with the parental worries about the child's body shape, weight, appearance, and fitness. Many parents mention here their schemas for which characteristics constitute children's wellbeing, based on their experience and values:

> For me a fat child is the scariest thing in the world. I'm scared to death he will be fat. Especially as a child. I know what it's like to be a fat child, and that is one of the most horrible experiences a kid could have.[1]

Many parents are concerned about whether their fears surrounding their child's weight and the dieting terminology they use to describe their child is healthy:

> My older daughter, I think her weight is higher than it should be . . . I think about it a lot and talk to myself a lot about it. I tell myself "She's only a child, what do you want from her? Put her on a diet already?" I remember with sadness myself her age.

Both parents often describe their concern of their child's growing curiosity for and response to parental eating behaviors:

> Rather than I will supervise my five-year-old's eating at dinner, she joins my husband in monitoring me; asks me what did I eat today, urging me to take one more bite. This feels twisted, like it should totally be the other way around.

Our experience working with parents with eating disorders is that they all do not want their eating disorder to negatively affect their children's behaviors, and they are highly motivated to gain skills and capabilities to diminish unhealthy eating patterns in their children.

In families where the parent with the eating disorder is the one who is responsible for most of the feeding interactions, sometimes partners may not be aware of the extent of parental control that could be exerted during feeding in some families. As a result of a great concern for the child's shape and weight, parents with eating disorders have been found to monitor and restricting their child's intake, more than parents with no eating disorder history: having short meals, delaying the introduction of solids, postponing autonomous eating (for instance, by spoon-feeding children who are able to eat independently), avoidance of social events that are overflowing in foods, etc. The therapist helps both parents express their attitudes toward these behaviors and explores their connection with the parental eating disorder and additional family characteristics. For example, in the presence of existing overweight, life-threatening allergies, or significant developmental problems, some of these abovementioned behaviors make sense and would be advised.

The cognitions and behaviors that are associated with the parental eating disorder and the spouse's reactions to them may be difficult for many parents to acknowledge. However, these are the targets of Parent-Based Prevention! The therapist should facilitate this discussion in a tactful and respectful manner, trying to understand the meaning and the function of certain thoughts and behaviors. Such an approach could later assist the therapist in addressing similar issues effectively, by providing relevant information and helping parents develop the capabilities of minimizing the influence of the parental eating disorder on their child's eating and development.

Goal: Distinguish the Parent's Eating Disorder from Other Aspects of Parental Functioning

Why?

In this step, the therapist helps the parents differentiate between their concerns and behaviors that are more strongly associated with the parental eating disorder and those that are not. The therapist uses the information gathered in the session to separate the eating disorder from other aspects of the parents' and child's functioning and behaviors. The therapeutic stance of Parent-Based Prevention asserts that every parent is a whole person; although the eating disorder may affect some aspects of parental functioning, certainly both parents are devoted to assuring their children's wellbeing, health, and prosperity. This intervention is designed to help the parents achieve this goal and make sure their children thrive in an environment that supports healthy growth. This part of session 1 is critical because it aims to reduce parental guilt by amplifying the more functioning aspects of each parent (i.e., the child-rearing beliefs and practices that are not compromised by the eating disorder). By reducing guilt, parental empowerment is enhanced. This approach should also reduce the spouse's criticism of the "target" parent for their eating disorder and model uncritical acceptance.

Another benefit of separating parental functioning from the illness is to normalize and validate certain conditions that would commonly be stressful for most parents, not only those with an eating disorder history. Here are a few examples to demonstrate this: severe and life-threatening allergies in children would be upsetting to all parents, regardless of their eating patterns; a father whose siblings and parents have obesity could have a realistic worry if his four-year-old's weight is in the 100 percentile; and a mother with a history of child sexual abuse could be rightfully anxious when her daughter is invited to a sleep-over at a friend's house. These contexts could be all daunting to many parents. The therapist should explore if and how the parental eating disorder exacerbates family members' responses to these situations.

The therapist should also highlight that the goal of Parent-Based Prevention is not to intervene directly in the parental eating disorder symptoms, as this concern might overwhelm them and shift the parents' focus to themselves as individuals instead of the family functioning. Rather, the purpose of the treatment is to limit the impact of the eating disorder. Our experience working with families affected by parental eating disorders is that when following the respectful discussions that separate the eating disorder from other dimensions of parenting, most parents independently acknowledge a gap between their desire to model healthy eating habits for their children and their difficulties in modifying problematic behaviors.

How?

In collaboration with the parents, the therapist seeks to distinguish between common difficulties that are not associated with the parental eating disorder (such as the costs of child care that burden the family, discomfort when the living room is untidy at the end of the day, etc.), unique challenges that are not part of the eating disorder but may affect the family, and issues that appear to be aggregated by the eating disorder history. The therapist asks the parents if there is any additional important information she should know about the family, and if there are any special circumstances at this time of their lives. As happens in life, people experience situations that affect their ability to put themselves fully into the intervention, such as losing a job recently, dealing with debts, a recent loss of a parent, a recent suicide attempt of the second parent, a medical procedure planned in the near future, a change of living environment soon, a jail history, legal problems with an ex-spouse, etc. The therapist should hold an uncritical and accepting attitude toward both parents, their individual symptoms, and their difficulties in feeding their child. At the same time, the therapist should display her care for the family by emphasizing that there are some areas of the parental functioning that need to be changed to enhance and reinforce a healthier lifestyle. This is not to say that the therapist should treat lightly regarding any of the problems that are expressed or acknowledged in the program, but she should attempt to understand if it is the eating disorder overpowering parenting in any given scenario, and continuously teach the parents the distinction. Importantly, collaboratively creating working hypotheses per the unique impacts of the parental eating disorder is a potent means of further individualizing the intervention to the family and increasing parents' awareness. A useful metaphor to illustrate this distinction appears in Box no. 2.

The therapist should pay attention to the partner's understanding of the behaviors that may be significantly associated with the parental eating disorder and which behaviors are less connected with the disorder. The therapist should provide many examples of related parental cognitions and behaviors, and explore relevant issues, including feeding habits, eating style, activity level and its purpose, who eats with the child, when and where, and so on. For example, the therapist may say something along the following lines:

> In some families that I work with, one parent is motivated to minimize the child's exposure to foods that are high-fat, high-carb, while the other parent believes these foods should not be restricted. Sometimes one parent feels that the family meals are so stressful that they eat alone prior to arriving home. Does anything like this happen in your family?

Box no. 2 "The Updated GPS Unit"

Therapists can use this metaphor to demonstrate to the parents the eating disorder's impact on the parental approaches and behaviors, and how Parent-Based Prevention addresses it:

> I would like to use an analogy to a GPS navigation device to explain better the goal of this program. Remember those old GPS units used in cars years ago? They used a predetermined map that was built into the unit. It could lead you from point A to point B according to its calculations, but with complete disregard for changing circumstances or roadblocks. More recent navigation apps on your smartphone respond to the environment and are continuously updated. This can explain how the eating disorder models your parenting. The old, eating-disorder-oriented mindset navigates your parenting, grounded in the roadmaps of the eating disorder. Here in this program we work to broaden your

(continued)

(continued)

mental map system so that your parenting is guided not only by your concerns, but prominently by your overarching values, your knowledge of children's development, and your co-parenting decisions. Even if you think that the eating disorder is your default, we can practice ways by which you are mindful of the effects of this type of programming, and actively choose the non-eating-disorder parental navigation.

Goal: Focus the Parents on the Individualized Goals of the Program

Why?

By this point of the session, the Parent-Based Prevention therapist should be able to identify the fundamental problem and future risk areas of the family. The therapist might also have some hypotheses on the cognitions and behaviors that should be targeted first in the treatment, in order to precipitate additional progress in related areas. Although the foci of the program on healthy eating are the reason the parents have initially enrolled in the treatment, it is the personalization of the objectives that can help maintain motivation over time; the more the parents feel that Parent-Based Prevention is tailored to their unique characteristics and needs, the more they will remain engaged in and between sessions.

How?

After listening to the parents' account of how the parental eating disorder is associated with their child's eating and family structure, the therapist should summarize the problem areas that the parents have identified and help the parents prioritize them. This is an active and collaborative process where the therapist confirms that both parents have expressed their beliefs and goals, and then provides feedback before the personalized targets of the program are defined. The therapist models the Parent-Based Prevention approach that focuses first on changes that are within the sphere of eating and are more easily achievable, and consequently transitions to broader difficulties, where the seeds of changes can be sowed toward the tail end of the program. A representative dialog could sound like this:

So if I understand correctly, both of you would like your family meals to be more pleasant and less conflictual. Danna, you would like to be able to take the entire family to your office events without being anxious that the kids would freak out in the sight of the buffet. Tom, you want to feel more effective at home, and that neither Danna nor the kids override what you say, because it is very off-putting for you and you avoid their company. Does this sound like a good summary of the issues you have both mentioned? How would you prioritize them? [*The therapist listens to the parents' response.*] I recommend that we begin by focusing on what happens around mealtimes, first at home and later in social events. Then we will shift gears to talk about improving your co-parenting collaboration. We will learn what transpires in these interactions, and then develop strategies to make Tom feel more significant, and consequently more motivated to engage. This approach dovetails the outline of this program, and I believe that changes in the earlier issues will mitigate changes in the later issues. Does this plan make sense?

Goal: Ensure That Both Parents Understand Their Importance in This Therapeutic Approach

Why?

The therapist works to repeatedly engage the spouse in the conversation by encouraging him or her to express the concerns he or she has. Engaging the spouse persistently sends a clear message that for change to occur, both parents must be involved in the process. Many times, this is a challenging task, especially when the equilibrium in the family is based on refraining from conversing about the role of the eating disorder in the family life. Many partners, motivated to support their spouse, avoid any conversations that could be stressful or rub the other parent the wrong way. Participating in Parent-Based Prevention necessarily requires that the couple learns new, additional ways to converse about the different perspectives that guide their parenting, including the parental eating disorder. By arriving together at the first session, the parents have already taken the first step in the process, and the therapist amplifies this good will and interest in the process.

How?

With the intention of reinforcing the importance of both parents' active participation in the program and in the behavioral changes that will take place at home between sessions, the therapist acknowledges this directly (i.e., verbally referring to the spouse's central role in the child's healthy development) as well as indirectly (for instance, by continuously involving both parents in the discussion). For example, the therapist may say something along the following lines:

I know that you may be afraid that the eating disorder takes over you entirely and will not allow you to provide your children the amount and variety of food they need for healthy development. It is our job here to make sure that both of you parents take charge of feeding your children according to their needs, even if the eating disorder will try and convince you to avoid these changes at home.

Or:

I've noticed that when Diane was talking about her fear that your child will over-eat unless you force him to stop, you started looking at your phone and seemed a bit detached. I am wondering if this is something that you noticed too.

Many spouses may feel overburdened by the expectation to co-manage a problem they were not responsible for creating; further, some feel that they have done a good job *avoiding* any discussion of their spouse's eating disorder and would like to maintain this status quo. In these cases, the therapist should remind the parents why their collaboration is important to curtail the parental eating disorder, but at the same time keep an optimistic tone and highlight some of the strengths and positive details she already knows about the family that would enable the parents to leverage the intervention. Parent-Based Prevention aims to unite the parents and alienate the parental eating disorder which is perceived as having only partial impact on the family relationship and functioning. Amid an evident gap between the parents, the therapist can mention that in Phase Three, issues that are relevant to the parental collaboration could be addressed, if deemed appropriate to Parent-Based Prevention: "Further down the road, we could work on practicing additional ways for you to support each other as parents."

Goal: Prepare the Parents for the Family Meal

Why?

The next step before transitioning to the individual part of session 1 is to provide instructions for the family meal that will take place in session 2. The therapist invites the family to arrive at the next meeting with their children and have a meal together in the session. The parents are asked to bring a meal that is suitable for all family members according to their judgment and based on their collaborative thought. The therapist explains to the parents that in order to learn more about their family in Phase One, observing the family in a meal creates a unique opportunity for real-time assessments.

Interestingly, the majority of parents are thrilled by the opportunity to share this challenging part of their routine with the therapist, and they are intrigued to hear what she learns about the family in this *in vivo* observation.

How?

The therapist explains that a prerequisite step to further individualizing the goals of the intervention for the family is observing a family meal that will be held in the therapist's office. The therapist can explain this, using the language below:

> This will be a learning opportunity for all of us to understand more about your family transactions and patterns during a meal. It will also be my one chance to meet your children and observe how the matters you have mentioned are expressed. I ask you to bring a meal that is closest to what you would have at a similar time at home.

The therapist helps the parents to plan when is the best time to have this meal so that the children are exuberant and ready to eat. She also clarifies that she will not be eating with the family.

The conjoint part of session 1 should end with the parents' appreciation of the urgency of revisiting the family structure and communication around food so that their child develops healthy habits. The therapist also verbally acknowledges that this meeting has probably not been easy for the parents and instills hope and optimism that they will be able to work out a way to achieve the goals set in the session.

Goal: Collect Sensitive Information about the Family and Individual History and Functioning and Their Likely Impact on Feeding Behaviors and Child Eating

Why?

Once the parents know which types of challenges in feeding, eating, daily routines, and additional developmental aspects may be associated with the parental eating disorder, the therapist tries to further evaluate how the family's unique characteristics and coping styles are linked to difficulties and dilemmas around feeding and eating. Although the skilled therapist should be able to create good rapport with both parents, in order to create a comprehensive formulation that integrates the parental eating disorder with the characteristics, background, and concerns of each family member, the therapist talks with each of the parents individually.

The goals of the individual segments of session 1 with each of the parents are to help them reflect on and express their fears and dilemmas regarding the parental eating disorder as well as additional qualities of the family. Each parent has an opportunity to openly share with the therapist his or her feelings and thoughts without being afraid of hurting their spouse's feelings or creating more stress. With these benefits in mind, the therapist should always remember the caveats in holding separate meetings in a parent-centered intervention context. The therapist should clarify to both parents the nature of confidentiality in these conversations and how the material discussed in the individual meetings will be handled. As one of the program's aims is to support spousal communication, both parents are encouraged to share the content of their individual meetings with their partner.

How?

When laying out the agenda for session 1, the therapist should inform the parents about the structure of the meeting and that it includes a conjoint and separate conversations. After planning the family meal that will be held in the next meeting, the therapist lets the parents decide in which order they would like to talk to her alone. In each individual conversation, the therapist tells the parents that she is interested to hear about their personal history, if there are important things they did not feel comfortable sharing in the presence of their spouse, and if there is anything additional she needs to know to make the intervention as successful as possible. The therapist clarifies that the information shared in this one-on-one conversation is private and will not be discussed with the other parent; and that before the meeting concludes she will consult with the parent on what is helpful to share with the partner and what should be kept confidential. Sometimes the parents need some prompts to begin this part of the session, and the therapist can say something along the following lines: "Let's shift gears. Now that you know more about the focus of this program, is there anything additional that you think I should know in order to help you guys make the most out of this program?"

The therapist points out that any additional issues the parents believe may be linked to difficulties in child feeding or eating should be brought to discussion. The therapist may explain this in the following way:

> I would like to understand more about the effects of your (or your spouse's) eating disorder, and maybe other aspects of your family life, on your child's eating habits. Whatever we talk about today will help us better support the intervention process so there is a potential benefit to talking today openly and privately. This conversation is about digging deeper into your perspective of what affects your child's eating and attitudes about his or her body. What you will tell me can help us build a better action plan for you at home.

The therapist should make clear that it is preferred that the topics discussed between each parent and the therapist will be shared with the partner. However, the parent is to decide if and to what extent the issues will be shared outside the therapist's office. The therapist could propose the following explanation:

> If what we talk about today is about a personal issue you have, it stays between me and you. But if you tell me things about your own or your partner's behaviors or concerns that may be relevant to your child's eating, I advise you will share them with your partner. At the end of the session I'm going to list out the things that I would like to be able to discuss with your partner. However, I will not share with your spouse anything you will ask me not to.

The therapist allows the parents to openly express their views in a noncritical atmosphere, by using a matter-of-fact tone and composed reactions, and avoiding criticism.

The therapist can further encourage the parents to communicate openly on relevant themes and reflect on their views and worries by suggesting a few conditions common in the families of parents with eating disorders which may interfere with the child's development of healthy eating habits. These general prompts are scenarios that are common amid parents with eating disorders, their children, and their spouses. The scenarios are presented to the parents as open-ended questions. The following questions serve as an anchor and the attuned therapist should add more prompts according to his knowledge and clinical impression of the family:

> Are there any additional influences of your eating habits (or your spouse's) on the family? Is there anything else you would like to mention on the thoughts, feelings, and concerns you or your partner have regarding eating, shape, and weight that affect the feeding of your child? Do you have any additional concerns about the eating habits in your family? Is your spouse aware of your current symptoms? What are your own weight and shape concerns regarding your wife or children? How do you feel about your spouse's looks? What kinds of dilemmas do you have in sharing your perspective on your husband's attitudes and behaviors with him?

Common issues that both parents are likely to discuss in the individual part of the session pertain to "typical" spousal difficulties, such as monetary and child-rearing differences, the involvement of the origin families, and the quality of the spousal relationship. Often these are issues that the parents have not shared with anyone before because they often felt that they were too personal, embarrassing, or idiosyncratic, or they did not want to expose their family's challenges to people outside the family. Universal themes raised by parents with eating disorders include disclosure that their current eating disorders symptoms are more severe than they have exposed to their partners (more frequent binges and purges, nocturnal eating, compulsive exercising, co-occurring psychiatric symptoms, a more intense preoccupation with the shape, weight, and eating of themselves and of their children, etc.), or that they are frustrated that their spouses do not understand or share their concerns about child feeding. Some spouses feel much guilt and shame about their distress and feel that they overburden their spouses with their difficulties. Many mothers with eating disorders who are the primary caregivers of their toddlers, or stay-home moms, often mention feelings of loneliness and stress that exaggerate their eating disorder. The spouses (i.e., the parents with no eating psychopathology) frequently express their concern for their spouse's wellbeing, especially in light of recent relapses the other parent has undergone. They may share their dilemmas regarding how to approach their partner's eating disorder in a supportive and not demeaning way. Some partners feel that the family is more affected by the comorbid problems of either parent, such as anxiety, mood intolerance, and substance abuse. Some partners share their own eating, weight, and shape concerns regarding themselves and reflect how some behaviors affect the parent: calorie counting, excessive exercise, daily weighing, rigid food preferences or rituals around eating, and binge eating. It is also not uncommon that partners – now that they have learned more about the nature of eating disorders – revisit negative comments they have made over their spouse's appearance and eating behaviors that unintentionally may have caused further stress. Before summarizing the personal interview with each parent, the therapist reviews with them the key points that she takes from the conversation and verifies what could be addressed in the conjoint meetings.

When session 1 is completed, the therapist reviews Form no. 1 and adds any relevant information and key intervention goals that she was not able to record during the meeting.

Common Therapist Dilemmas in Session 1

The Therapist Is Worried That the Therapeutic Alliance Is Not Positive Enough

Addressing their own mental problems or any difficulties in their child is undoubtedly upsetting for any parent. Parents may become defensive if they feel that the therapist is being judgmental or if they have the idea they may unintentionally contribute to child feeding difficulties. Often, while the person with the eating disorder has some prior experience of being in treatment, for their spouse this is the first time in a treatment setting, which could be very anxiety-provoking. Further, due to lack of knowledge or misinformation regarding eating disorders, some parents can become quite protective of their spouse and feel that the focus on the parental eating disorder does not perceive them as a whole person and undermines their recovery thus far. It is the therapist's responsibility to create a therapeutic bond with the parents and make sure that a practical working atmosphere is generated. The therapist should stress that they believe that parents are well-intentioned and wish only the best for their children, and that Parent-Based Prevention is geared to help the couple expand their knowledge and competences in promoting their child's wellbeing. In addition, the therapist should compliment the parents for the positive and adaptive parenting behaviors that she had recognized during the meeting – the positive parental attitudes toward the child or the healthy practices the parents report. We also recommend discussing the therapeutic alliance in supervision should this be deemed necessary.

The Parents Do Not Reach an Adaptive Anxiety Level

Managing appropriate anxiety levels of clients is a delicate task for any therapist. The therapist should confirm that the parents are driven to take action and change their behaviors to support their child's healthy eating. However, their worries should not be too intense and overwhelming; nor should these be too low and decrease parental motivation for the intervention. It is recommended that the therapist addresses this issue using direct and circular questioning to both parents, in an attempt to create an atmosphere of shared responsibility and motivation to change.

The Non-Affected Partner is Less Engaged in the Intervention

The spouse who does not have an eating disorder may feel that although this preventive intervention is important, it is less relevant for them as they are not the "affected parent." Some partners may claim that only if the other parent treats their eating disorder will other problems be resolved as well. This is another opportunity for the therapist to educate the couple about the importance of both parents to shaping, feeding, and eating practices, or work through difficulties in couple communication. The therapist should stress that both parents play a prominent role in supporting the development and maintenance of healthy eating and self-regulation. Additionally, the therapist points out repeatedly that the parental eating disorder is an enduring coping style that is not going to be emendable through this program and trying to change it may undermine the intervention.

The Parents Do Not Agree on Common Goals

It is common that parents find it difficult to agree on what they want the intervention to focus on. This discrepancy between the parents is often created when there are unresolved issues between them that one parent wishes to explore during the program, while the other does not. For instance, one parent feels that an older stepchild's eating habits impede their toddler's healthy development while the other parent is not open to revisiting this issue; or one parent is interested in having a regular family dinner, while the other maintains they cannot leave work early enough. There may be also diverse goals concerning the context of feeding and eating practices or the spousal communication and relationship. The therapist should openly discuss these differences with the parents and help them reach mutual objectives regarding the overarching goal of behavioral focus on their child's eating and behavioral changes.

The Parents Focus on Personal, Marital, or Parental Issues That Have Little to Do with the Links between the Eating Disorder and Child Feeding

Every family unit faces challenges that are not associated with a parental eating disorder or comorbid difficulties, and many times parents are interested to work through these additional issues that burden their family, such as: financial issues, problems with an extended family, infidelity, etc. However, unless these types of problems compromise the development of healthy eating habits among the children, they are typically outside the scope of the current intervention. Should such issues arise, the therapist will direct, re-direct, and focus the discussions on the family's eating behaviors, with an emphasis on the child and how the eating disorder and other family characteristics may affect healthy feeding and broader aspects of development. The therapist should emphasize that the goal of the program is to prompt a continuous evaluation of the family's organization, management, and concern around food, eating, and weight, and the traits and habits of each family member and their influence on feeding. If the parents discuss an issue that is of less relevance to the intervention, the therapist should align them back to the goals of the intervention.

The Parents Are Uncertain about the Urgency or Long-Term Effects of Parent-Based Prevention

Motivating people to participate in a prevention program is always a complicated task as most individuals tend to act in the face of concrete or foreseeable demands. Parents of young children may particularly find it difficult to allocate time and effort to the program due to scheduling difficulties and other responsibilities, although they feel it is important. The therapist should use a serious and professional tone and explain to the parents that maladaptive eating behaviors are most easily shaped during early childhood. Although the therapist cannot evaluate accurately the risk of their child developing an eating disorder, the consequences of underestimating this risk may be prevented. The therapist should further explore with the parents any scheduling concerns they may have and work through these difficulties. However, if the parents choose not to enroll in the program, the therapist should leave the door open and maintain that the parents are invited to reach out to her when participation is more feasible.

Note

1 Some of the quotes used in this chapter are adapted from Sadeh-Sharvit et al. (2015).

References

Sadeh-Sharvit, S., Levy-Shiff, R., Feldman, T., Ram, A., Gur, E., Zubery, E., . . . Lock, J. D. (2015). Child feeding perceptions among mothers with eating disorders. *Appetite*, 95, 67–73. doi:10.1016/j.appet.2015.06.017.

Sadeh-Sharvit, S., Zubery, E., Mankovski, E., Steiner, E., & Lock, J. D. (2016). Parent-based prevention program for the children of mothers with eating disorders: Feasibility and preliminary outcomes. *Eating Disorders*, 24(4), 312–325. doi: 10.1080/10640266.2016.1153400.

11 Session 2

The Family Meal

In session 2, all family members are invited to participate in a family meal meeting that is held at the therapist's office. At the end of the first session, the parents were instructed to bring a meal for their children and themselves that they perceived as appropriate for the family's nutritional needs. The family meal meeting is therefore an opportunity for the therapist and the parents to assess the family's conversations, non-verbal transactions, and coalitions around feeding and eating, as well as to recognize parental strengths and their children's competence.

Most interventions with individuals with eating disorders do not typically involve food or eating at the therapist's office. Eating during a session is outside many professionals' comfort zone, due to schemas of how "talk therapy" works that are embedded in psychological approaches, which emphasize the therapist's neutrality, verbal discussions versus acts, and the standard setting of sessions. Yet observing a family meal at the clinic provides both the therapist and the parents with important information about the family's interactions around feeding and eating. The family meal session is an opportunity to assess the transactions, coalitions, and communication patterns between family members in a semi-naturalistic setting. When working with young children who cannot always articulate their eating-related attitudes and habits, a family meal in the session not only deepens and broadens the therapist's understanding but is also an opportunity to directly support the family during mealtime.

In Family-Based Treatment (FBT) for eating disorders, the therapist systematically uses the family meal as an opening to evaluate the family and educate and train the parents in their attempt to renourish their child (Lock & Le Grange, 2013). Since inclusion criteria for Parent-Based Prevention is a parental eating disorder history rather than active symptoms in the children, the children participating in it are not perceived as patients and may not have existing symptoms. Therefore, parents are guided at the outset of the family meal session to talk about issues that are appropriate to discuss in their children's presence. For example, if the therapist observes coalitions in the family, such that the mother and the two children exclude the father, refuse his attempts to communicate and collaborate, and eat different food than him, this is likely a very important issue for the therapist to consider exploring prior to introducing the behavioral intervention. However, in most circumstances we would recommend that this observation will be shared with the parents only. Similarly, some families engage in "fat talk," i.e., commenting on people's body weight, body type, and eating – with heightened criticism of those who are overweight or obese. As discussed in Chapter 4, these conversations are associated with adverse weight, physical activity, and psychological wellbeing outcomes in children. Nonetheless, therapists are advised to postpone discussing this interaction style with the parents until the next session. Occasionally the parents are reminded of a concern following the interaction with their child during the family meal. For example, a parent may turn to the therapist and say: "You see, it is just impossible to feed him, he is the most stubborn kid possible," or they would criticize their partner: "Everyone in your family is overweight, and if you continue buying this fast food your son will be obese as well!" Although the material may be of important relevance for the intervention, in session 2 we suggest that the therapist point out that whatever the parents may be interested in sharing can be explored in the subsequent meeting (session 3), which only the parents attend.

Session 2 typically lasts between 45 to 60 minutes; after the family finishes eating, some unstructured conversation and interaction between the therapist and the family may continue, provided that the meeting can extend (i.e., children are not too tired and can play or chat with the therapist). As mentioned above, conversation topics in this session should be limited to those appropriate in the children's presence, excluding discussions on parental criticism of the child's eating preferences, body type, and weight, parents not being unified in their approach, the parental eating disorder, parents' early feeding and eating histories, and the like.

The major goals for session 2 are:

A   Observe the family discussions and behavioral patterns around food preparation, food serving, and eating.
B   Assess the family structure and its likely impact on the parents' ability to successfully feed their children in age-appropriate amounts and encourage autonomy.
C   Identify family members' cognitions and behaviors as manifested in interactional practices, feeding rituals, and communication that potentially influence the child's cognitions and behaviors. These beliefs and thoughts are the targets of the intervention.

By the end of session 2, the therapist should be able to expand the formulation from the first session regarding the family's competencies and challenges in terms of interactional processes, feeding rituals, and parental attitudes and concerns that could have an impact on feeding their children. In session 3, the therapist will share with the parents his or her observations

Form no. 2 A therapist's worksheet for session 2, Phase One

Dimension	Information gathered	Possible targets of PBP
1 Concrete aspects of the family meal		
2 General qualities of feeding and eating practices		
3 Transactional patterns in the family that are beyond food and eating		

Note: the therapist should use Form no. 2 to record important data that surfaces in session 2 and note possible targets for the intervention.

and insights, listen to their concerns, and further individualize the program to match the family's needs by helping the parents to identify which behaviors and attitudes should be prioritized during Phases Two and Three.

The interventions the therapist uses in order to accomplish these goals are delineated as follows:

1 Instruct the parents to serve the meal and eat it as closely as possible to how it would be in their home environment.
2 Observe the family patterns, transactions, and discussions around food preparation, food serving, and eating, especially as they relate to the child.
3 Close the session with a simple summary and plan the next meeting.

In addition to the prescribed steps, there is also a proscribed behavior, and that is to avoid therapeutic discussions in the presence of the children; at the end of the session, the therapist informs the parents that observations made during this session will be discussed at their meeting the following week, and asks them to think about what they have learned from the meeting. Since this program is designed to be support the parents as their family's agents of change, discussions and interpretations will be held with them only.

Hereinafter, the therapist's interventions during session 2 are elaborated.

Goal: Instruct the Parents to Serve the Meal and Eat It as Close as Possible to How It Would Be at Their Home Environment

Why?

In session 2, the therapist hopes to increase understanding of the family's unique risk factors for feeding and eating difficulties in their children, as well as additional potential adversities in self-regulation, socio-emotional functioning, and parent–child interactions. The therapist also aims to improve parental insight of these factors. The assessment of the family is not a single occurrence; rather, further understanding will unfold throughout the sessions. With the family meal, though, the therapist wants to start his assessment of the family's transactional patterns around feeding and eating in a setting that attempts to be as close as possible to a naturalistic observation.

How?

At the end of session 1, the parents were instructed to bring in a family meal that they felt met the nutritional requirements and preferences of all family members and was as representative as possible for a typical family meal. The therapist reminds the parents that the goal of the meal is to help them and the therapist learn more about the types of interactions that family members have with their children about food and eating, and how they acknowledge hunger and satiety. At the meeting, the therapist guides the family to take a seat around a table that is as similar as possible to a dining table and allows parents to sit comfortably and close to their children. The therapist must be able to observe and take notes while not interfering with the family's usual mealtime practices as much as possible: he sits close to the family in a location that allows him to hear their verbal communication and observe their behaviors and non-verbal communication. However, the therapist does not participate in the meal itself. Further, it is advised to schedule this session at a time that the parents perceive as challenging, to maximize their and the therapist's learning. Most parents report difficulties managing dinners, therefore meeting them for lunch (or when their children are not typically fed) would likely provide less information.

Goal: Observe the Family Patterns, Transactions, and Discussions around Food Preparation, Food Serving, and Eating, Especially as They Relate to the Child

Why?

The family meal provides the therapist and the parents with a strong, unique exposure to the family's organization. This is a rare opportunity for real-time assessment of the family structure – i.e., the often-repeated patterns of communicating, controlling, nurturing, socializing, forming boundaries, making alliances and coalitions, engaging and disengaging from certain interactions, solving problems, etc. The family meal, therefore, offers the therapist an opportunity to observe these family processes *in vivo*, specifically as they are brought to the forefront during mealtimes. Ultimately, the hope is that the therapist can use these observations to further individualize the goals of the program for this family, as many of the aspects of parental functioning and child behaviors may become better defined. Subsequently, clearer understanding of the potential effects of the family patterns improves the therapist's effectiveness in facilitating family changes. The generalization of the interactional patterns observed on one occasion may often be erroneous. Therefore, the therapist should validate with the parents if the issues he notices are typical or not, and get both parents' perspectives (in session 2 or in session 3, as appropriate) per his observations.

How?

In order to evaluate the nature of the family's potential risks for present and future eating psychopathologies, the therapist studies the attitudes and behaviors of family members via his observations and by asking questions to assess and refine his hypotheses. Here is a breakdown of several aspects that the therapist should consider during session 2, which the therapist lists on Form no. 2. The therapist should use discretion when determining whether to seek further information from the family during the session (i.e., in front of the children) or defer until the next session with the parents alone. The following excerpt explains more about potential problems that might ensue if topics are brought up at the wrong time:

> Sam and Barb are the parents of Joanne, a 5-year-old girl. In session 1, the parents described their concerns about Joanne's great fondness of sweets, and their fear that this tendency will result in overweight and health problems as well as stigmatization by her environment. The parents mentioned that members of their origin family are obese or have diabetes, and that they wish a different fate for their daughter. In the first session, the therapist observed that both parents value appearance and have internalized the thin ideal. During the family meal meeting, Joanne ate the dinner her father had prepared and then asked him if there was any dessert. Sam turned to the therapist and said angrily: "This is the perfect example. Her 'sweet tooth' is becoming terrible. Maybe you can talk some sense into her, because I am worried and tired of these fights." Joanne started crying: "Stop saying 'sweet tooth,' 'sweet tooth' all the time!" The therapist replied: "I sense that conflicts over dessert may be something that your family is frustrated about. But I think it would be better to postpone discussing this topic to next week, when we might feel more comfortable examining it."

Some issues, however, could – and perhaps, should – be explored during the family meal session. For instance, when Levy and Shoshana, parents of 7-year-old Dan and 15-month-old Maddie, attended the family meal with their children, the therapist explored how the parents had agreed on the type and amount of foods to bring to the meeting. He also asked how many family meals they have each week, who attends most meals at home, and whether family members eat the same things or have different meals. Dan actively participated in the conversation: "Mom serves cauliflower, which I hate! Only she likes it. Why can't we eat normal food like fish and chips?" The therapist followed up with another question: "What is it that you hate about cauliflower?" Dan responded: "I agree to eat it once a week, and that's it. But for every time I eat cauliflower, I wish we could have fish and chips the next day." In the following session, the therapist used this exchange to explore relevant issues such as the (un)varied diet provided to the children, how the parents respond when their children resist certain foods, and how the parental interest in reducing their children's risk of obesity may inadvertently compromise children's balanced eating habits. As a rule of thumb, the older the children, the more likely that they have some insight about the parental eating disorder, and therefore more open discussions in the children's presence should be facilitated.

In addition to the explicit information gathered by interviewing the family members in attendance, the family meal provides an opportunity to collect non-verbal data that will be meaningful throughout the intervention. We have identified three types of information the therapist could uncover by observing the family meal, and we provide hereinafter a few examples of possible scenarios. Only a few behaviors may be present during this particular session, and the therapist can interview the parents (and the children, as appropriate) to learn about their existence elsewhere or lack thereof.

A   Specifics of the family meal:

1   Who decided what to bring to the family picnic, and is that typical of the pattern at home? (For example, one parent is surprised to discover which food is served; the parent responsible for bringing the food says they ran out of important ingredients; the family orders take-out to bring to the therapist's office that includes foods that some family members do not eat.)

2   Do the types, varieties, and amounts of food the family brought represent the kind of meal they would have had as a family meal at their home? (For example, there is a significantly larger amount of food than usual, or too little food, and the children do not receive a second serving if they request it, or one parent does not eat since there is not sufficient food for everyone.)

3   What is the children's response to the food offered? (For example, the child refuses to eat and cries in tears: "I told you a million times I hate hardboiled eggs!" or children ask for additional helpings of the food.)

4   Who among the family members was expected to eat, and who is eating? (For example, one parent feeds the child and does not eat their own food, or mom prepared a meal for the children only, and dad eats their leftovers.)

5   Is the child being fed, or does he/she eat autonomously? (For example, a 2-year-old's eating behavior could be composed of one, or all, of the following: food is chosen by the parent and the child is spoon-fed; parents provide finger food; and/or the child eats independently using their own tableware.)

6   Does the child choose what to eat? If not, which parent feeds the child or puts food on the plate, and is there any communication about this food? (For example, the parents fill the child's plate without asking about the type and amount of foods he or she would like to receive; a child receives a large pizza box she is expected to finish.)

7   Is food being offered in response to the child's hunger cues? (For example, the children run in the therapist's office or are engrossed in another activity while the parents insist that the meal starts promptly; the parents planned the meeting to fit the family's dinner, but the child was very hungry earlier and received his meal prior to their arrival at the session; a child fell asleep on the way to the meeting, and does not seem interested in food but the parents offer it regardless.)

8 Does the meal end when the child indicates a decreased interest in food? (For example, children are asked to finish the food on their plate regardless of their behaviors.)

9 How do the parents respond when a child refuses to eat, and how do they encourage their child to eat more? (For example, do the parents use coercions, sanctions, incentives? Do they appear aligned, or does only one parent engage in communicating with the child about their intake?)

10 How do each of the parents respond to the child's attempts to share food with siblings, feed the parent, taste the parent's food, etc.? (For example, do they end up eating together or in turns from the same plate; or forbidding the child to touch another family member's food.)

11 Do all family members eat the same food? (For example, are there two or three distinct meals – the child eats pizza, one parent has salad, and the other parent eats a burrito?)

12 Is there any discrepancy between the content of the verbal interaction regarding food and the non-verbal gestures and behaviors? (For example, the parents tell the child that everyone can eat whatever they want, but repeatedly urge him or her to finish their vegetables.)

13 How do family members respond to leftover food? (For example, one parent eats the leftovers, either because the amounts brought to the meeting were too little or because they feel compelled to consume available food.)

14 What is the therapist's impression of the atmosphere during the meal? Is it conversational? (For example, the family eats in silence; family members share stories from their day; the meal is perceived as a pleasant experience.)

B General qualities of feeding and eating practices. Some of the answers to the inquiries below can be gathered from direct discussions with the parents (and their children, as appropriate). Some of the information has already been collected in session 1, and the missing information will be collected in session 3:

1 How is the schedule of feeding set (according to a pre-planned routine, the child's requests, one of the parents' time of arrival at home, etc.)?

2 Who typically eats with the child?

3 How often do family meals take place?

4 Do the parents or other family members eat at the same time as the child?

5 Do the parents or other family members eat the same food as the child?

6 How many times a week does the child eat meals with all, or most, family members present?

7 Where do the meals usually take place?

8 Is there a family dining table in use or another space where everyone can eat at the same time?

9   How do the parents decide on the amount and type of foods their child should eat?

10   Who prepares the food at home?

11   Are there any food preferences, allergies, etc., in the family? How do they affect child feeding?

12   Who shops for food and ingredients?

13   Is food being used for non-nutritional purposes, and in which cases?

14   In case the parents have children of both sexes, do they see a difference in food provision, available choices, and comments they provide between their daughters and sons?

C   Transactional patterns in the family that are beyond food and eating:

1   What is the family environment like during the session? How do the parents describe it later (e.g., tense, flexible, accepting, playful interactions)?

2   Do transactional patterns differ between feeding and non-feeding interactions? (For example, the parents are quite strict when they feed their children, but once the meal is over, the communication feels more spontaneous and pleasant.)

3   How do parents communicate over child feeding in comparison to other tasks? (For example, one parent is mostly responsible for encouraging the child to eat while the other parent is the one comforting the child or asking about their day at school.)

4   Are there any coalitions? (For example, children turn to a specific parent for comfort or emotional refueling; when a parent refuses a request, a sibling intervenes.)

5   Do parents ask one another for help, and if so, regarding which issues?

6   Do the things that are said and the way that they are being expressed match or differ?

7   Do family members express much self-criticism or comment on each other's behaviors? (For example, a parent verbally scolding themselves for forgetting an item, an older sibling making fun of a younger one, several family members criticizing another.)

Throughout the session, the therapist observes the family members' behaviors and interaction patterns and asks them for further clarifications as needed. This additional inquiry augments the therapist and the parents' understanding of what potential changes in these aspects are advised. Examples of the therapist's questions may include the following:

- Who normally cooks?
- Who cleans up afterward?
- Do you guys always eat healthfully?
- Is this meal/interaction representative of what goes on typically?
- I see that Mom and Dad are not agreeing on whether your daughter should finish the food or not; how do you usually manage your disagreements?

Goal: Close the Session with a Simple Summary and Plan the Next Meeting

Why?

By the end of the family meal session, the therapist should have developed more tailored understandings of the family's risk factors. The therapist should also have several customized, operational behavioral changes to discuss with the parents in the next session. The parents also use the family meal as an opportunity to reevaluate the patterns in their family, but they typically would need the therapist's encouragement and concrete ideas on how to spearhead the change. Although many parents welcome the opportunity to share with the therapist how difficult feeding might be for their family, the family meal session may also elicit in the parents feelings of embarrassment, guilt, shame, or self-blame. Relatedly, the parents may be triggered to share with the therapist issues that may be less appropriate for this meeting. Therapists should use their clinical judgement and delay some conversations to a later session, when the children are not present and the therapist feels that he can interview the parents more openly about the situation he witnessed. As a rule of thumb, clinicians rarely regret interpretations or feedback they have not said, but could gladly retract a question or an observation said prematurely. Thus, the therapist should conclude the meeting in a very general manner with an optimistic tone and should not go into specific evaluations of his interpretations.

How?

Session 2 concludes with a short summary during which the therapist asks the parents about their experience: Did the meal that took place during this session represent a typical or average meal at their home? Did the meal go according to plan or the way they imagined it would? The therapist should note there will be an opportunity to talk openly in the next session with parents alone, so this is not an occasion for a full discussion. The goal of the questions asked in this session is to help the therapist get to know the family better and to prompt more reflective thinking among the parents regarding family feeding and eating habits. The therapist tells the parents that a summary of observations will be provided during the following week's session and asks them to think about what they have learned from the meeting. The parents are asked to reevaluate the meal experience, think of any additional concerns or dilemmas they have about feeding their child, and bring those in for discussion during the next meeting. Finally, the therapist should finish the session by pointing out the family's strengths and acknowledging instances of adaptive decision making, proactive spousal communication, and healthy child behaviors that were evident in the meeting.

The following example depicts the therapist handling a summary of session 2 with parents presenting with significant anxiety:

Dr. Gonzales met with Jody and Al and their twin toddlers for the family meal. In session 1, he observed that Jody tends to criticize herself in very harsh words, and that Al responds to this self-consciousness with feedback that amplifies Jody's guilt and shame. Jody – who was responsible of preparing and bringing the meal to the session 2 – went very hard on herself for forgetting milk and napkins, saying tearfully: "I am so stupid!" or "I am very sorry to have forgotten the milk the kids drink every evening." As the therapist wrapped up the session, Jody mentioned that the therapist might have criticized her for her forgetfulness. The therapist then responded: "You know, Jodi, these kinds of things happen to everyone, so please do not beat yourself hard for it. Parenting is essentially work in progress. In our next meeting we can discuss how you both plan and get ready for your responsibilities, and whether you should test a few tweaks to the current way your tasks are shared, if necessary." Jody looked relieved hearing the therapist's comforting words, and Al did not respond. When the family left, the therapist added a few comments in his notes: explore whether Jody's self-criticism also affects her sense of low parental self-efficacy, explore Al's reactions in these situations, discuss with the couple the potential impacts of parental self-criticism on their children, and provide strategies for self-compassion and spousal support.

Common Therapist Dilemmas in Session 2

The Parents Do Not Bring Food for the Whole Family to Eat Together

The goal of the family meal is to help the therapist and the parents assess the feeding relationship and learn more about mealtime interactions: what are the different roles family members take as they dine together, do the parents eat at the same time as their children, what do their discussions about food look like, who controls the initiation and termination of eating, etc. When parents fail to prepare enough food for all family members or bring food that is not typically eaten by everyone, this can invite an open discussion and be used as a learning opportunity for the parents. Planning or preparing a meal that fits everyone's preferences can be posed as a future goal in the program, and the therapist can add a second family meal in the clinic, when suitable.

The Child Refuses to Eat

The family meal session should be scheduled to a time when the child typically eats. Sometimes, young children arrive to this meeting when they are evidently not interested in eating. Perhaps the time slot that was chosen for the meeting is not congruent with their eating routine or the parents had to feed the child on their way to the meeting, and now she is not hungry. Some children may become overly excited, uncomfortable, or anxious about eating in an unfamiliar context. The therapist should observe how the parents manage this conundrum, and if possible use the meeting for chatting with all family members to collect more information to extend his working hypotheses from session 1. Further, the therapist can use this meeting or the following one to discuss with the parents why their child was reluctant to eat, learn more about the daily schedules and the typical eating habits of the child, and how the parents typically manage similar scenarios, as leverage to learn more about the structure and planning of meals specifically, and the family routine in general. For example, if the parents state that the child is frequently unwilling to eat, the therapist should propose setting regular eating or parental coaching to address picky eating as specific goals of the program. The parents can later schedule a family meal session at the therapist's office should they feel they need one. Alternatively, the parents can record another meal held at their home and share the video with the therapist.

There Is No Conflict during Mealtime

When the family meal "runs smoothly," this does not pose a problem by any means. The therapist should inquire how typical this situation is and how often they all get to eat together as a family. The therapist should acknowledge this example as reflecting one of the family's strengths, and reinforce the parents' healthy feeding behaviors, encouraging them to continue providing age-appropriate, varied foods, maintain a pleasant atmosphere during mealtimes, etc. In many cases, collecting additional information, preferably in session 3, on the parents' beliefs and attitudes toward feeding can be worthwhile, as the therapist can uncover more feeding-related parental concerns and maladaptive beliefs that were not expressed during session 2 for various reasons.

The Therapist Identifies an Important Issue That May Be Outside the Scope of the Parent-Based Prevention Program

The therapist uses clinical judgement and discretion to evaluate additional aspects of the family system that he observes but extend beyond the sphere of eating and food. For instance, the therapist may notice that a parent appears depressed or responds very angrily to his family, that a child behaves defiantly with one parent or oppresses the siblings, that the parental behaviors are very authoritative, and so on. The therapist could note other issues that are mentioned in the session, such as a parent's long commute to work that affects his or her emotional availability during dinner or his or her eating patterns, the family's financial difficulties, a child being bullied at school, and so forth. In the case that the therapist thinks that these issues may be associated with greater risk for the children's development, these should be explored tactfully with the parents in session 3 and later in the program. Some issues could be addressed as part of the intervention. The therapist could reflect on other challenges, validate them, and teach the parents about their importance. The therapist can also refer the parents to a professional who could help them work though this issue later.

Not All Family Members Attend the Family Meal

The family meal is the therapist's sole opportunity to observe all family members and study their unique characteristics and interactions with one another around food and eating as well as in non-food-related situations. Identifying relationship and communication patterns, therefore, requires the participation of all family members. Hence, partial attendance may impede the learning from the family meal. The therapist should highlight that all family members must participate in session 2. One caveat to this rule should be mentioned: if a family member is regularly not present at home – for instance, an older child who is in college – holding the family meal without their attendance is reasonable. Should the parents inform the therapist in advance that one family member cannot be in attendance, the meeting is to be rescheduled. Further, if the entire nuclear family does not arrive at session 2, the therapist should explore with them how typical is the family meal in the absence of the person not present, and offer another family meal session, as needed.

Reference

Lock, J., & Le Grange, D. (2013). *Treatment manual for anorexia nervosa: A family-based approach*. New York: Guilford Press.

12 Session 3

Embracing Change

Session 3 marks the end of the First Phase in which the customized goals of the program as they apply to the unique case of the family are defined and addressed. In session 3 the therapist and the parents conjointly analyze the family meal and their previous discussions and create a work plan to challenge the identified cognitions and behaviors by devising their first operational behavioral experiment.

There are five main goals for session 3:

A Utilize the data from the family meal to enhance the insights from session 1 and reassess the goals of the intervention.
B Reinforce the Division of Responsibility model as a framework for the behavioral experiments around feeding and mealtimes.
C Prioritize the intervention targets and inform the parents of how these map onto the structure of the intervention.
D Help the parents plan their first behavioral experiment.
E Prepare the parents for the individual sessions during Phase Two.

Below are the interventions used in session 3:

1 Engage both parents in defining their goals for Parent-Based Prevention.
2 Facilitate parental agreement on the individualized goals.
3 Prioritize the targets of the intervention and identify those that can be worked on in Parent-Based Prevention.
4 Reinforce parental discussion of the Division of Responsibility in Feeding.
5 Help parents formulate their operational goals and plan their first behavioral change.
6 Prepare the parents for the structure of therapeutic interactions in Phase Two.
7 Summarize Phase One in an optimistic stance.

The therapist's interventions during session 3 are detailed below.

Goal: Engage Both Parents in Defining Their Goals for Parent-Based Prevention

Why?

In a focused intervention program such as Parent-Based Prevention, the therapist should maintain a flexible consultative stance – identifying the prominent challenges for the family, but at the same remaining respectful of the parents' insights, preferences, and existing coping strategies. To guide the parents in their application of the program to their family's unique case, the therapist helps them review the observations and insights gathered in the two meetings thus far, and formulate and refine the focus of this preventive intervention. The therapist assesses the risks for the children, given the information she has gathered thus far. This risk assessment may include present feeding problems, such as poor nutrition and body talk or fat talk (i.e., conversations on people's shape and size), danger of future eating disorders, expressed emotion between family members, and other factors the therapist perceives as associated with negative health and psychological outcomes in the children. This risk assessment incorporates data from several sources: the information provided by the parents, the therapist's observations during the family meal, the therapist's knowledge of the treatment of eating disorders and child development, and her clinical experience and skills.

How?

Prior to meeting the parents in session 3, the therapist uses Form no. 3 to summarize her assessment of the family's individual risk factors, as defined by the parents and the therapist in the first session. Outlining the key concerns identified, the therapist also integrates observations from session 2. Employing a consultative stance for collaborative decision-making, the process underscores that the parents are ultimately those responsible for ranking the targets of the program, based on their values, habits, and additional stressors.

The therapist begins by asking the parents how they perceive the family meal in light of the program's goals and invites them to openly share their thoughts and reflections. Interestingly, some parents do not remember the family meal or do not know exactly where to start. In this case, the therapist can expand the scope of the questions and interview the parents about their experience feeding their children in the past week, asking whether they have noticed anything different. Often parents have trouble labeling and sharing their feelings and observations due to feeling uncomfortable about their family's meal interactions, or since they do not know whether their family's experience is different than others'. We found that the following opening statement helps parents articulate their thoughts more easily despite of these barriers:

> I am an expert in eating disorder prevention. You are an expert for your own child and the dynamics at your home involving food. I can help you identify your strengths as a family and revisit some possible challenges on which we can work collaboratively.

Referring to their familiarity with their own family and implying that the parents are integral to their children's health often encourages parents to reflect on their concerns and dilemmas and to identify potentially problematic behaviors. The therapist and the parents engage in a discussion that clarifies their concerns about feeding their child, the child's eating habits, spousal collaboration regarding food and healthful lifestyle, and any additional spheres of family functioning. For instance, a father experiencing frequent conflicts with his children around their food choices may express interest in reducing these interactions. Similarly, a mother with binge-eating history may set a goal of reintroducing food that was labeled as "forbidden" out of fear that it would trigger loss of control of her own eating.

When prompted to share their insights, many parents are not sure where to begin. They may find it helpful when the therapist starts by sharing her professional observations and recommendations. The feedback should always begin with acknowledging the family's strengths, including the parents' commitment to their children's wellbeing as demonstrated by their initial enrollment in this treatment. Next, the therapist incorporates the parents' insights with the potential targets she has already listed in Form no. 3. The therapist then leads a discussion about these targets, and whether they should be tackled in Phase Two, Phase Three, or post-intervention. The therapist also helps parents break down the challenges (i.e., interfering or maintaining factors) and the strengths (i.e., facilitating factors) that are related to this risk. The therapist can also add suggestions for changes for the parents to consider related to the family's behaviors and transactions as these ideas can help facilitate the parents' decision-making process. Using her records on Form no. 3, the therapist integrates information from various sources: details shared by the parents in previous meetings, information gathered through the self-reported assessments they completed upon entrance into the program (if these are used; for further information, see Chapter 8), and the family meal meeting. The therapist should also discuss any observations about the role of the child's temperament and additional family characteristics that may become relevant to the family's risk assessment. The therapist structures the discussion around child healthy eating patterns and the parental behaviors associated with positive outcomes.

The discussion should cover aspects of family structure that are relevant to the prevention of feeding and eating problems, including (but not limited to) the following: parents' attitudes toward eating, food, shape, and weight; parents' sense of self-efficacy; additional/comorbid parental difficulties; child temperament; and spousal communication patterns and problem-solving skills. The therapist should then offer specific solutions that may improve the child's resilience against feeding and eating problems.

Form no. 3 The therapist worksheet for session 3, Phase One

PBP target	To be addressed in Phase Two, Phase Three, or post-PBP?	Related challenges	Related strengths	Possible operational changes	Priority (1st, 2nd, 3rd . . . issue to tackle)

Note: Form no. 3 is used for summarizing the goals of the targeted intervention. As such, it should first be completed prior to meeting the parents in session 3. Additional information may be written on this form during the session, reflecting parents' foci of interest and their ranking of the urgency/importance of the change.

Nevertheless, due to Parent-Based Prevention being a short-term intervention, some challenges may not be easily addressed within this framework. These may include, for instance, a parent's tendency for self-criticism, a parental child abuse history and its possible effects on the child's trust in the world and independent endeavors, parental difficulties in managing a zestful preschooler with hyperactivity and attention deficit disorder, and so on. When these issues are perceived (by the parents or the therapist) as impacting the parenting and feeding practices, they should be addressed within the program. However, if these characteristics or concerns are not directly influencing eating behaviors, they may be targeted during the Third Phase or in another intervention. For example, when Chantelle mentioned that her trauma history, particularly the flashbacks she has been experiencing recently, are compromising her functioning at work, the therapist replied, empathetically:

> I am sorry to hear about how things have been difficult at work recently. This must be very concerning to you, and debilitating. As you know, since this is a time-limited program we are targeting a few issues we think are affecting your family's behaviors and relationships around food. Therefore we will not be able to address your trauma history. But I care for you and for your overall wellbeing, and am wondering if I could recommend some therapists that specialize in treating trauma? Would this be OK? Is there anything else I can do to support you at this time? And is it OK if I ask your partner now how she can best support you?

Goal: Facilitate Parental Agreement on Individualized Goals

Why?

In sessions 1 and 2, the therapist and the parents developed insights regarding the transactions between family members concerning food and eating, and the broader challenges for children's healthy development. In session 3, the therapist coaches the parents in identifying the operational, tailored goals of the program and spearheading the changes in their family's attitudes, behaviors, and transactions. These are derived from their improved understanding of the effects of the parental eating disorder on child feeding and eating and on their general family structure. But before moving forward to planning the behavioral experiments the parents commit to trying, the therapist should verify that both parents agree with the formulations and the individualized goals of the program. This step is crucial, as the behavioral changes planned throughout the intervention will be designed in accordance with the parents' shared insights. The parents are not expected to agree on every observation or suggestion their partner or the therapist offers. Instead, it is the discussion process that improves parental communication and promotes better understanding of each family member's perceptions. Nevertheless, the therapist should help the parents reach consensus regarding the aspects of the parental eating disorder, family structure, and family members' characteristics that may maintain existing maladaptive patterns or precipitate future adversities they will target in the Parent-Based Prevention program.

How?

Assessment of family functioning is an ongoing process. At each meeting, the therapist and the parents enhance their understanding of the family structure and its associations with the child's risk for eating problems and developmental difficulties. By session 3, the parents have become more attuned to the possible routes by which the current or past parental eating disorder models their parental functioning. Therefore, they should feel ready to begin working on the set of targeted goals. Through a series of both direct and circular questions, the therapist helps the parents clarify their viewpoints and their partners' perspectives on the issues raised. Direct and circular questioning were introduced in Chapter 8. To recapitulate, this is a form of interviewing used in couples' counseling and family treatment; direct questions solicit the patients' understanding of themselves; for instance: "What did you feel when your daughter refused the second slice of pizza you offered?" However, circular questions are used to increase awareness of other family members' mental state, emotions, and needs; for example: "When your daughter refused your husband's encouragement for more food, what type of support did you think your husband wanted you to offer at that time?" When both types of prompts are used, they augment collaborative understanding of subjective states and mental processes each family member undergoes.

The therapist delicately and tactfully acknowledges any discrepancies between the parents' perspectives and facilitates spousal communication about them. As needed, the therapist reminds parents of the family's strengths and mentions that other families have overcome similar challenges. Further, she encourages parents to empathize with others' perspectives (the children as well as the other parent, should he or she exist), and promotes greater understanding of how the parental eating disorder and parents' additional characteristics, histories, and preferences affect their perceptions and behaviors. For example, one parent's greater sensitivity to negative cues from the environment increases their agitated responses; a child with a tendency to overeat could elicit responses from his parents that might increase the child's pre-existing risks for unhealthy eating attitudes and behaviors; or a personal history may impact a father's use of food for non-nutritional purposes and for regulating his children's stress.

The following clinical vignette may be useful here in illuminating how the therapist helps the parents reach an agreement on their personalized goals:

> When Dr. Garth met with Nicole and Connor for session 3, the couple appeared to concur with one another that they should make some changes in their feeding practices. Both partners appeared eager to

experiment with new methods of providing food to their children. However, they were not in agreement about the order in which they should make these changes. Both parents believed that addressing their food-monitoring comments around eating as well as their food policing behaviors was important. However, Nicole believed that if they started by improving structure of the child feeding schedule and reducing between-meals and snack-time eating, they would be able to reach more quickly their goal of reducing negative comments, while Connor thought that beginning by enhancing parental modeling of healthy eating practices would spearhead further lifestyle changes in their children. Dr. Garth shared with the parents her observation: "I see that both of you are on board and are interested in testing out some changes in your family's eating behaviors. But you differ in the routes through which these changes will occur. I am wondering how it would best make sense to prioritize the targets of the intervention. Both targets you mentioned appear relevant, and I have written them down on my notes. But we may want to begin with a behavior that can be modified with relatively little effort. Which of the targets you mentioned could be changed more quickly – following a feeding routine or adapting your eating habits?" Both parents looked at one another and then Nicole responded: "I guess that changing the meal routine is right now easier for me than changing my own eating. This will take some time. What do you think, Connor?" Her partner replied: "I see what you are saying here. But the routines are completely your responsibility; I am not home early enough so really feel like I cannot contribute then. I understand why beginning to tackle the routine is important, so if you tell me how I can be helpful, I am happy to help out."

As the conversation becomes more specific and focused on the family's distinctive patterns around food that illustrate their strengths and difficulties, it is important that the therapist remains attuned to the parents' guilt, shame, and self-blame, because these feelings may compromise their ability to engage in and perform the behavioral experiments. The therapist tries to ensure that the parental anxiety is in an optimal range for learning; not too intense and overwhelming, but high enough to motivate positive behavioral change.

Goal: Prioritize the Targets of the Intervention and Identify Those That Can Be Worked on in Parent-Based Prevention

Why?

Parent-Based Prevention offers a modular approach that helps parents identify and work through risk factors that could compromise their children's development. Once some targets of the intervention – adapted to the specific family – are recognized, the therapist guides the parents in choosing which challenges they would like to focus on first. Strategizing which behaviors to initially tackle requires consideration of a number of important factors. The therapist should first explore what were the concerns and dilemmas that initially brought the parents to the intervention. Typically, these are related to their concerns that their child eats unhealthily and/or that a prolonged parental eating disorder is negatively impacting parental efficacy. As a result, the parents may be particularly motivated to make a change in these areas. Targeting these issues first may result in the greatest stress reduction. As an example, parents who seek treatment because their child is a picky eater would benefit from focusing first on the child's eating habits. Other common sources of stress are a disorganized schedule and a parental experience that they cannot predict their child's eating and sleep habits. Evidently, better management of the family schedule can create a greater sense of parental efficacy. Therefore, addressing the family's routine (and most importantly, the meal schedule and sleep hygiene) could be prerequisite steps. Most importantly, the therapist should help the parents to focus on behavioral changes that are feasible and will motivate the parents to continue their progress. In general, the therapist should support ideas that are easier to actualize rather than bigger modifications that require more time and confidence.

How?

The therapist asks the parents to brainstorm ideas as to which behaviors should be targeted first. As always, the therapist includes both parents in the conversation, points out differences in perspective, and attempts to build a cohesive narrative of their problems, the order of importance or urgency of these problems, and how the parents can join forces in targeting them. As insights unfold, the therapist expresses confidence that the concerning behaviors can improve. The therapist can help to instill hope in the parents by highlighting the protective factors she has identified in the family, and focusing the discussion on resilience and capabilities. The therapist further reminds the parents that early childhood is the ideal time for a Parent-Based Prevention, because the children's patterns are not yet fixed. Moreover, any changes implemented by the parent now could reward the family in years to come.

At this point, the therapist could say:

> So please let me see if I got it right. In the first session when you both mentioned that there is a lot of tension around the dinner table, and we listed this as a primary goal of the intervention. Ashlyn often refuses to eat many kinds of food. You, Nicole, are mostly engaged in feeding the baby and you, Sydney, are very worried about Nicole's and Ashlyn's eating, as well as problems in the projects you are in charge of

at work. With everyone so worried and agitated at dinnertime, maybe we should first focus on making your meals more pleasant and less stressful. I also heard you guys saying that Ashlyn's difficult transition to a new school stresses you out very much. Nicole, if I understand correctly, you feel that the stress associated with the thoughts of how Ashlyn is doing at school leads you many times to binge and purge before pick-up time. And Sydney, you said your method of dealing with this stress is to ask Ashlyn at dinner to tell you everything that happened at school today. While you may feel that this solution helps you be an involved parent and support Ashlyn, these questions are often experienced by your daughter as overwhelming and they increase her food avoidance. By dinnertime, you, Nicole, feel "very tired and resentful," in your words, after spending a long day with the kids, and you also feel like you can't think of any proactive idea to help Ashlyn and Sydney. Is this a fair description? How would it be for you if we decide to focus first on building and improving your eating routine, and then see if we can address your parental concerns and exhaustion, and figure out if you can support Ashlyn differently?

Goal: Reinforce Parental Discussion of the Division of Responsibility in Feeding

Why?

Parents of young children are often uncertain of how to feed their children healthfully. They are exposed to opposing information on the types and quantities of food that they should offer, the number of meals their children should have per day, whether the parents or the child should be in charge of eating, and how to address requests for sweets and processed foods. In session 1, the therapist introduced Satter's Division of Responsibility in child feeding (Satter, 1986, 1990) as an anchor for making basic decisions about their children's eating. To recap, this model provides guidelines for feeding practices that support gradual evolution toward autonomous eating which relies on the child's self-regulation, within the structural boundaries that the parents define. In essence, the parents are responsible for *what* the child is offered to eat, and *when, where,* and *in what way* feeding takes place, and the child is responsible for *whether or not* they eat, and *which* and *how much* food will be eaten. The parents serve as leaders within an authoritative parenting framework, wherein the child is encouraged to act with age-appropriate autonomy. In our experience, many of the difficulties in child eating that parents express in the beginning of the Parent-Based Prevention program are instigated by an inaccurate division of responsibility. Although this model was presented to parents in the first meeting, reiterating it in session 3 helps design behavioral experiments that address key problems in the feeding relationship.

How?

The therapist reminds the parents about the Division of Responsibility model and reviews its importance in regulating children's eating. The model is explained verbally in an age-appropriate manner. The therapist also provides the parents with a handout of the model for children of different ages (see Handout A: Division of Responsibility below).

The therapist first asks the parents to list all the things they consider when they want to feed their child – how they decide when it is time to eat, what will be served, who will eat with the child, where the meal will take place, when the feeding should be stopped, etc. The therapist validates and reinforces adaptive parental feeding practices that are already in place, and educates the parents about the Division of Responsibility guidelines, drawing their attention to existing gaps. The therapist makes an effort to understand and champion the parents' large, but often unused, set of skills and store of knowledge regarding healthy eating, sufficient amounts of food, and particular characteristics of their own child. Simultaneously, the therapist and the parents should also discuss how the ongoing aspects of the parental eating disorder model their perceptions and behaviors regarding their feeding practices. The therapist addresses any reactions and dilemmas elicited by these guidelines, including current feeding habits that the parents believe are in accord with the Division of Responsibility model. The following excerpt illustrates a typical discussion on implementing the Division of Responsibility at home:

> Mateo and Martin sought treatment to help them reduce what they described as a "constant battle over second and third servings of food, another cup of milk, and candy" with their five- and eight-year-old children. During the family meal, the therapist observed that Mateo – who had anorexia in his teens and who was described as the parent who is responsible for most of the feeding at home – offered the children a small avocado sandwich and some cucumbers. When the children requested more food, he took out of his picnic cooler other food items, such as a hard-boiled egg, cherry tomatoes, and canned tuna fish. Mateo offered each of these items separately, and only after the children had said they were still hungry and requested additional food. All through this meal, Martin had hardly spoken a word, but when the meal – which lasted about 50 minutes – ended, he was much more verbally engaged with his family. In session 3, when the therapist presented the Division of Responsibility model in feeding, the parents expressed some reservations. Mateo said: "I have heard similar ideas in the past, also from our pediatrician and from a child nutritionist we once consulted with. Maybe it can work well for families where kids are not super eager to eat sweets and non-nutritious food, but if I let my children eat whatever they want, they will eat enormous amounts of food and their choices will be problematic, to say the least." Martin coincided: "I think this model is expecting Mateo to provide all the types of foods without commenting. I am not sure this would

fly in our family." The therapist said: "So please let me explain the model a bit more. The idea is that the parents set the stage for the family's eating habits. You decide which foods will be served, when, and where, and you choose foods that you think are nutritious, appetizing, and that your children will enjoy. Then, when you do serve them, you allow your children to eat until they feel satiated. But the goal is to reduce grazing between meals and to provide dessert items in moderation. Does this make sense?" Mateo responded: "And what might be the risk of us continuing the same practices we have been carrying out until now?" The therapist replied: "I was wondering when we met whether the current feeding practices were slightly restrictive. I understand that you are concerned your children will become overweight if you do not monitor their eating carefully. But there is data to show that the more children feel their eating is restricted or controlled by parents, the more these 'forbidden foods' become more appealing. Why don't we try out this Division of Responsibility model this week and see how it works for your family? There is little chance your children's weight will change dramatically during this time-frame. Is this something you are willing to consider?"

Many families are interested in receiving tools and ideas on serving a "family-style" meal, in which the food is served on the table and each participant can choose their own plate. Therefore, the therapist may provide basic dietary instructions and coach the parents on their feeding skills and the difference between their preferences and their children's nutritional needs. Handout B outlines some dietary instructions for parents. Should the therapist feel that planning meals or providing a varied diet remains a challenge beyond the scope of the program, referral to professional dieticians with whom the Parent-Based Prevention therapist can collaborate will likely augment the parent learning in the intervention.

Handout A   Division of Responsibility in Feeding

ELLYN SATTER'S DIVISION OF RESPONSIBILITY IN FEEDING

Children have natural ability with eating. They eat as much as they need, they grow in the way that is right for them, and they learn to eat the food their parents eat. Step-by-step, throughout their growing-up years, they build on their natural ability and become eating competent. Parents let them learn and grow with eating when they follow the Division of Responsibility in Feeding.

(continued)

(continued)

The Division of Responsibility for Infants

- The parent is responsible for *what.*
- The child is responsible for *how much* (and everything else).

Parents choose breast- or formula-feeding, and help the infant be calm and organized. Then they feed smoothly, paying attention to information coming from the baby about timing, tempo, frequency, and amounts.

The Division of Responsibility for Babies Making the Transition to Family Food

- The parent is still responsible for *what*, and is *becoming* responsible for *when* and *where* the child is fed.
- The child is *still* and *always* responsible for *how much* and *whether to* eat the foods offered by the parent.

Based on *what* the child can *do*, not on how *old* s/he is, the parents guide the child's transition from nipple feeding through semisolids, then thick-and-lumpy food, to finger food at family meals.

The Division of Responsibility for Toddlers through Adolescents

- The parent is responsible for *what, when, where.*
- The child is responsible for *how much* and *whether.*

Fundamental to parents' jobs is trusting children to determine *how much* and *whether* to eat from what parents provide. When parents do their jobs with *feeding*, children do their jobs with *eating*.

Parents' Feeding Jobs

- Choose and prepare the food.
- Provide regular meals and snacks.
- Make eating times pleasant.
- Step-by-step, show children by example how to behave at family mealtime.

- Be considerate of children's lack of food experience without catering to likes and dislikes.
- Not let children have food or beverages (except for water) between meal and snack times.
- Let children grow up to get bodies that are right for them.

Children's Eating Jobs

- Children will eat.
- They will eat the amount they need.
- They will learn to eat the food their parents eat.
- They will grow predictably.
- They will learn to behave well at mealtime.

For more about raising healthy children who are a joy to feed, read Part Two, "How to raise good eaters," in Ellyn Satter's *Secrets of Feeding a Healthy Family*. For the evidence, read the Satter Feeding Dynamics Model at http://ellynsatterinstitute.org.

Reprinted with the permission of Ellyn Satter Institute ©.

Handout B   10 Tips for Feeding Kids Healthfully

Food should be a pleasant, nourishing, and interactive part of your family's routine. Healthy lifestyle and weight management optimize your child's development, and are factors of eating habits as well as issues such as physical activity, screen time, sleep hygiene, and coping skills. Here are some issues to consider:

1 Make sure kids are having three square meals and 2–3 nutritious snacks a day.

Regardless of your own meal preferences, children need to eat regularly throughout the day: breakfast, lunch, and dinner as well as 2–3 snacks. Make sure there are at least one-hour gaps between meals, but no longer than three hours.

(continued)

(continued)

2 Have a daily routine around food.

Eating at regular times throughout the day is a healthy habit to teach your kids. Children are accustomed to having a regular routine and most of them thrive when the expectations are simple and clear.

3 Make sure your kids do not miss out on key nutrients.

Nutrient-dense food provides important vitamins, minerals, calcium, potassium, and dietary fiber. Essential fatty acids and carbohydrates are important for your child's developing brain and body; therefore you do not want to eliminate them from your child's diet. Reduce your child's consumption of saturated fats, sugars, starches, sodium, and sweetened beverages.

4 Trust your children's hunger and satiety cues.

Children mostly know when they have eaten too much, too little, or just enough. If your kids say they are full before all of the food on their plates is gone, that is OK. If your kids ask for seconds and thirds, that is also OK – remember that children should learn to self-serve appropriate portions. Children are also capable of adjusting their energy intake across successive meals. Pressuring or restrictive feeding practices have been found to undermine children's self-regulation.

5 Plan to have at least one family meal per day.

Meals are a wonderful time for family members to unwind and bond with one and other. These experiences help kids develop a healthy, positive attitude toward food and better diet quality. Family meals are a fantastic opportunity for discussing daily events and reinforcing adaptive coping skills that will reduce a future abuse of food to regulate stress and emotions. Engaging your kids in obtaining, preparing, and serving food is both important for their future eating habits and is fun!

6 Sweets and treats are fine, in moderation.

Let your kids know how many salty snacks, candy, desserts, and sweetened beverages they can have in a week, and help them to space out these items.

7 Kids should not be dieting.

Kids' bodies are growing and changing, so putting them on a diet, or allowing them to eat according to your diet, is likely not good for them.

Make sure there is non-diet food in the house and that they are eating adequate portions at meals and snacks.

8 Stick to a set bedtime.

Getting enough sleep is important for maintaining a healthy relationship with food. Adequate sleep helps with digestion, and in avoiding erratic cravings and being in touch with your bodily sensations.

9 Endorse flexibility.

Unplanned social gatherings, trips, and spontaneity also call for unregulated behavior and more eating out. In the event that your plans get derailed, embrace the new opportunity and resume your routine when appropriate.

10 Be a role model around eating.

Children make meaning of the world not only from direct messages they receive from parents, but also from by watching their parents' actions and observing their conversations and interactions with others. If you demonstrate a healthy, relaxed attitude around food, it will encourage your kids to treat food in the same way. Avoid using certain "dieting" language (like "calories," "lose fat," "good" vs. "bad" foods, etc.) which could be repeated and over-valued by children.

   If you feel that you have been practicing these recommendations and still experiencing challenges or dilemmas about your children's eating, development, and health, please consult with your Parent-Based Prevention therapist, your pediatrician, or a child nutritionist.

Goal: Help Parents Formulate Their Operational Goals and Plan Their First Behavioral Change

Why?

After carefully reviewing the family's competences and difficulties in regard to feeding, the therapist helps the parents to operationally define the aims they would like to achieve. Both the therapist and the parents should bear in mind that Parent-Based Prevention is a short-term program during which not all desired changes can be achieved. The therapist should help the parents focus on operational goals that are:

(a) Related to existing or potential feeding and eating difficulties the child may have;
(b) Reachable within the framework of the intervention; and
(c) Preferably demand the collaboration of both parents.

The overarching aim is to focus first on behavioral experiments (i.e., a series of behavioral changes the parents make, which are analyzed in the following session and refined) that strengthen parental efficacy and set in motion further changes in the feeding relationship. The more successful the parents feel in their first attempts to create change, the more motivated and effective they will be to generalize their achievements to future challenges, during the intervention and following its conclusion. Therefore, the conversations between the therapist and the parents about appropriate goal-setting are impactful. The therapist models a scaffold approach, beginning by addressing daily eating routines, and moving forward as early change is secured. Usually this concrete discussion covers ideas for necessary modifications in the planning, preparation, and provision of foods. Later, when the habit of a less stressful family meal is reinforced, the parents can test additional ways to offer healthy food choices to their child.

How?

Once the parents have become more informed about the risks for feeding and eating problems in their child and have committed to changing specific, potentially-maladaptive behaviors and attitudes, the therapist charges the parents with the task of deciding on the first behavioral change they will carry out. The therapist facilitates holding an experimental mindset, in which they both try to understand whether a modification in their current attitudes or behaviors leads to a desired outcome in their child's behavior. In the next session, the therapist will help the parents evaluate the behavioral experiment and refine their responses when necessary. This behavioral experiment mentality reduces parental judgement and frustration.

Parents may choose to set complex goals, such as avoiding commenting on the child's culinary choices, or may begin with simpler tasks; for instance, having a few family meals a week. Common goals that parents define repeatedly converge into four categories. The first is expanding the child's food consumption: adding more nutrients; foods rich with calories, carbohydrates, or fat; more meals per day, etc. The second is challenging the parental control needs: allowing the child to decide what and how much he or she eats, offering foods that likely involve messy eating, experiencing social situations in which the child may eat different foods, etc. The third category includes minimization of the child's exposure to the parental eating disorder: eating with the child more frequently, discontinuing any binges or purges that were done in the child's presence, and abstaining from commenting on and criticizing the child's, the parents', or other people's looks, eating, and weight. Finally, the fourth category comprises goals related to improved spousal communication and involvement around child feeding: having more family meals, communicating about the parents' concerns and dilemmas over the child's shape and activity level, requesting help around food preparation and provision, and collaborating better in social events that include eating.

At this point, discussions may become very concrete and specific. Although the therapist should defer the decisions as to how to accomplish the goals to the parents, it may help to offer them some ideas to consider; e.g., organizing the family meals in advance so that they can feed the child more effectively, planning the schedule for the week ahead of time, and deciding on the partner's role in exposure to new foods. The therapist should emphasize that for the next few weeks of the program, it may be necessary that they reserve cognitive, emotional, and time resources to achieving these goals. In addition, the goals should be defined as clearly as possible and include identified outcomes. For instance, if parents are interested in allowing more carbohydrates in their child's diet, a desired outcome may be defined as "eating pasta or couscous for dinner three times a week." Some parents may be worried that these prescribed changes will not be effective. The therapist should, as always, underscore her belief in both the Parent-Based Prevention program as well as the parents. She can respond to such a concern with:

> You have tried all sorts of things to develop healthy eating habits in your child. Some techniques have worked well and we would like to continue using them. Here we have an opportunity to add some new tools to your parental tool box, in a safe and supportive environment, where you support one another.

The following case description illustrates one parent's process in deciding on her first behavioral experiment:

> Maggie has been struggling with binge-eating disorder for about ten years. A single mom for twin toddlers, she was motivated to find ways to reduce the risk of eating and weight management problems in her children. During the first and second sessions, Maggie and her therapist, Dr. Williams, have been discussing the lack of structure in feeding and the absence of family meals, due to Maggie's stressful, demanding work and her childhood experiences growing up in a family that did not hold family meals. In session 3, when asked by Dr. Williams to plan her first behavioral experiment, Maggie mentioned a few practices she would like to change: "I frankly do not know where to start. There are so many things I'd like to change that it feels a bit overwhelming, to be honest." The therapist replied: "Could you list them? Then we would

brainstorm what your first behavioral experiment should focus on." Maggie responded: "OK, let's see. I'm definitely interested in changing the way we eat, and having more family-style meals with the kids. I think that I should do something to add diversity to our meals. I cook a few quick things or order in food, but I feel that we are eating mostly carbs, which may trigger my night binging. But this may be another issue. When we do eat, I'd like to teach the kids how to slow down their eating, and make dinnertime more conversational. Sometimes I feel like we consume our food very quickly and the meal ends abruptly. See, I've told you that there are a zillion things to change." The therapist smiled: "I understand why these issues may sound like a lot to handle, but I actually think they are related with one another. Let's focus on the low-hanging fruit. The idea is to tackle first something that will be relatively achievable within the following week, and that will motivate you to move forward with additional changes. Of the few things that you have mentioned – having family meals, allowing the children to serve themselves, encouraging them to slow down their eating, and revisiting what you guys eat – where would it make most sense to begin?" Maggie thought for a while, and then replied: "I guess that I would start with having regular family meals." The therapist replied: "Yes, this sounds like a good plan. When we have these family meals established, we could move on to targeting another behavior, such as helping each child plate their meal or teaching your kids how to slow down their eating. Now, let's try and set a reasonable expectation. If I remember correctly, currently you have family meals occasionally, but not on a regular basis. How many times a week would it be feasible to hold such meals?" Maggie responded: "I was thinking of arriving home every day at 4pm from here on, spending time with the kids and cooking for us fresh food we'd all enjoy." "Could you please remind me what is your typical time returning home currently?" asked Dr. Williams. "I usually get home by 6:00, 6:30pm, sometimes later. Four days a week I have the babysitter there, and once a week my aunt helps me with the kids," replied Maggie. The therapist continued: "I am wondering whether moving from arriving home around six o'clock to cutting two hours of your work day, each day, is a bit of a stretch. This is a big shift in your routine. I am worried whether you are setting yourself up for failure. Maybe you are better served aiming at having family meals twice a week, one on a weekday and one on a weekend? I am concerned that if you have too many barriers to succeeding in this behavioral experiment, you might feel less motivated to carry out additional changes in the future. Does this seem sensible?" Maggie smiled: "I am known for my overachieving, but I don't think it serves me as a parent. Maybe I could arrive home earlier on Tuesday, and plan one family meal on Saturday evening. I am not sure, though, when will I have time to cook for the Tuesday dinner. Any suggestions here?" The therapist replied: "What do you typically provide for dinner? Is there anything that is relatively easy and that the three of you enjoy?" Maggie answered: "Pasta marinara usually works for all of us. I can prepare it the night before if it makes more sense." "That's a great idea, Maggie!" smiled Dr. Williams. "It sounds like a terrific first behavioral experiment. But please remember, it is just an experiment. If it does not work out as planned, we re-evaluate it here on the next session, and make any adaptations needed to bring your family closer to where you'd like them to be."

Goal: Prepare the Parents for the Structure of Therapeutic Interactions in Phase Two

Why?

After the parents agree on the specific goals of the intervention, the therapist helps both of them understand the following phases of the program and how they should best prepare to utilize this short-term program. The therapist delineates an outline for the following nine sessions. The therapist should explain that during Phase Two, the meetings will be held mostly with one parent with the eating disorder history, and emphasize that both parents are expected to increase mutual support for achieving their goals. Additionally, the therapist discusses another possible consequence of the program, which is a temporary relapse in parental symptoms, as the changes encouraged can be stressful for some individuals and temporarily worsen their difficulties. However, the preliminary data of Parent-Based Prevention suggest that although some parents reported increased symptoms, completion of the intervention was associated with an overall improvement in their eating and mood (Sadeh-Sharvit, Zubery, Mankovski, Steiner, & Lock, 2016).

How?

The therapist describes the structure of the following two parts of the program: Phase Two focuses on the behavioral experiments around eating, and Phase Three includes conjoint sessions that expand the focus from eating to additional risk factors. The therapist confirms that the parents are knowledgeable about the purpose of the assignments they will perform, and that the spouse's role is to support their partner while they are leading the adaptations of the family environment. The therapist underscores that part of the parents' process will be learning to encourage and respond to each other with proactive problem solving. Phase Two includes one conjoint session scheduled between the four individual sessions with the affected parent. The couple could utilize the conjoint meeting to consult with the therapist on how to best reinforce spousal communication and support in achieving their goals.

The therapist also delineates some of the "side effects" of the program, namely a possible, transient deterioration in the eating disorder as a consequence of the increased attention to the parent's eating, shape, and weight concerns for themselves and their child. Of note, in a pilot study testing Parent-Based Prevention in sixteen mothers with eating disorder histories and their families, participants reported a temporary increase in their eating disorder symptoms, but ultimately a reduction of symptoms and improved wellbeing at the end of the program (Sadeh-Sharvit et al., 2016). Consequently, the therapist may consider sharing this information along the following lines:

> Different families experience this program differently, and some may feel their own family's problems are more difficult to address. This program should help you to better take care of your child's eating. We do not know how it will influence you. On the one hand, directing a lot of attention to your family's eating can intensify your concerns. It is also possible you will temporarily feel more stress. People react to stressful situations in many ways, and one of them is to resort back to coping patterns that have reduced their stress in the past, even if these tools are not effective in the long term. It may be that the things we discuss here, or your behavioral experiments, will trigger urges to use eating disorder behaviors. However, this is not always the case. We have found that some parents experience some deterioration in their management of their own eating disorder symptoms, but for the most part this was temporary. So, there isn't any reason why this program would result differently for you, but you should let me know if this is occurring, so we can discuss whether additional help might be needed.

Goal: Summarize Phase One in an Optimistic Stance

Why?

Primiparous parents and parents of young children in general are often unsure how good a parent they are. The parents participating in the Parent-Based Prevention program may be especially anxious or insecure about their behaviors and their child's development. The focus during Phase One on the family's problems and challenges may leave the parents feeling pessimistic and discouraged about their ability to support the development of healthy eating habits in their child. For this reason, the therapist takes a nonjudgmental and optimistic stance that addresses resistance to change and instills faith in the parents' ability to overcome identified barriers. The therapist emphasizes that the parents are the best resource for feeding their child well, because they know their child best, are most invested in the child's wellbeing and future health, and have demonstrated good parenting in feeding- and non-feeding-related parental functioning.

How?

The therapist concludes session 3 in an optimistic and cheerful note, highlighting the family's strengths and competencies. The therapist makes a case for the family being the major resource for their children's health. The therapist carefully approaches the parents' possible challenges by first identifying their good care for their child and their dedication to him or her. The therapist motivates the parents to focus their efforts on preventing potential problems in their children, rather than overwhelming them with the risks and challenges their child may face. The parents should feel welcome to express their concerns about their or their partner's ability to accomplish the operational goals defined, utilizing the nonjudgmental atmosphere the therapist encourages. Although it is important that the therapist provides some positive feedback, it is also a good opportunity to train the couple to instill hope in each other about the healthier track their family can maintain.

Common Therapist Dilemmas in Session 3

The Parents Differ in Their Understanding of Risk

Parents could have contradictory views on their family's functioning, their children's development, and many other aspects of their lives. Each parent may understand some characteristics of the parenting style or of the child's behaviors differently. For instance, a mother may believe it is important to educate young children on the dangers of being overweight, while her husband might think it is too early to discuss these issues; or, the partner could feel that complete abstinence of sweets is advised for their children, while the mother would want to practice the incorporation of feared foods in their diet. In the case of such divergence between the parents' attitudes and concerns, the therapist should encourage spousal communication through circular questioning and weighing the pros and cons of each decision. The therapist also serves as a professional who specializes in the prevention and treatment of eating disorders, and as such she should provide relevant research findings about the possible role of certain behaviors and reactions, including preoccupation with eating, high expressed emotion, too few family meals, etc.

The following vignette illustrates this scenario and how it was handled:

> Patty and Elizabeth both reported a lifelong history of being overweight. Patty grew up in a household where there was no guidance or supervision around food, while Elizabeth recalls her parents "lecturing me about healthy eating, clean eating, and all that jazz. We had zero access to sweets, salty snacks, or soda." When the couple met in college, they connected on account of their nocturnal eating and their midnight trips to a convenience store nearby. They reported presenting to the study due to their concern that their children (a 6-year-old boy and a

4-year-old girl) "will end up like us" and struggle with their weight. They expressed concerns about their daughter because she says she "is never full" and has a "strong sweet tooth", and about their son since he avoids almost any type of physical activity and often requests to extend his screen time. However, the parents had significantly opposing perspectives on how to go about reducing their children's risk of unhealthy lifestyle choices: Patty thought that the best way to achieve the goal of developing healthy eating and exercise habits was by limiting the children's constant access to snacks and electronics, and creating a table where the children recorded their daily exercise; Elizabeth, however, believed that if snacks, sweets, and sodas were available and in her children's reach, these items would gradually become less appealing and the children's interest in them would eventually wear out. Consequently, in session 3, the parents asked the therapist to weigh in on the matter. The therapist replied: "I am very glad that you guys openly communicate about how your own experiences have affected your current beliefs and attitudes regarding your children's eating, exercise, and TV watching. I want to share with you my perspective and explain the rationale and the research behind it, if that is OK." As both parents nodded in agreement, the therapist continued: "I think that what we know from studies on developing healthy habits in families is that one might not want to push too strongly in either direction. On the one hand, having a dieting mentality could unintentionally develop a sense of deprivation that could backfire if kids do not have any access to certain types of food. On the other hand, an important part of parenting is educating children to make healthy choices in complex situations, and modeling such healthy choices. Throughout the thousands of interactions you will have with them about eating, about screen time, and about physical activity, you teach your values and agenda. Therefore, I would like to propose a middle ground for you to consider. Having strict rules in either direction is not recommended. There are research data to show that once you restrict children's eating too much, they will tend to overeat when given the option. Likewise for physical activity. On the other hand, you probably do not want to avoid setting any boundaries around undesired behaviors. But there is a lot that you can be doing that is less strict, and at the same time provides structure and clarifies your expectations from your children. Research has shown that when you use language that endorses moderation, this is likely more suitable for children. Does this make sense?" Patty asked: "But we differ so greatly from one another in these areas, shouldn't just one parent take the lead on this?" The therapist responded: "I think that children easily grasp it when their parents are not unified in their approach. I believe you can find a common ground, or at least try out a few strategies that we can revisit here later." The parents concurred and, with the help of the therapist, continued exploring strategies to nurture healthful behaviors in their children.

The Parents Find It Difficult to Define Operational Goals

Viewing one's family from a prevention mindset is a developing skill. Often parents may experience child-rearing concerns that are well within the normal range of development. Other parents will have trouble imagining how their parenting practices and interactions with their child could be different. In these instances, we recommend that the therapist gives the parents some ideas for their targeted goals, based on her assessment and professional experience. The therapist provides feedback on possible goals, such as having meals at the dining table instead of in front of the TV, avoiding direct comments on the child's eating, and broadening the menu at home. It is often helpful to advise the parents to "look at this from 500 feet up" or think of how they would counsel a friend or a family relative to respond in a similar situation.

The Parents Do Not Understand the Rationale for the Individual Meetings during Phase Two

Some couples will ask to continue working together with the therapist in conjoint meetings. This may be due to a good therapeutic alliance with the therapist and/or both parents' realization of the challenges ahead. However, other parents may feel uneasy about the individual sessions, because they fear that the intervention will become focused on them instead of the child. Similarly, the spouse may be uncomfortable with the partner meeting alone with the therapist and possibly leaving him or her out of the loop. The therapist acknowledges these reservations empathically and respectfully and explains the reasoning behind having individual sessions with only one parent. The therapist also emphasizes that this is important due to the potential for enduring effects of the current or past eating disorder on feeding. It might be noted as well that it is a strategy aimed at helping families to be able to attend Parent-Based Prevention by diminishing the difficulties in scheduling twelve meetings with two parents of young children. However, should the parents insist on meeting together during Phase Two, there is no reason to object to their preferences and assess their progress in the program after two sessions (i.e., at the end of session 5).

References

Sadeh-Sharvit, S., Zubery, E., Mankovski, E., Steiner, E., & Lock, J. D. (2016). Parent-based prevention program for the children of mothers with eating disorders: Feasibility and preliminary outcomes. *Eating Disorders*, 24(4), 312–325. doi: 10.1080/10640266.2016.1153400.

Satter, E. (1990). The feeding relationship: Problems and interventions. *Journal of Pediatrics*, 117(2), S181–S189.

Satter, E. M. (1986). The feeding relationship. *Journal of the American Dietetic Association*, 86, 352–356.

13 Phase Two

Distinguishing the Parental Eating Disorder from Parental Functioning

Phase Two is the time where the therapist facilitates the active development and maintenance of healthy feeding and eating habits in the children of the participating parents by expanding, reinforcing, and repeating some of the tasks introduced during the assessment period in Phase One. Both parents are expected to engage in behavioral experiments through which they test new skills and techniques in feeding their children, and experiment with different ways to manage their worries about the child's eating, shape, and weight. Phase Two consists of five sessions – four individual sessions with the affected parent alone, and one conjoint session for both parents that is scheduled in between the individual sessions. Each session begins with a review of the adaptations the parents have initiated in the time since the last meeting, and ends with a decision on a behavioral experiment the parents will undertake during the following week. The conjoint session (session 6) also serves as a mid-intervention evaluation when the therapist and the parents discuss strategies through which the parents can support one another.

The therapist repeatedly reviews with the parents their attempts at feeding their child according to the Division of Responsibility guidelines. Further, the therapist systematically advises the parents on how to proceed in inhibiting the influence of the paternal eating disorder on child feeding and related behaviors. The sessions may be characterized by some reiteration of the defined goals of change by addressing them from different angles and adding variations. The therapist also reviews the same steps weekly in order to help the parents be more consistent in their management of the child's eating behaviors, while utilizing approaches that help the parents reach their goals in previous weeks. Throughout Parent-Based Prevention in general, and in Phase Two especially, the tasks are introduced in a graduated difficulty that allows for positive reinforcement of all family members.

The Goals of Phase Two

A   Extend the parents' understanding of the effects of the parental eating disorder and of family members' additional characteristics on child feeding practices.

B Focus the discussions on the operationalized ways in which the parents can support the development of healthy eating habits in their child.
C Plan the behavioral experiments that the parents would like to try at home, and evaluate their execution and the goals achieved.

Phase Two is also characterized by three main structural aspects:

- **The therapist guides the parents in the operational changes that were decided on during the assessment period, through a series of behavioral experiments.**

Following the assessment in Phase One and the goals set together by the parents and the therapist to address the family's risk model, the parents are encouraged to actively adjust their behaviors so that they fit better with their children's needs. These adaptations are accomplished through small, gradual changes in parental behaviors, and they are also agreed upon and discussed during the session. The therapist may consider with the parents the pros and cons of each alternative, the consequences of choosing different courses of action, and possible challenges that may arise. Discussions could often be quite specific and concrete. For example, when planning the types of food to offer at specific meals, the parents and the therapists may delineate the exact time, and by whom the meal will be provided, which food is offered, etc. Parents often refer to these tasks as "homework." As described in chapters 2 and 9, we frame these tasks as behavioral experiments, a term that is associated with a greater sense of control by the person and the lack of immediate penalties once initial efforts fail. The therapist clarifies that the change of maladaptive feeding behaviors is expected to be gradual and that he is there to support the parental efforts.

Discussions may be characterized by a considerable degree of reiteration as the therapist and parents may address the same challenges week after week. This type of work is important in order to create sustainable change that allows the parents to overcome their difficulties in facilitating transformations in the home. At the same time, the sessions should end on an optimistic note, acknowledging parental endeavors and motivation, and amplifying their actual success and efforts. The therapist should be mindful of the parental hope and engagement in the process so as to uncover any interfering schemas.

- **Phase Two is composed of mostly separate interactions between the therapist and the affected parent that replace the couple meetings.**

Following the formulation of an agreed, specific work plan in session 3, the therapist holds four weekly individual meetings with the affected parent and one conjoint session including both parents. The rationale for conducting individual sessions lies in the preliminary justification for the parents' participation in the program, which is the eating disorder of one of the parents. Evidence indicates that a parental eating disorder is associated with developmental adversities in their children, and that interventions that are matched to the type and stage of the eating disorder are linked with an improved outcome (Treasure, Stein, & Maguire, 2015). Hence, the affected parent should receive greater therapist time to uncover and attend to the explicit and implicit mechanisms by which the eating disorder may impact parental functioning, including the concerns, emotions, comments, and child feeding practices which have been identified as risk factors in the development and perpetuation of eating disorders (Ogden & Steward, 2000). At the same time, the therapist constantly mentions the spouse and encourages the affected parent to think about engaging both parents in behavioral experiments at home in order to enhance spousal support.

- **The discussions during Phase Two concentrate on feeding-related concerns, dilemmas, interactions, and behaviors while other important issues are deferred to Phase Three.**

Parent-Based Prevention is designed to reduce the possible negative outcomes that the offspring of parents with eating disorders may endure. Consistent with the targeted goals defined by the therapist and the parents, Phase Two focuses on the fundamental level of risk, namely feeding and eating problems in the children. Given the short-term nature of this program, the additional risks for difficulties in other aspects of self-regulation and social-emotional maladjustment are deferred for later discussion (during Phase Three). Examples of this include spousal communication, and the role of anxiety and avoidance in the family life. Both the therapist and the parent may acknowledge these concerns, and it is the therapist's role to explain why certain issues cannot be attended to in this part of the intervention and to focus the conversation back on the goals suitable for Phase Two. If any additional novel and important topics do arise, the therapist can review Form no. 3 and add them to the list.

References

Ogden, J., & Steward, J. (2000). The role of the mother–daughter relationship in explaining weight concern. *International Journal of Eating Disorders*, 28(1), 78–83. doi: 10.1002/(SICI)1098-108X.

Treasure, J., Stein, D., & Maguire, S. (2015). Has the time come for a staging model to map the course of eating disorders from high risk to severe enduring illness? An examination of the evidence. *Early Intervention in Psychiatry*, 9(3), 173–184. doi: 10.1111/eip.12170.

14 Sessions 4–5, 7–8

Individual Sessions with the Affected Parent

The overarching goal of the individual meetings with the affected parent in Phase Two is to increase their understanding of the contribution of the eating disorder to their parental feeding practices and in turn to the child's eating behaviors, as well as to develop skills, tools, and capabilities to change behaviors. The affected parent – through whom the family enrolled in Parent-Based Prevention – receives more therapeutic contact and support than the spouse, in an effort to promote earlier changes in the family dynamic and structure. However, the therapist's perspective remains systemic as they strive to understand and respond to each member while keeping the family structure in mind.

Sessions 4 and 5 are held with the affected parent alone. In session 6 the couple meets with the therapist together for a conjoint meeting. Finally, the therapist meets the affected parent for two additional individual meetings (sessions 7 and 8). The meetings in Phase Two follow a less systematic structure, and may not always adhere to a pre-specified order. The sequence of the interventions and the time dedicated to each of them varies according to the topic at hand; however, regardless of the specific path in each meeting, the therapist should help the parent uncover a mechanism that maintains the effects of the parental eating disorder on the child's healthy eating, and helps the parent target it through a behavioral experiment.

Goals for the Individual Sessions with the Affected Parent

A Assist the parent in identifying specific ways in which the parental eating disorder and family members' related characteristics affect child feeding practices.
B Plan and review the behavioral experiments the parents will test at home.
C Increase parental self-efficacy and help the parent feel more confident in their ability to nourish their child without the interference of the eating disorder.

In order to achieve these goals, the therapist will need to undertake the interventions that are listed below. Of note, the same interventions are prescribed for the individual as well as the couple meeting, with the exception that the steps involving spousal communication (i.e., steps 5 and 6 below) are composed of parent–therapist discussions when only one parent is present, whereas when both parents participate they are encouraged to practice in the session how to initiate conversations on the matters at hand.

1   Focus the discussion on the challenges the parent has in feeding the child.
2   Identify parental concerns on how the eating disorder affects the child's eating.
3   Challenge the parent's observations to promote greater parental self-inquiry.
4   Plan and review the behavioral experiments the parents will test at home.
5   Identify the specific spousal support that may be helpful to the affected parent and facilitate requesting and accepting it.
6   Write down, together, the issues that the parent will discuss with the spouse.
7   Summarize the meeting in an optimistic note.

Hereinafter the therapist's interventions during sessions 4–8 are elaborated. For the therapist's convenience, these interventions are outlined in Form no. 4.

Goal: Focus the Discussion on the Challenges the Parent Has in Feeding the Child

Why?

Parent-Based Prevention directly targets one of the main fears of parents with eating disorder histories: that their own difficulties in eating, body image, and co-occurring symptoms will negatively impact the wellbeing of their children. Many parents have not shared these worries with anyone prior to their participation in the program. Moreover, many parents with eating disorders have never been in treatment for this problem! The invitation to meet alone with the therapist, and reflect on their parental schemas and how their eating disorder might model their parenting practices, could be experienced by some parents as overwhelming and anxiety-provoking. In the pilot study testing Parent-Based Prevention, maternal anxiety remained high during the program in contrast to the significant improvements found in maternal eating-disordered and comorbid symptomatology (Sadeh-Sharvit, Zubery, Mankovski, Steiner, & Lock, 2016). It could be that the psychological distress that is associated with parenting young children – together with the intervention setting – accentuates parental guilt, memories of past experiences as a child, negative views of self, and pessimism. These feelings, although alleviated temporally, are indeed

Form no. 4 The therapist interventions in Phase Two

PBP individual meetings interventions	Information gathered	Possible behavioral experiment/follow-up
1 Focus the discussion on the challenges the parent has in feeding the child		
2 Identify parental concerns on how the eating disorder affects the child's eating		
3 Challenge the parent's observations to promote greater parental self-inquiry		
4 Plan and review the behavioral experiments the parents will test at home		
5 Identify the specific spousal support that may be helpful to the affected parent and facilitate requesting and accepting it		
6 Write down, together, the issues that the parent will discuss with the spouse		
7 Summarize the meeting in an optimistic note		

Note: the therapist should use Form no. 4 to plan the session, record important data, and note possible targets of the intervention.

distressing. Understandably, the parent could be overwhelmed and wish to consult with the therapist about these issues. However, the therapist should be cognizant of the need to focus and redirect the conversations in Phase Two on the child's feeding and eating. Other concerns the parents have are verbally acknowledged by the therapist, who empathetically realigns the parent on the goal of the intervention and of Phase Two specifically. The therapist is to explain compassionately that a more comprehensive discussion of these issues may be postponed until Phase Three. Alternatively, if the therapist feels that the level of distress reported by the parent is very intense (or that there are important issues that demand an immediate response), they could help the parents find additional relevant resources in the community.

How?

The therapist begins the session by setting the agenda for the individual meetings of Phase Two. The therapist continues by asking the parent if there is anything that resonated with them from the last meeting until today's meeting, if the discussions in the past few weeks have made the parent think differently about things, and if the parents' behaviors at home have changed in any way. These questions allow the therapist to evaluate the family's readiness for the planned changes, and indicate for the parent that Phase Two is mostly about translating their insights to modified feeding-related behaviors at home. The therapist listens to the parental account and provides feedback in a nonjudgmental, professional, and supportive tone. The therapist keeps in mind the importance of prioritizing the issues raised into three groups: first, those which are highly relevant to the focus of Phase Two on the regulation of feeding practices and child eating habits. These include feeding practices and dilemmas on how to respond to the child's eating, physical activity levels, or weight. Second, issues that may have relevance to the child's mental, cognitive, and socio-emotional development, or to other aspects of family or spousal functioning; for instance, difficulties in social interactions or highly critical and conflictual interactions between family members. These should be postponed for discussion during Phase Three, in which the parents have a conjoint meeting with the therapist. Third, issues that are less relevant for the focus on child's healthy development of eating and related behaviors, such as parents' career dilemmas, work–home balance, marital difficulties that are less related with child-rearing, etc. The therapist shares his considerations in prioritizing the challenges with the parents, and suggests that by the completion of this short-term program, the parents could further explore these concerns in another consultation.

Prioritizing these three groups of concerns is based on the therapist's clinical judgment and experience. For example, it the parents work late hours in a very demanding job, this may indicate that they cannot be present in an adequate number of family meals to try out new techniques in feeding their children differently. The stressful working situation can also worsen the parent's eating disorder – an important issue to address, although it should not be managed in Parent-Based Prevention. Thus, the therapist openly discusses these issues and clarifies their approach in prioritizing which challenges are addressed.

The excerpt below illustrates how this scenario was managed:

Seth, a man with a history of anorexia nervosa, is married to Angelina. The couple adopted three children, whose ages range between 1 and 5 years old. The couple sought Parent-Based Prevention as they were hoping for guidance on feeding their children and preventing future weight-regulation issues. In session 3, the couple had decided on a plan for when and how they will provide their children access to food they deem as less nutritious (such as items high in sugar, fat, or sodium), in line with the Division of Responsibility model. When Seth arrived at session 4, the therapist was expecting to hear about how the past week has gone, and whether the parents were able to meet their behavioral experiment goal. However, when Seth entered the room, he looked very troubled. He disclosed he had just met an acquaintance from high school, who served as a psychiatrist at the same outpatient program where the therapist worked and the intervention was provided. Although this woman was kind and polite and had not asked Seth about the reasons for his visit to the clinic, Seth felt disheartened and discouraged, saying: "I am probably the least successful graduate of North Valley High. Everyone in my town hold great careers and have great families, and I am such a failure." The therapist had observed before that Seth tends to express black and white thinking and that he has very low self-esteem. However, the therapist was not sure how to address this in the context of the Parent-Based Prevention program. Therefore, the therapist remained silent for five minutes, while Seth detailed his negative perceptions of himself, the terrible career decisions he had made, in his opinion, and other self-critical descriptions. The therapist realized that unless he intervened in a way that would be supportive and yet decisive, Seth and Angelina might not reach the goals they had set for this brief intervention. Therefore, the therapist said: "I see how dismayed and disappointed you are by this few minutes' meeting. And I understand that some things can trigger a wave of negative thoughts and feelings in you, Seth. I care for you, and I would like to help you feel better about yourself. However, I am also thinking about the goals you and Angelina have set for this program. If we speak about important issues such as your self-esteem, we might not be able to follow through with the aims of this program and, as such, exacerbate your concern about not being efficacious also in your role as a parent. Therefore, I suggest that in the next few sessions we will focus on identifying how your self-defeating thinking affects your parenting practices, particularly with how you go about feeding your children. But I'd like to leave maybe 10 minutes of today's session to explore with you some options for additional support for you, beyond your parenting role. Does this sound like a good plan?"

Goal: Identify Parental Concerns around How the Eating Disorder Affects the Child's Eating

Why?

In Phase Two, the parent is encouraged to reflect on the links between the eating disorder and the risk to the child of feeding and eating problems. Some of the themes that emerge in the meetings are common to many parents with eating disorders. (A wide range of families, challenges, and parental dilemmas are described throughout this book.) However, every family has an individual organization that interweaves the unique characteristics of family members and the family structure. Based on his acquaintance with the family, his clinical experience, and the information gathered throughout Phase One of the program, the therapist adds his perspective to augment the parent's self-inquiry.

How?

The therapist attempts to focus the parent's attention on the behaviors that may be mostly linked with negative outcomes in the child, as the foundation of the targeted behavioral experiments. When appropriate, the therapist reflects on the enduring aspects of the eating disorder and their likely impact on parental functioning and feeding practices:

> Your eating disorder can be perceived as an entrenched strategy to manage stress, negative experiences, and, as a parent of a young child, possibly also fatigue. However, there is a discrepancy between your old habits and what you may want for your child. This program is designed to help both of you manage this gap. I invite you to bring your concerns and dilemmas about these issues to these meetings.

These discussions are delivered openly and in a nonjudgmental manner. In addition, the therapist also continues to educate the parent about healthy feeding by reinforcing the Division of Responsibility model for child feeding that was discussed in the previous sessions.

The therapist clarifies the limits of confidentiality by assuring that the parent that meetings are confidential, but that in order for the program to be effective some of the discussion should be shared with the spouse. The therapist clarifies that by the end of the session, they will review the issues that were examined and communicate with the affected parent the points or topics that would be beneficial to communicate with the spouse.

Goal: Challenge the Parent's Observations to Promote Greater Parental Self-Inquiry

Why?

The therapist directs, re-directs, and focuses the conversation on the family's eating behaviors and organization around food preparation and provision, and the family meals. The meetings should concentrate on the parental eating disorder and additional parental and child characteristics that may affect the attempts at normalizing feeding, and acquiring healthy eating behaviors. The therapist encourages an ongoing evaluation of the links between the eating and the family's organization, management, and concern around food, eating, shape, and weight, as well as the traits and habits of each of the family members. This is a dynamic process in which the parent mentions a concern, the therapist asks for clarifications of the nature of this concern, the parent reflects on it more, and the therapist replies with additional observations and feedback about how the parental eating disorder may compromise the child's healthy development.

How?

As the parent expresses their difficulties, worries, and memories, the therapist demonstrates his interest in comprehending their experience and in understanding the influence that the eating disorder has on parenting, and on feeding in particular. In these four individual sessions, the therapist should first help the affected parent explore this issue by asking him or her to express thoughts, dilemmas, and past experiences spontaneously. Gradually, the therapist leads the conversation to the targeted goals that were decided on in session 3. Helpful prompts to steer the conversation could include the following:

> You mentioned that you are very concerned that your child overeats, although he is in a normal percentile for his age and has followed the same growth trajectories since he was born. How do you understand this gap? How do you know that your child overeats? Are you certain that he overeats or are you concerned he may overeat unless you closely monitor his eating?

Some parents can identify with general examples from other families:

> Many parents that I work with say that they find themselves overly criticizing their family members' eating habits. Some become very upset during mealtimes, although they do not necessarily think it is a good thing. Is this something that happens to you?

Here are some examples of typical challenges experienced by parents with eating disorders and ideas of how the therapist can expand the parent's insights regarding how the eating disorder interferes with parenting:

- "My child has the same body shape as I had when I was her age. She is chubby, and I can't stop thinking about how unhealthy this is."

  Therapist: "What makes you be unable to stop thinking about this? Are you 100% sure that having this body type is synonymous with being unhealthy?"

- "I get very anxious to see how many candies they collected on Halloween. I've been talking with them about practicing moderation since the school-year started, and this just made them even more eager to go trick-or-treating. Every night after the kids go to bed, I count how much more candy is left in the cupboard."

  Therapist: "What are you really worried about? Could you consult with your spouse how to form rules about similar social situations in a way that is aligned with the Division of Responsibility model?"

- "When I washed my four-year-old last night, she pointed at her belly and said that her tummy was huge. She was laughing and playing, but I was instantly thrown thirty years back when kids made fun of my body. I could not stop crying last night."

  Therapist: "I am so sorry to hear this, it sounds like it might have been a very difficult experience for you. Must have been hard to be reminded of these painful events from your childhood. Is it OK if we explore this a bit, and try and think about what you know of your daughter's experience with her body? I am asking how she feels about her body, because not all the kids her age have internalized a 'fat stigma'. Is this fair to say? Would you like us to work on ways through which you can nurture your child's self-love and self-acceptance? How do you think that your spouse would have reacted if it had been him there in the bathroom with her?"

- "I dread dinnertime. Already by 3pm I get almost possessed with thoughts about what I could serve for dinner. And I find myself unsure whether to give them a small snack at 4pm or not, and how to prepare dinner when they want to play with me. I feel like this whole dinner thing really ruins our evenings at home."

  Therapist: "This sounds very intense. I can almost feel the stress you've described in my body right now in the session. Let's try and unpack this. Is it the difficulty finding ideas what to serve at dinner? Is it your concern that if your kids eat a snack after school they will not be hungry enough for dinner? Could it be that you are just exhausted by the evening and it's difficult to think straight after the baby kept you up all night? Or is it a combination of a bunch of things?"

Goal: Plan and Review the Behavioral Experiments the Parents will Test at Home

Why?

As the parents develop and enable healthier feeding practices that will nourish their child, every session should end with a detailed plan for the behavioral experiment the parents will test at home. The behavioral experiments should be designed in gradual difficulty and urgency – after identifying which current challenges are most troubling to the family, the change should target a goal that is achievable until the next session, and one that has the potential to empower the parents in consecutive adaptations.

In the majority of families, behavioral changes around better structuring the meal routine and reducing mealtime conflicts are most appealing to parents. These challenges are often interrelated, and they are associated with insufficient planning, avoidance of handling food, and skipping earlier meals and snacks in the day. Interestingly, parents experience the most feeding problems in late afternoon and evening, when the parents themselves are exhausted and distracted. Despite many parents' demoralization, some simple modifications in these areas improve the atmosphere at home, the eating environment, and all parties' distress.

Regardless of the issues confronted, the therapist should instigate self-inquiry, selection of realistic goals, and proactive problem solving, using varied techniques and strategies. The parent should remain with the experience that he or she has developed important skills and abilities to navigate the feeding relationship and cope with related challenges.

How?

The therapist and the parent first analyze the issues raised in the session in light of the operational goals that were determined by the end of Phase One. Then the parents choose one specific thing that he or she would like to work on this week. The therapist and the parent discuss in detail when, where, and how the behavioral experiment will take place, the expectations of how different family members will react, possible scenarios, and expected responses of each family member. During these conversations, the therapist encourages the affected parent to anticipate any barriers to change and unplanned reactions, and think of pragmatic solutions. The ways in which parents can request and receive their spouses' support in these behavioral experiments are considered as well and the parent is encouraged to converse with the spouse in advance about making any changes and explore how they could help one another. In the following meetings, the behavioral experiments are analyzed and modified, as needed.

Eating disorders are characterized with low self-efficacy and pessimistic attributions of success and problems. In order to "unplug" the parental

eating disorder mindset and contextualize children's responses, the therapist provides the parent with constructive feedback that strengthens their
mastery and sense of competence. The therapist also presents important
information on developmentally-related considerations that could affect
children's responses to the desired changes. In their analysis of challenging scenarios while testing the behavioral change, the therapist also helps
the parent differentiate between difficulties that can be attributed to the
adverse effects of the parental eating disorder, and challenges that reflect
normal-range child-rearing experiences. For instance, for a parent who
tends to attribute problems to their own behaviors, trying to maintain
a planned schedule of meals with a toddler who responds with a temper
tantrum could be disheartening. The therapist should identify the assumptions the parent has on their ability to lead their family, and empower them
to acquire and practice necessary tools to achieve change.

The next vignette illustrates how the therapists help the affected parent formulate the behavioral changes to be tested, and how the assessment
process occurs in the session:

> Elaine, a single mom whose daughter was 7 years old, had already
> received four sessions of Parent-Based Prevention. She first worked on
> a better division of responsibility in feeding, in line with the model the
> therapist had presented early on. The changes she wanted to implement
> appeared to be effective, and mealtimes became much less conflictual
> and less stressful. Further, Elaine identified a close friend from work who
> was a single parent of two older children, and was willing to provide
> support in helping troubleshoot problems and contingency planning.
> Now, when Elaine described her child's routine, the therapist identified
> that Elaine often skipped breakfast herself, and her daughter had been
> avoiding breakfast some days as well, mirroring her mother's behavior.
> When the therapist provided psychoeducation about the importance
> of breakfast, especially for children (i.e., better concentration at school,
> improved metabolism, and preventing subsequent overeating and
> binge-eating), Elaine expressed her desire to model healthy behaviors.
> However, she endorsed cognitions in line with the dieting mentality
> and expressed uncertainty about the importance of breakfast consump-
> tion. Despite these challenges, Elaine decided to work on adding back
> breakfast and to follow up with her close friend for support in doing so.
> The therapist suggested that Elaine detail her plan for the behavioral
> experiment the following week, but she said she would figure it out
> later. The therapist maintained that the more detailed the plan was, the
> greater the chance that it would be carried out. So, Elaine planned offer-
> ing breakfast to her child on Tuesday and Thursday the following week.
> When the therapist inquired about the barriers to following through
> with her plan, Elaine acknowledged she was not sure exactly which
> food she could offer her daughter. After generating some ideas with

the therapist, Elaine decided to let her daughter choose between eating cereal and milk or an omelet. The following session, Elaine informed the therapist that she had offered her daughter breakfast food, but the latter refused, saying that if her mother was not eating breakfast, she was not eating it either. Her daughter also expressed concerns about "getting fat" if she ate breakfast. The therapist reflected on how difficult it might be for both Elaine and her daughter to introduce breakfast to their routine. Then, he helped Elaine identify, examine, and challenge maladaptive cognitions related with the number of meals. The therapist encouraged the mother to model eating breakfast once a week, possibly on the weekend when Elaine felt less stressed. Further, the therapist encouraged Elaine to share her concerns with her friend and seek more concrete advice and instrumental support, as needed. In the next session, Elaine was very proud to report that her child began eating breakfast once she re-introduced breakfast into her diet. The therapist complimented her for her persistence in building a healthier lifestyle in her daughter, and her flexibility in adapting her own behaviors so that they better model the habits she wants her daughter to develop.

Goal: Identify the Specific Spousal Support That May be Helpful to the Affected Parent and Facilitate Requesting and Accepting It

Why?

Most parents arrive at Parent-Based Prevention after they have tried numerous ways to feel less preoccupied and stressed about their child's eating. In many families, although the parents with the eating disorder understand that their attitudes and responses are often nonadaptive, they struggle with how to change, and are not sure how to request and accept their spouse's support. A detrimental part of an eating disorder is the secrecy it involves and the immanent difficulty to share how deeply ingrained are the fears of gaining weight, the binge–purge cycles, and other symptoms. Additionally, many couples have developed a delicate couple's dance (metaphorically) in their avoidance of communicating directly on the parental eating disorder. Spouses have tried in the past reaching out to their partners about their difficulties, but too often the communication resulted in misunderstandings, conflicts, and greater stress for both parties.

We frequently hear from couples in Parent-Based Prevention that they are very pleased with their relationship, communication patterns, and parental collaboration in areas that do not involve eating, child feeding, and the parental eating disorder. They are happy and content with their ability to support each other in educational, monetary, household, and extended-family dilemmas. But they still feel they need the therapist's support in improving their communication skills regarding their children's healthy eating and development. Following a long time when these issues were not verbally discussed, the therapist could help the couple reconnect.

How?

After designing a behavioral experiment that the affected parent wishes to try out at home during the next week, the therapist reviews the types of support resources they can rely on while implementing this change. Then the therapist prompts the parent to think about some ways to utilize their spouse's support. At this point parents could benefit from some concrete ideas concerning how to communicate with their partners, and the emotional and practical support their spouse can provide. The therapist can offer a few suggestions that could expand the parents' repertoire and be useful also on later occasions. Requests for support from the spouse could include: planning together the meal schedule of the family, shopping for groceries, returning home earlier to participate in mealtime, cooking at least one more meal a week, engaging the child in more physical activity, etc. The therapist may practice with the parent different techniques of requesting the type of support needed in an engaging manner.

Goal: Write Down Together the Issues That the Parent Will Discuss with the Spouse

Why?

Each of the four individual sessions with the affected parent should conclude with a brief summary of the matters that were discussed, and the targeted plan for the behavioral change that the parent will test in the following week and that will be analyzed in the following session. The therapist encourages the parent to share their self-inquiry and anticipated changes with their spouse to the extent of self-exposure they are comfortable with. The therapist informs the parent that in the next session, not only the results of the experiment but also the communication with the spouse will be reviewed and analyzed. This information is later used to further identify the strengths and challenges of the family unit and to individualize the intervention even more.

How?

The therapist asks the parent during the session what they have learned about themselves and the behavioral experiment they would like to try in the following week. The therapist reviews the central issues that have been discussed and examines whether the parent is willing to share any of them with their spouse themselves, if he or she would like to do it with the therapist's support during the conjoint spousal meetings, or if he or she would like to continue contemplating for a while what are the most appropriate way and setting to converse with their spouse on these topics. Two examples can highlight this part of the meeting:

> One father chose a behavioral experiment that is related to having a family meal a couple of times a week. Even if he feels confident that he can manage the preparations alone, his wife's knowledge and support of this goal are invaluable, even if she cannot attend these meals.
>
> Another mother feels that since her binges had recently increased, she has been more impatient with her family. Therefore, she decides to ask her physician for medication. Her husband's knowledge of her experience is thus very important; the therapist can discuss with the mother the benefits of discussing with her partner any of these issues – her increased stress, the increase in binges, the idea of medication – or all of them.

Without a planned tactic about how to communicate difficult issues that pertain to child feeding and wellbeing, the affected parent may feel alone and disempowered, and the other parent might become disengaged and disheartened. Facilitating the parents' continued conversations between sessions is, thus, an important strategy to keep the treatment's momentum going.

Goal: Summarize the Meeting in an Optimistic Note

Any change the parents do during Parent-Based Prevention is likely associated with some ambiguity and stress. Before the parent embarks on this change, the therapist should reiterate the behavioral experiment mentality and convey the message that the parents can bring their family closer to the desired outcomes. The therapist encourages the parent to experiment with different attitudes, behaviors, food, and spousal collaboration, and reassures them that in the following session they will be able to reevaluate their thoughts and actions with the support of the therapist.

Reference

Sadeh-Sharvit, S., Zubery, E., Mankovski, E., Steiner, E., & Lock, J. D. (2016). Parent-based prevention program for the children of mothers with eating disorders: Feasibility and preliminary outcomes. *Eating Disorders*, 24(4), 312–325. doi: 10.1080/10640266.2016.1153400.

15 Session 6

A Conjoint Meeting with Both Parents

During this meeting that is scheduled in the middle of the individual sessions, the parents' understandings and efforts at reducing any negative impacts of the parental eating disorder on their children's eating are reunified. The goals of the conjoint session are as follows:

A Work through both parents' understandings of how the parental eating disorder, along with both parents' additional characteristics, affect child feeding practices.
B Plan and review the behavioral experiments the parents tested at home.
C Encourage positive parental self-efficacy and normalization of common feeding interactions.

The structure of this conjoint session is similar to that of the individual sessions during Phase Two. However, more time is dedicated to recapitulating both parents' views of the process thus far and encouraging emotional and practical support, active listening, and couple co-regulation. The therapist facilitates the discussion between the parents and guides them toward finding the communication styles and the problem-solving techniques that are useful and effective for their family.

Common Therapist Dilemmas during Phase Two

Parents Would Like to Focus on Personal, Marital, or Parental Issues That Have Little Relevance to the Links between the Eating Disorder and Child Feeding

People respond differently to psychological interventions, depending on their personalities, period in life, support resources, and additional factors. Parent-Based Prevention may be perceived by parents as an outlet to vent or discuss other concerns and dilemmas they may be having. For instance, the recent transition to parenthood may have elicited in the parent memories and conflicts that are more related to the origin family and the parental identity, or the partner may be struggling with guilt about his relationship with his children of a previous marriage. Nevertheless, the therapist should keep parents focused on the program's objectives, which are predominantly reducing the risk of feeding and eating problems in their child. A possible response in such a situation would be to sensitively share with the parent the therapist's view of this discrepancy, along these lines:

> I hear that this issue is very important to you and troubles you greatly. And I understand why you bring it here. This intervention is about adapting what you would do with your child, and the issue you have just described may indeed make things a bit more complicated. How do you think this will affect your ability to feed your child differently (or: help your spouse 'lower the volume' of their eating disorder)?

The therapist reassures the parents that in the closing session they will be able to discuss referral to other services if indicated and if the parents would want it, including an eating disorder treatment, couple therapy, individual psychotherapy, and career counseling.

Parents Misattribute the Reason for the Added Individual Sessions with the Affected Parent

Some parents erroneously think that the fact that in Phase Two the affected parent receives four individual sessions, while the spouse attends only one session, indicates that one parent is more responsible for any difficulties than the other parent, or that the affected parent should work harder with the child, or that the goal of Parent-Based Prevention is to reduce the symptoms of the parental eating disorder. All of these assumptions are not true. The parents are enrolled in Parent-Based Prevention due to one parent's eating disorder and its association with feeding and eating difficulties in their children. Therefore, it makes sense that the affected parent will receive more interaction with the therapist in order to clarify these associations. However, this intervention holds a systemic approach and works with both parents to learn about their contribution to the current difficulties as well as their strengths in supporting healthier habits. Since the spouse does not have an eating disorder history, she or he can make use of the program with less contact with the therapist during Phase Two. The therapist should emphasize to both parents that the partner is expected to be highly involved in implementing the changes at home and collaborating with the affected parent in their joint efforts to facilitate the development of healthy eating in their child, as illustrated in the following example:

> When Kiomi contacted the therapist to inquire about Parent-Based Prevention, she queried about the meeting schedule, saying that her

partner, Abner, travels for work several times a month. Therefore, she was wondering whether she could receive the intervention on her own. The therapist, Julie, explained why – in families headed by two parents – involving the partner is key to the intervention's success. She also mentioned that the intervention is designed to adapt to the scheduling difficulties of young parents. Therefore, the therapist encouraged Kiomi to speak to her partner about the program. After a few days, Kiomi called back to schedule the first appointment. During Phase One, the therapist observed that Abner was somewhat reserved. He frequently looked at his cell phone, or gazed randomly in the room, avoiding eye contact with Julie. She felt that her efforts engaging him more in the intervention were not fruitful.

Kiomi expressed concern around balancing her children's different nutritional needs and the parental messages about healthy habits, given the children's different biological sex, body shape, and physical activity habits. Specifically, she reported that the couple's youngest daughter is overweight, the middle son is underweight, and the eldest daughter is normal weight but expressing concern with the number on the scale and placing a great deal of emphasis on comparing her body shape and weight with those of her teenage friends. When prompted, Abner admitted that he was slightly worried about these things, but reiterated that he would have never sought treatment unless Kiomi had pursued it. At the end of session 3, and after learning the Division of Responsibility in Feeding model, the couple set the behavioral goal of allowing their children to serve themselves at dinner this week, instead of their parents plating their food for them. In the first meetings of Phase Two, the therapist noted that Kiomi spoke in the first person about her implementation of the Division of Responsibility model at home. When the therapist asked about Abner's involvement, Kiomi mentioned that he was traveling a lot during the week, and hence was not involved.

After the parents asked to postpone session 6 a few times (to which they were supposed to arrive together), both attended the meeting. The therapist was wondering whether Kiomi had trouble arranging the conjoint session. She decided to raise the issue of Abner's involvement tactfully during the conversation. Ten minutes into the session, the therapist observed that Abner looked quite disengaged, and she turned to him: "Abner, I am not sure exactly what is going on with you at the moment. Would you mind sharing with us what your thoughts are right now?" Abner appeared indifferent: "I really don't think I can help here. I have no issues with the way I – or my kids for that matter – look, eat, or feel about our bodies. I am happy to support Kiomi, but don't know what I can do. I understand where she is coming from and why it is difficult for her when one is underweight, one is overweight, and so on, but these are things she needs to figure out herself." The therapist asked Abner: "You mentioned that you are happy to support Kiomi. What kind of support you think Kiomi needs from you in order to make changes?" Abner replied: "Probably to not have an eating disorder." The therapist smiled: "That is an interesting take. Can you please expand?" Abner responded: "I was half joking, but if her mind automatically says the eating disordered thing about our children I guess I can say the opposite? I am not really sure how this works." The therapist replied: "Why don't you ask Kiomi what kind of help she needs from you?" Abner bent toward Kiomi and asked: "Do you need any help?" Since Kiomi did not respond, the therapist commented: "I see that it is not easy for Kiomi to answer your question, Abner. There are many types of involvement. You can provide instrumental support, technical support, emotional support, or anything else that would help Kiomi feel more effective in her role as a parent. For example, when you are away, maybe just checking in with her after the kids go to sleep is enough for her. The thing is that if you want this program to be effective in facilitating long-term benefits to your family, you can make it more effective and relevant to your family if you both find a way to communicate with one another and collaborate. I think that we can also be open here about your potential barriers for open communication, especially about topics such as body image, eating, shape, and weight." The therapist felt that the two parents were contemplating what she said. Then, Kiomi spoke, turning to Abner: "There are some things I struggle with, that I feel uncomfortable sharing with you. I wish I could be more open with you, but your tone of voice, facial expressions, and even posture, prevent me from reaching out for help." Abner replied, thoughtfully: "I can solve a problem if you present me with one. But from the way that you present your worries, I can't understand what it is exactly that you want me to say or do. I can be more involved if I receive simple instructions how to help." The therapist responded: "I think that this is a good start. I observed in our meetings that both of you are committed to fostering better eating habits and body image in your children. Maybe I can provide some information on improving spousal communication strategies?" The parents spent the remainder of the session coming up with techniques to engage Abner more, in a way that would not undermine Kiomi. The therapist provided more information about how a parental eating disorder may hinder the affected parent's confidence around feeding and eating, and Kiomi was better able to concretely define the types of aid she needed. Over the next sessions, the parents significantly improved their communication and support, and Abner has become more engaged in his family's eating.

Parents Insist That the Parental Eating Disorder Is the Key Problem That Should Be Resolved Prior to Additional Changes in Family Routines

Some couples feel that the parent's eating disorder is the main barrier for change and hence should be first worked out before the family can move on to overcome another challenge, i.e., feeding. The therapist stresses that while improvement in parental symptoms is always advised and is viewed as an important future goal, the parents should stay focused on the task of promoting age-appropriate eating habits and healthy attitudes toward shape and weight in their child.

The Parent Experiences Greater Eating Disorder Symptomatology as the Intervention Progresses

Parent-Based Prevention, being a short-term program that targets the identified risk factors through a series of changes in child feeding, may naturally elicit some distress in the parents. In addition to the necessity to adapt quickly to the demands of the program – a structural demand that is stressful by itself – parents are invited to face their greatest difficulties, which are handling and providing food for their children, and disconnecting the association between their concerns and their behaviors. Naturally, some parents may resort to a coping style that was effective in reducing immediate anxiety and tension in the past (e.g., binge-eating, purging, compulsive exercise). In these cases, the therapist should discuss the triggers for this lapse with the parents, and reiterate that in a pilot study of Parent-Based Prevention, some mothers reported a temporary increase in their symptoms, but by the end of the program there was a decrease in their self-reported eating psychopathology. If the deterioration in any of the family members' condition persists, the therapist must use their clinical judgement and experience, and refer the parents to relevant services, should it be deemed necessary.

16 Phase Three

Enhancing Parental Efficacy
and Family Resilience

Phase Three of Parent-Based Prevention focuses on bringing both parents back together for conjoint meetings, with the intention of reinforcing the changes that have been achieved by now, broadening the discussion of additional risks to their children, and adapting the spousal communication skills to better support the behavioral experiments and parental adaptation. In addition to the continuing assessment of feeding and eating and co-occurring behaviors, the therapist and the parents also evaluate the role of other targets of prevention that are related to healthy child development and improved parental communication: the child's sleep habits, stress levels and stress reduction, and physical activity. The meetings in Phase Three are held twice a month. The goals of Phase Three are:

A   Facilitate parents' learning from the behavioral experiments;
B   Reinforce parents' efforts in regulating child eating patterns;
C   Focus the parental behavioral experiments on broader risk aspects of parental and child functioning; and
D   Improve spousal communication over child healthy development and resilience.

To achieve these goals, the therapist makes the following interventions:

1   Assess the parents' success thus far in reaching the desired changes in their parenting practices and their child's behaviors;
2   Expand parental attention to additional risk areas;
3   Facilitate prioritization of the additional challenges for the child;
4   Encourage parental communication about their concerns and behaviors regarding the additional risks;
5   Support parents in planning the next behavioral experiments; and
6   Conclude the meetings with an emphasis on the family's strengths.

In this chapter, the therapist's interventions during Phase Three meetings 9–12 are detailed. For the therapist's convenience, these interventions are also outlined in Form no. 5, which should be used throughout the sessions.

Form no. 5 The therapist interventions in Phase Three

PBP individual meetings interventions	Information gathered	Possible behavioral experiment/follow-up
1 Assess the parents' success thus far in reaching the desired changes in their parenting practices and their child's behaviors		
2 Expand parental attention to additional risk areas		
3 Facilitate prioritization of the additional challenges for the child		
4 Encourage parental communication about their concerns and behaviors regarding the additional risks		
5 Support parents in planning the next behavioral experiments		
6 Conclude the meetings with an emphasis on the family's strengths		

Note: the therapist should use Form no. 5 to plan the session, record important data, and note possible targets of the intervention.

The therapist's interventions are elaborated in the following section.

Goal: Assess the Parents' Success Thus Far in Reaching the Desired Changes in Their Parenting Practices and Their Child's Behaviors

Why?

One of the overarching goals of Phase Three is to strengthen and boost parents' learning from the behavioral experiments, i.e., generalize the effects of the intervention across settings. Parent-Based Prevention, being a short-term program, is not intended to cover all aspects of risk in the child. Instead, participation in the program can help the parents not only become more educated about the potential risks to their children, but also enhance spousal communication and mutual support in the transition process. Discussions are oriented toward facilitating and evaluating changes in parental and child functioning beyond the sphere of feeding and eating. Therefore, the therapist reinforces parental self-reflection as well as spousal communication on the changes that were achieved to this point. In session 9, which is the first conjoint meeting after the conclusion of Phase Two, the therapist encourages a collaborative review of the parents' attempts in fostering healthy feeding and eating practices at home, through which the therapist and the parents identify effective and ineffective parental behaviors. The explicit changes the parents report, and their view of these changes, direct the therapist's interventions in this session. In case the family presents a significant improvement in feeding, a greater proportion of the meeting in dedicated to the additional developmental risks of the children. If the child's eating habits are not stabilized or the parents do not indicate their ability to collaborate well about eating, then session 9 is mostly focused on feeding and on galvanizing the parents' understanding of the Division of Responsibility model. However, the focus of the intervention gradually shifts to additional aspects of parenting and child functioning. In the next two meetings (sessions 10–11), the therapist and the parents continue generalizing their progress around the additional risk aspects identified.

How?

As in Phase Two, each session in Phase Three begins with a concrete appraisal of the behavioral experiments the parents decided on in the preceding week. The therapist helps the parents review the process in light of the goals defined earlier in the program. The therapist uses direct and circular questioning to learn about the effects of the parents' attempts to adapt their behaviors (may that be feeding-related practices or behaviors that have to do with additional risk areas): how did each family member respond to the behavioral experiments; what has gone as planned versus the unexpected surprises; which actual, tangible changes were achieved at home; how did the parents support each other in the behavioral experiments; which further actions the parents think are needed to reinforce and expand their achievements, etc. The therapist uses this information to help the parents summarize what they have learned from these behavioral experiments in regard to the effects of the parental eating disorder, the child's reactions, their parenting role, their spousal communication skills, and ways they can further mutually support their spouse's initiatives. The therapist's feedback should praise the parents for their efforts, and empower them by emphasizing their achievements. The therapist should also coach the parents to lean more on the **parental subsystem** by providing constructive feedback and emphasizing parental efficacy.

After reviewing the parents' individual and shared processes in facilitating the development of healthier eating patterns in their children, the therapist asks the parents to define what will be their focus of Phase Three. The therapist states that in these conjoint meetings the behavioral experiments discussed should include both parents, in contrast to the changes in feeding during Phase Two, that could have been potentially led by one parent exclusively. The therapist may present this shift in the following way:

> The goal of the next few sessions is to empower you as a family, and to concentrate on developing the abilities and communication patterns that would ultimately be more helpful for your child. You had an opportunity to practice some important changes in feeding your child and in his/her eating habits. Now we shall apply what we have learned to additional areas, to foster additional changes that will support your child's wellbeing.

Hereinafter is an example of how the therapist and the parents evaluate how the parents accomplished implementing their behavioral experiments in a more age-appropriate and age-effective way:

> Dr. Cohen has been working with Taylor and William for eight weeks now in Parent-Based Prevention. The couple, presenting to treatment due to Taylor's history of bulimia nervosa, which was followed by morbid obesity and diabetes and finally a bariatric surgery, are the parents of two teenage girls in middle school. From the outset of the program, Taylor and William have been highly motivated to change the eating patterns they identified in their children. Throughout the meetings of Phase One and Two, Dr. Cohen has observed that the couple possess many strengths, including high

motivation, seemingly very little defensiveness, high openness to receive feedback, and a strong sense of responsibility for change in their family. They also expressed optimism about the program's potential to help them reach their goals.

In earlier sessions, the parents have set the goal of increasing the diversity of their children's diet. They have worked through increasing the girls' contact with food by inviting them to participate in food preparation process for one meal per week. This participation included giving each child a task in helping to prepare the food. The parents were very pleased with the progress both their daughters made, and demonstrated good collaboration and effective spousal communication skills. Therefore, when Dr. Cohen asked Taylor and William at the beginning of session 9 about their perspective of the process up until now, William replied: "We did accomplish some of the things we wanted, but we talked on our way here about some issues that we were not able to make progress with." When Dr. Cohen asked William to expand, he responded: "Involving the girls in food preparation was a good strategy to help them experiment with more varied types of foods. I might even say that the cutting, chopping, cooking, baking, etc., went well and were pleasurable experiences to all of us. However, when we do sit down to eat, the atmosphere returns to being very tense. The girls pick on one another; they are often very aggressive and mean to one another and even to us at times." Taylor added: "I noticed this is happening mostly during and after dinner, but at other times they can hang out with each other for a while without any fights. So I am not sure whether these conflicts are part of the eating experience in our home, or something that all sisters engage in. I have been reading on adolescents' developing brains and their lack of inhibitory mechanisms, and I was wondering if this is what's been going on." Dr. Cohen responded: "Thank you for bringing this up. I think that the more detailed your description is, the more we can learn from it. First off, I want to highlight your accomplishments. You were concerned about your daughters' lack of diversity in eating, perhaps even some rigidity in their intake. I observed you collaborating very nicely with each other, supporting one another, and making progress with your family's eating habits and healthy lifestyle. I know what an undertaking this process is, and I am very proud of you for making such incredible progress. Now, if we thought that was enough, the treatment would have ended. But thankfully we have Phase Three to address other issues that may be relevant with the eating habits, or unrelated to them. Before I ask more questions about the issues that bother you now, I want to emphasize again that you have achieved your earlier goals. In Phase Three and the next few sessions, we will capitalize on the skills that you have utilized so nicely earlier, and come up with strategies to reinforce positive behaviors in your children."

Goal: Expand Parental Attention to Additional Risk Areas

Why?

The developmental risks for the children of parents with eating disorders are unfortunately not limited to eating-related behaviors and attitudes. Data suggest that a parental eating disorder is linked with compromised mental development, greater psychopathological symptoms in children, and difficulties in the parent–child relationship. Some children may be more reactive to anxious or controlling parental behaviors, and consequently may have difficulties in acknowledging their needs and preferences adaptively or finding an appropriate solution for them. In addition, mothers with eating disorders have greater comorbid symptoms as well as greater stress associated with their maternal role (there are currently no available data on fathers with eating disorders, but there is evidence that the presence of a paternal mental disorder compromises the experience of parental efficacy). Thus, any preventive intervention program should assess and address the impact of these co-occurring challenges on the parenting practices and child outcomes. These broader risks become the focus of sessions during Phase Three, although the management of feeding and eating is still discussed.

The therapist's role is threefold. First, to educate parents on the broader risk aspects for their children – problems in managing important bodily functions, as sleep and emotion regulation, maladaptive behaviors associated with co-occurring parental symptoms, and additional unique characteristics. Second, to help parents identify the potential relevant risks for their child, based on their knowledge of their child, themselves, and their family functioning. Third, to facilitate parental ability to prioritize and decide risks to concentrate on. It is likely that some parents may not be aware of or concerned about some of these additional risk factors, or that the parents are not aware that these issues may be associated with the eating disorder or the comorbid conditions. In these cases, the therapist educates the parents about the risks and applies his understanding of the family and his clinical expertise to make the conversation more concrete and relevant to their lives.

How?

The therapist explains that the focus of attention now shifts to additional aspects of child resilience and healthy development. The therapist introduces the role of daily routines in young children's wellbeing and the possible impacts of the co-occurring symptoms on parental functioning, and asks the parents to express their thoughts, behaviors, and concerns regarding this topic. Common additional potential concerns of parents with eating disorders and their spouses include: difficulties in sleep regulation (i.e., difficulties in falling asleep, frequent waking up at night); parental anxiety that interferes with the child's age-appropriate, autonomous behaviors; social inhibition of the parent and its potential effects; high parental sensitivity to criticism and its impact on parenting, etc.

One approach to addressing the impact of any parental difficulties on parenting practices is to present the parents with a series of open questions about situations and processes that characterize families in which a parent has an eating disorder. The therapist may phrase this in the following way:

> As we have discussed in session 3, our work in this part of the program is going to focus on additional challenges that are related to parenting your child. Identifying them can further strengthen your child's resilience and prevent future difficulties that are linked with eating and mental problems. Some parents that I have worked with were concerned that they were highly self-critical, and were interested in learning ways to help their children feel better about themselves. Do you think this applies to you and your family?

Or:

> Throughout our interactions I have noticed that you, Mickey, tend to speak your negative self-talk out loud. You did it when you forgot to bring the cheese sticks that you had planned for the family meal. You were really hard on yourself also when there was no parking outside the clinic and you needed to park in a remote lot. I am wondering how the kids feel when they hear you scold yourself like that, what do they learn from that, and what kind of self-care do you want them to imitate?

Often, parents' responses to this set of questions stimulate a discussion. The therapist tries to clarify both parents' perceptions of themselves and their spouses, and how they perceive any effects on their children. Then the therapist provides psychoeducation about the importance of predictable daily routines and the potentially adverse effects of parental symptoms on the child. These psychoeducational explanations should be very brief, tailored to the child's age and personality as well as to the variety of possible lifestyles. The conversation should be very concrete and relatable to the specific family. If the therapist feels that the discussion develops into a general conversation about children and families, she should ask the parents for more concrete and personal examples.

Goal: Facilitate Prioritization of the Additional Challenges for the Child

Why?

Although Parent-Based Prevention is designed to address different aspects of child development and of parental functioning at different times, the parents do not typically differentiate between concerns and issues they have about their children. It is not unlikely that the parents have a different agenda than the individualized goals defined in session 3. Some parents may have also changed their perspectives following Phases Two and Three, and they are now considering other things as more urgent. The therapist models and explains to the parents how to approach identifying and ordering the challenges to address. Initially, these priorities are risks related to feeding and eating. Then, the focus may shift to important other dimensions of self-regulation (sleep hygiene, self-soothing skills, etc.). Finally, broader aspects of the child's functioning that are mostly impacted by parental practices can be focused on.

How?

Following their discussion, the parents are guided in selecting the specific risks for their children and in communicating about the behavioral experiments they choose to continue with. The parents are encouraged to choose three issues to be addressed in Phase Three. The therapist stirs the discussion, integrates the parents' perspectives, and weighs in input from informed psychoeducation (including professional literature and handouts she can share with the parents). In case sleep issues do arise as a concern, they should be dealt with first, given their strong link with eating regulation and dis-regulation. Some parents may have trouble focusing on only three things. The therapist may respond along the following lines:

> Many of the issues you have discusses cannot be completely resolved in this program. However, you have now an increased capacity to solve problems. We are going to work on sleep hygiene and we will use that as a leverage to practice new tools and skills.

There are parents who find it easier to focus on each of their children separately, in consecutive sessions. The therapist can approve this approach and connect it to the goals of Phase Three:

> If I understand correctly, you have different concerns and dilemmas with each child. With your 2-year-old girl, you are unsure how to manage her stress levels and emotional outbursts. But with your 5-year-old boy, you are more worried about his behavior problems and

his separation anxiety at the beginning of every week. There could be some things that connect these challenges, and I also understand why it could make more sense to devote a separate session to talk about each child. I will be mindful of the connections, though, and note them occasionally. I also think that the skills and insights that you gain with one child will expand your parental tool kit and empower your interactions with the other child.

Goal: Encourage Parental Communication about Their Concerns and Behaviors Regarding the Additional Risks

Why?

One of the goals of Phase Three is to improve spousal communication and problem-solving skills. The therapist reinforces spousal listening, reflection, and support about the issues at hand. The therapist concentrates on fostering effective communication that will eventually facilitate an agreement between the parents on their behavioral experiment at home. These discussions are also an opportunity to support effective negotiations between the parents on their parenting practices and on their collaboration in encouraging a family environment that supports child healthy development.

How?

The therapist asks each parent to communicate his or her thoughts, beliefs, and dilemmas regarding the issues at hand. Circular questioning – an interviewing tool to explore family members' understanding of each other's perceptions and to enhance communication skills – can be a helpful strategy as well. Only when the parents have carefully listened to each other does the therapist express her perspective, her impression of the family structure and functioning, and some of the issues that have been mentioned during the individual sessions. The therapist provides feedback after the parents communicate their thoughts, concerns, and dilemmas. The therapist asks for clarifications about the similarities and differences in parents' approaches to the issues at hand:

- What would you say is your wife's greatest concern now regarding your child's development, besides his eating and weight?
- In what ways do you think your partner would want to be more involved when it comes to putting your child to bed?
- What do you think that your partner is most concerned about when he thinks of the adult your child will become?
- It sounds like your son's social functioning bothers you, Venessa, very much, but you, Fiona, do not seem to think this is a problem. Is this fair to say? What do you make of this gap?

Goal: Support Parents in Planning the Behavioral Experiments

Why?

After the parents and the therapist acknowledge the changes the parents would like to achieve in regard to their children, the therapist leads the parents in the task of deciding on a behavioral experiment. The parents (both, in non-single-parent families) should agree on the desired changes and on a division of labor and responsibilities between them. Although parents may have a few ideas for changes they want to implement with their child, they should choose just one behavior each session for the following week. In case the parents indicate that their child's sleeping habits could benefit from more management, the first behavioral experiment should involve regulating sleep. The therapist facilitates this process by training the parents in relevant spousal communication skills around these issues. As in the Division of Responsibility model of feeding that encourages age-appropriate autonomy in the child, the therapist should point out the reasonable expectations of children, given their age, sex, temperament, and personality (based on the therapist's impression as well as information provided by the parents). Again, the therapist leverages earlier insights and successful experience in helping the parents generalize their capabilities into the additional behaviors they attempt to change in their children.

How?

The therapist encourages the parents to communicate and understand each other's perspectives and impediments for change, and what each parent needs from their partner in order to succeed in the behavioral experiment that targets the matter at hand. The discussion is often very detailed and requires the therapist's involvement in concrete aspects of the family lifestyle. The behavioral experiments may include issues such as working hours of the parents outside the home, arrangements necessary to make sure that both parents are at home before the child's bedtime, the levels of neatness and cleanliness of the child in different situations or times of the day, planning adaptive exposures to people outside the immediate family, timing of play-dates with peers, communication between parents, and mutual help when one of them struggles with their child, etc. The therapist urges the parents to discuss the desired, expected, and realistic results of the behavioral experiment, and to make contingency plans when possible.

Since these are the final meetings in the short-term program, the therapist nurtures greater parental self-efficacy. The therapist focuses on the positive and adaptive aspects of parental functioning and keeps an optimistic tone.

In the subsequent sessions, the therapist analyzes the behavioral experiments together with the parents. Often, the parent who is more anxious, has more trouble with organization, or tends more to be over-controlling, needs the therapist's approval and support in order to rely more on their partner to make the changes this parent still finds difficult. A therapist intervention that is both mutative and motivating is arguing that child development and parent–child interactions are ongoing processes during which parents and children have many opportunities for practice, re-evaluation, and reparation. In regard to the parental collaboration on mutual goals and on role division in the behavioral experiment, widely used intervention strategies such as active listening, proactive problem solving, or collaborative dialogue may be helpful. The therapist should emphasize that the parents are expanding their problem-solving skills, and that their collaboration will serve as an asset when they face future problems.

The next case illustration demonstrates how the therapist helps the parent(s) prioritize their Phase Three goals:

> Halid, a single parent with two children, thought he would benefit from participating in the Parent-Based Prevention program. Recently widowed from his wife, Halid was encouraged by the counselor who helped him and his children process their grief and adapt to their new life situation. Before his wife passed away, she was responsible for feeding their children, and Halid – who has been struggling with both binge-eating disorder and generalized anxiety disorder – was less involved in this dimension. During the First and Second Phase, the intervention concentrated on introducing more structure to the eating routine, reducing snacking between meals, and stopping to use food for non-nutritional purposes when the children were upset. Now, in Phase Three, the therapist and Halid were assessing his success thus far in reaching the desired changes in his children's eating behaviors. Halid reported meeting his goals from last session, including maintaining the nutritional behavioral change goals and reducing his and his children's mindless eating. He expressed his interest in helping build better emotion regulation skills in his children.
>
> In session 9, Halid decided to focus his first behavioral experiment of Phase Three by starting discussions on identifying and naming emotions with his children. Halid discussed with the therapist his experiences growing up, when he relied on eating to regulate adverse emotional states. Through this discussion, the therapist observed that Halid was expressing catastrophic thinking about the possible consequences should his children not learn emotional regulation skills. The therapist thought that he might want to reinforce Halid's previous accomplishments in the program, and use cognitive restructuring to dispute the relevant maladaptive thoughts. With this therapeutic

goal in mind, the therapist shared her observations with Halid, and reminded him that he had expressed the same cognitions when they were discussing the behavioral experiments to reduce grazing: "I remember that when we talked about helping your children eat more mindfully when they feel hunger, you had similar worst-case scenarios. You claimed 'being 95% confident' that you will not be able to beat your children's mindless eating habits. But you crafted very nice ideas to remove grazing, and these changes were effective. Do you remember this?" Halid responded: "Yes, I remember saying something about being 95% sure. I am happy I was wrong then, but teaching my kids to cope with difficult emotions is much harder." The therapist replied: "It is not an easy task, I agree. However, I believe that you have already demonstrated the skills to help your children regulate better. Let's think what worked well then, OK?" Since Halid agreed, the therapist reinforced his earlier work outside the session and discussed ways to build from what he was already doing at home. Halid explored some options, e.g., getting an emotion chart to post at home; talking with his brother for support in managing his anxiety when his children looked troubled, prior to speaking with them; and adding more opportunities for family physical activity, as he acknowledged its positive effect on him and the children. Finally, he decided to focus on correcting the children's misperceptions of parental emotion by naming and identifying his own feelings when they were misread by the children. The therapist assisted in planning in detail this experiment.

In the next session – which was held after two weeks, according to the schedule of meeting every other week in Phase Three, Halid informed the therapist that this behavioral experiment has worked out well. He also started implementing the additional changes he had mentioned in the previous meeting. In the current session, he expressed his interest working on the parental anxiety affecting his children's development. Halid mentioned his fear of taking the children to places outside the home due to concerns related to being too far away from home, especially when driving in unfamiliar places and crossing bridges. He also expressed his worry about his children misbehaving in public, and that others will develop negative perceptions of his parenting ability. The therapist provided psychoeducation on anxiety and appropriate skills for managing it, both cognitive and behavioral. Then, they collaboratively decided to focus on exposure activities, which included taking his children to the park to ride their bikes. The therapist discussed the importance of response prevention and ways Halid, who wanted to avoid social situations, could manage such urges. Finally, the therapist supported Halid in setting a goal of telling his brother about the exposure plan and asking for his help in following through with the plan if he attempted to avoid it.

Goal: Conclude the Meetings with an Emphasis on the Family's Strengths

As the therapist supports the parents in their efforts to minimize the effects of the parental symptoms, each session ends with a summary of the topics that have been examined and the behavioral experiment the parents will test in the following week. The therapist emphasizes the agreements and similarities between the parents, and yet acknowledges the discrepancies and possible ways of coping with them. The therapist compliments the parents on their collaboration in curtailing the parental eating disorder and comorbid symptoms and enhancing family resilience. It should be noted that although the therapist encourages relief of parental eating psychopathology, the parents also need to examine their family life with the view of the eating disorder as an ongoing state. The specifics of this process are highly individualistic and there is seldom a prescribed way how to proceed. However, encouraging open and supportive spousal communication about parental symptoms and their implications is an important step in the family's long-term adaptive functioning. The therapist maintains an optimistic stance toward the family's efforts to maintain healthy eating habits, reduce any adverse outcomes in the child, and promote resilience. The therapist also enhances parental self-efficacy and their sense of competence in achieving at least some of the goals set at the outset of the program, by accentuating their accomplishments.

Intervention Summary in Session 12

The last meeting of the program, session 12, is dedicated to summarizing the process the family underwent in Parent-Based Prevention. The therapist acknowledges and emphasizes the effective parental behaviors that were associated with improved eating habits and more general resilience. The therapist also shares an appreciation and respect for the parents' endeavors to enhance their spousal communication skills and congratulates both parents on successfully overcoming the challenges they faced in achieving the desired changes. The children's strengths, as manifested through the parents' report, and as observed by the therapist during session 2, are emphasized as well.

The therapist also educates the parents about potential future developmental risks for the child, and provides information about additional relevant services, if any are advised. The therapist congratulates both parents on successfully facing the challenges associated with the parental eating disorder. The therapist should request feedback about the intervention from the parents, and try to genuinely learn from their experience for professional growth. Finally, the therapist concludes the Parent-Based Prevention program with an optimistic outlook on the family to enable further confidence and optimism.

Common Therapist Dilemmas during Phase Three

Review of the Process in Phase Two Does Not Indicate Notable Changes in Feeding

Parents may have the experience that they have not achieved the expected changes, or that they have achieved some desired outcomes in the feeding relationship and related behaviors, but these changes were cancelled out after a while (for instance, a child who was already eating independently stopped doing so after a week when they were sick). A careful review of the process often indicates that there have been notable changes that the parents have trouble recognizing, sometimes due to low self-esteem, high demands of themselves and their environment, and/or a pessimistic outlook on life. In these instances, the therapist stresses the improved cognitions and functioning she identifies, and discuss with the parents the possible explanations for their difficulty in recognizing them. Additionally, the therapist and the parents should explore likely reasons for the lack of sufficient changes: little collaboration and disclosure between the parents, depleted parental mental resources to pursue the behavioral experiment plan, unexpected adverse reactions by the child, unique circumstances, etc. The therapist and the parents should then think of ways that some of the behavioral experiments could be practiced again with greater spousal collaboration and more adaptation to the family's individual structure.

Parents Would Like to Focus on Feeding Difficulties Instead of Additional Potential Problems

For some parents, the idea of possible adverse outcomes in their child's eating habits is understood more easily than potential future difficulties in other domains. In addition, the discourse on feeding and eating problems may connect with concerns that the parents have already had prior to the program and that brought them to Parent-Based Prevention in the first place. The therapist should stress that although they had not planned to work on some of the additional risk aspects, the parents could use this opportunity to do so while in treatment. The therapist should also reemphasize the overarching goal of Parent-Based Prevention to promote positive child outcomes and greater resilience, in order to align the parents on the goals of Phase Three of the program.

Parents Have Difficulties in Agreeing on Mutual Goals or Working in Cooperation

Some families may experience spousal difficulties that are not related to the eating disorder, but negatively affect parental communication and collaboration. The therapist should handle these types of impediments to the process very delicately and tactfully in order not to intensify the existing problems. The therapist should focus, direct, and redirect the parents on the goals of the program and on their child's wellbeing. At the same time, heightened spousal conflict should receive some attention and be brought to discussion, and may necessitate referral to marital counseling that is outside the scope of Parent-Based Prevention.

The following case description is intended to provide insight into how a therapist delivering the Parent-Based Prevention might respond when he or she feels that the couple's communication patterns impede the parents' ability to utilize the program:

> Paul and Susan are an unmarried couple who have been living together for the past few years. They have had one child together, a toddler boy named Oliver. Susan has had anorexia nervosa in her adolescence, from which she has fully recovered. However, since she became pregnant with her son, she has felt very concerned he will be overweight, and worried about whether he will have a large appetite or that his body will accumulate baby fat. Susan's concerns intensified when Oliver was born in the 99th percentile for weight, and he remained in it since. Conversely, Paul dismissed Susan's concerns, saying that he, too, was bigger than average until his teenage years, and has had normal weight since. In the initial session, the couple reported they have been struggling with open and effective communication, particularly about Oliver's eating and growth, but also on other topics.
>
> Throughout the sessions, the therapist identified that Susan and Paul had difficulties holding productive discussions. At times, he observed Paul engaging in invalidating statements over Susan's concerns, and Sue quickly becoming quiet. Susan, however, appeared to not be taking Paul's feedback into consideration and often not informing him of her decisions. Therefore, the couple's discussions were not effective, although they both indicated that they valued effective communication and wanted to improve their collaboration.
>
> In session 9, when the parents were not appearing to be listening to one another, the therapist inquired about their communication outside of session, and about other issues than their son's eating habits and other potential risk areas. This assessment revealed that both felt dissatisfied with the current status quo. Therefore, the therapist suggested dedicating Phase Three to addressing the couple's communication patterns, clarifying that improving those will help in maintaining the changes they had already incorporated in the earlier parts of the program.
>
> The parents expressed their interest in improving the quality of their conversations. Next, the therapist assessed each partner's

experiences in the situation, current interaction style, and its effects, while noting the negative emotional experience for both Paul and Susan. The therapist provided brief psychoeducation on effective communication and the importance of tact, tone, and timing. Further, the therapist proposed ideas for better dialogues, including (as a speaker) the importance of avoiding over-generalizations and confrontative argument, and (as a listener) the importance of putting oneself in another's shoes; demonstrating listening, not overinterpreting; and asking questions for clarification. The couple identified aspects they do well and where to improve; both named their need to adjust nonverbal body language (e.g., looking at each other, turning toward one another, turning off electronic devices while speaking). The therapist encouraged the parents to create a specific plan to try using these skills in the upcoming week once a day, during daily check-in, 20-minute conversations.

In the following sessions, the couple reported meeting their goal last session of adding in a daily check-in conversation, and using new communication skills, particularly around food preparation and eating. Both parents revealed surprise at their partner's change in behavior and satisfaction with new interaction patterns. Additional inquiry revealed that both Susan and Paul have been speaking with members from each origin family, who provided conflicting and contradictory advice. The parents reported being aware that involving extended family members was detrimental to their relationship, but expressed feeling uncertain they would be able to avoid involving their families in their everyday decisions. At the last meeting of Parent-Based Prevention, the parents said that overall they had a positive experience with the program. However, both Susan and Paul voiced their awareness that their current communication skills are inadequate. The therapist facilitated brainstorming on how the parents can continue cultivating a more effective communication style. Additionally, he suggested providing contact information for a few colleagues who work with couples and also have experience working with individuals with eating disorder histories.

17 Parent-Based Prevention in Action

Stacey and Rob

In Chapter 5 we presented two couples who sought treatment to help them resolve their feeding and parenting related concerns, given one of the parents' eating disorder history. We described the first session with both of these families and the therapist's thoughts and observations thereof. This chapter summarizes how Parent-Based Prevention unfolded with the first parent couple, Stacey and Rob, while Chapter 18 describes the intervention as delivered to the other couple. We outline the central concerns and dilemmas the parents disclosed, the therapist's guidance of the parents following the individualized plan, and how the parents and the therapist coped with roadblocks along the way. By describing this case in detail, we hope readers have a better grasp of common parental and therapist responses along the way, and how the Parent-Based Prevention program addresses such issues and challenges.

In session 1 Stacey and Rob described their reasons for seeking treatment. Stacey reported her anorexia nervosa history, and more recent obsessive-compulsive disorder diagnosis; her current symptoms include significant weight and shape concerns and a very limited diet. While she is concerned about the eating habits and future weight of her daughter Emma (age 5), she is not worried about her son Aidan (18 months old). Both parents wanted to focus on reducing amount of conflict during mealtimes and expanding their children's diet, but they both mentioned Rob's long work hours outside home and Stacey's stressful reactions around feeding as the main barriers for implementing change.

Stacey and Rob arrived with their children at session 2, a session that is focused on a family meal. Emma and Aidan were both very friendly and polite, and approached the therapist's office with age-appropriate behaviors: Emma looked quietly at the items on the therapist's desk while Aidan ran in the room, touched furniture and books, and was eager to play. When the parents were prompted to begin the meal, Stacey took out food from the cooler they brought, and Rob placed plastic plates, forks, and spoons in front of each child. The parents plated the kids' dinner – each child received half of a hardboiled egg, some cottage cheese, and fresh vegetables. Emma ate her food very quickly and requested more, asking her father, "What else do we have to eat?" Rob then turned to Stacey and asked: "What else do we have to eat?" Stacey took out another egg and two cheese sticks from the cooler and placed them on Emma's plate. Emma looked at the therapist and then whispered to her mom: "Did you bring anything else? I don't want any more egg!" Stacey responded: "These proteins are very healthy for your body. They will make you stronger!" During this time, Aidan used a fork to eat his food, and Rob added more cottage cheese when Aidan finished. The same pattern repeated itself another time; because the children ate their food rapidly, Emma again asked whether there were different foods than those provided. When the children received their third serving, the parents took out their own plates, put the same food on their plates as they had given the children and started eating. The family ate quietly for a few minutes and the therapist noted that the atmosphere felt quite tense. She recorded this observation on Form no. 2, planning to share it with the parents in the consecutive session and wondering if this family meal is representative. After a few minutes of silence, Stacey asked Emma: "Have you told Daddy how fast you ran today at school? Daddy, Ms. Lee said that Emma had run, jumped, and played hide-and-seek with Lara." Emma replied: "We did not run, we just played. I am still hungry!" Rob looked at Stacey and waited for her response. Stacey took avocado out of the cooler, and said: "Here, can I slice you some? I can squeeze some lemon over it." Emma smiled. After the family finished eating, the parents cleared the plates and food from the table. The therapist asked Emma a few questions about her favorite activities and the family chatted, appearing more relaxed after the meal for a few more minutes. Emma shared a funny story about something that happened at school, while Aidan got off his seat and ran around the office again. In session 1, the therapist informed the parents that since Emma was old enough to grasp some of the issues related with her mother's eating disorder symptoms, they would discuss these topics in session 3, so as to not expose Emma to contents that were not compatible for her age, like her mother's mental health problems. Therefore, the therapist decided to conclude the meeting a few minutes after the family meal ended, and scheduled the next session with the parents. When the therapist reorganized her office after the family left, she noticed a heavy feeling that she could not exactly label.

The parents arrived at session 3 the following week. The therapist asked if they had any thoughts about the family meal and both parents admitted to forgetting all about it. The therapist asked if they had talked about the meeting at all, and they replied they had not. Rather, they said, they were interested in the therapist's observations and advice. The therapist started by thanking the parents for bringing their children to her office, and said empathetically that sharing a very intimate event such as a family meal could be a difficult thing to do. Then she complimented the children by saying how sweet, polite, and kind they were, and that she enjoyed chatting with Emma and observing how energetic Aidan was, as might be expected for a child of his age. Then the therapist also complimented the parents for organizing a meal, and said she was wondering how they had decided what to bring. Rob laughed, "I arrived like a guest at this dinner. Every time Stacey leaned toward the cooler, I was curious to see what we she would pull out for us to eat. It felt like it's Mary Poppins' purse or something." Stacey replied: "How come you're surprised? We eat the same things almost every day. That is part of the problem." The therapist asked Stacey to expand on this observation, and she replied that she knew the kids were unhappy at being offered only few items, but she felt she needed help coming up with other kinds of food to offer. Rob added: "When I come to think of it, the kids are very eager to try new foods. Whenever we eat out or at a friends' house, they happily taste most of the foods they are served." The therapist replied:

> So, if I understand you correctly, one of the things that the two of you would like to achieve in this program is offering a more diverse menu. Let's make a mental note of this point and talk about it later toward the second half of the meeting.

Next, the therapist said:

> Another thing that I observed was that you offer your children food very gradually. It is indeed like Mary Poppins' purse, as Rob mentioned. My concern is that this leaves a lot of responsibility and control on your end, Stacey, but then you have less opportunities to nurture your children's ability to make healthy choices further down the road. You see, when parents let children experiment with making decisions about food independently, you can facilitate their learning how to respond to their body's hunger and satiety cues, how to slow down when eating, and what are the more nutritious choices for their bodies. I remember last week, Stacey, that you expressed your fear that if you let your kids, particularly Emma, eat whatever they want to eat, they will become overweight. So, I understand where you are coming from, but by serving different food items one at a time, they might become so eager to get to try the next food that they may eat with little regard to their bodily sensations. What do you think about this?

As the parents reflected and said they agreed with the therapist, Rob added:

> I was wondering if this was a practice that would be eventually disadvantageous for the kids. As you've seen, Emma refuses to go along with the way we do our dinners, but this has developed to such a big conflict I feel that it's either I side with the kids or I side with Stacey, and either choice makes me uncomfortable.

The therapist asked Stacey about her reaction to Rob's statement, and then Stacey noted:

> I am so used to doing things my own way that I do not want him to intervene. Although I was thinking that it would be easier for me if Rob takes some of the dinnertime workload off of me.

The therapist then turned to Rob and said:

> I know you are really grateful that Stacey does the lion's share of the household and parenting duties, Rob, and that you don't want to upset her in any way. But maybe your attempt to avoid more conflict prevents you from helping out more in ways that are useful for Stacey. Does this make sense?

As both parents nodded, Rob put his hand on his wife's shoulder and patted her. The therapist continued:

> So if I am hearing this right, and please tell me if you think differently, these are two goals that we've mentioned. The first is adding more variety to the kids' meals, and the second is involving Rob more, or in different ways than he'd been involved thus far. Is this a fair description of what we've discussed?

After the parents expressed their agreement, the therapist added:

> There is just one last thing about the family meal that I'd like to discuss with you two, and then we'll move to making a plan to achieve the goals we discussed. I noticed that the meal was very quiet. I did not know if this was typical or due to the fact you were being observed, but I felt some tension during the meal. Is this something that you guys also felt?

Stacey replied instantaneously: "Absolutely! I hate this about our meals. I really want dinnertime to be much more conversational and fun." Rob nodded and said:

> Now that I come to think of it, we laugh and goof around a lot as a family, but not during mealtimes. It's like when there's food around it freaks us out. When I bathe the kids, we sing and tell jokes and funny stories, but at dinner the atmosphere is not as light-hearted as I'd like it to be. But do you think this is something that can change? I thought our family is *just like this*.

The therapist replied:

> You know what? This is something we will learn together. I am posi-
> tive that this program can help the four of you feel less stressed out
> during meals and in the presence of food. Would you guys want to
> mark this as another goal?

As the parents nodded, the therapist made a mental note about a few observations she had not shared with the parents in order not to overwhelm
them at such an early stage of the intervention: the discussions of physical activity with their children, parents not eating at the same time as
their children, etc. These issues may or may not be discussed later in the
meetings, as appropriate, but could overwhelm the parents with things to
consider and change at this early stage.

Following the outline of session 3, the therapist went on to teach the
parents about the Division of Responsibility in Feeding. Next, the parents
decided to focus their behavioral experiment in the following week on eating what they labeled as a "family-style dinner", that is, with all the food
placed in bowls on the table and each family member choosing which food
they wanted. The therapist reminded them:

> Remember, this is just an experiment. If you see that the changes you
> are trying to implement this week do not result in the desired change
> in your children and the atmosphere around eating this week, we will
> review and revisit them in the subsequent session and make any modifi-
> cations needed. So make sure you maintain this experimental mindset!

Lastly, the therapist reminded the parents that this was the last session in
Phase One, and that the meetings in Phase Two would be held with Stacey
mostly – she would meet with Stacey, the affected parent, one on one for
two sessions, then would meet both parents for session 6, and then have
additional two individual meetings with Stacey, to conclude Phase Two of
the program.

The following week, the therapist met with Stacey alone, as suggested
by the treatment manual. Stacey reported that the family had been eating
family meals in the past week; Rob was able to dine with them twice a week
and over the weekend. The night they returned home from meeting the
therapist, the parents informed the children that "We are now trying to test
a new thing in our home! Mommy and Daddy are going to serve the food
in the middle of the table and each of us will choose how much we want
to eat!" Emma was very excited for this new arrangement, and asked about
it the next morning: "Is today the night of the new plates?" Stacey felt
slightly anxious prior to each meal, but was surprised that Emma took only
a second serving and then said she was full. Stacey also mentioned feeling

surprised that Emma was happy with the food that was served and did not ask for additional items that were not on the table. Rather, Emma and Aidan looked very pleased with the new dinner setting. Overall, Stacey felt very happy with the changes implemented in the past week. However, when the therapist tried to understand what Rob's role in the new routine was, Stacey remained quite ambiguous. In the interest of keeping the treatment momentum and reinforcing Stacey's improved self-efficacy, the therapist decided to hold off asking more questions about Rob and his involvement.

When prompted by the therapist to plan her next behavioral experiment, Stacey decided to challenge her own habits and expand the diversity of the foods her family atw. Nonetheless, she reported feeling "Totally stuck here. I have no ideas of anything I feel comfortable providing and that my children will like. What do people feed their preschoolers and toddlers?" The therapist thought that this was a good opportunity to help Stacey include Rob more in feeding the children. Therefore, she asked:

> OK, so you are saying that you would like to diversify your kids' diet but do not know where to begin, right? Do you feel it is knowledge of other foods that you are missing or is it something else?

Stacey responded:

> Well, I can go on websites and get recipes, but I feel that something is blocking me from trying them out at home. I calculate the calories in each serving, try and assess how much carbs, protein, fat you get, and it is so anxiety-provoking for me that I just withdraw.

As the therapist listened to Stacey, she felt that Stacey's ongoing eating-related preoccupations were making it difficult for her to accomplish this goal. She chose to suggest involving Rob, so that Stacey might be more able to try out new modes of feeding. And so, the therapist responded softly:

> This sounds hard. I get it. Is there any way you could involve Rob more in this process? When you talk about feeding your kids, I often hear you speaking in the first person, and maybe if you felt it was Rob's and your responsibility to think about what your children are eating, maybe it would have been easier.

Stacey described her feelings of shame and guilt whenever she reached out to Rob for support regarding child-rearing issues:

> We made this decision that I am a stay-home mom, and he works so hard supporting us. Therefore I am always reluctant to ask him for anything . . . I am not sure even what to say – 'Please help me find ideas for meals'? It sounds a bit silly, doesn't it?

The therapist responded: "How would you react if Rob had said, 'I am feeling kind of stuck with something, do you have some ideas?'" Emma smiled: "Oh, he does that all the time. He is under enormous pressures at work and every night we analyze what has happened that day and what his is his to-do list for the following day." "I am glad to hear that you are able to communicate so openly and effectively on other matters, Stacey," the therapist said. "Is there any reason you will not be able to do this when it comes to preparing meals?" Stacey looked puzzled: "I guess not. I guess that he shares some stuff happening at work that could be embarrassing but I do not judge him. He can definitely help me with the mealtime dilemmas." Then, the therapist and Stacey defined her behavioral experiment for the following week. In discussing options for the behavioral experiment, several possibilities were considered, including how Rob might be involved. The therapist helped Stacey explore how she could communicate to Rob a route that would be supportive, rather than threatening, to Stacey. Finally, Stacey decided to ask Rob to brainstorm with her ideas for expanding the types of foods offered to the children during mealtimes and adding to dinners one item that the family has not eaten in a while.

Due to child care problems, it was two weeks before the next meeting with Stacey. Given her earlier experience providing Parent-Based Prevention, the therapist knew that these kinds of scheduling issues arise with parents of young children. As Stacey arrived at the therapist's office, she looked very worried and tired. When the therapist asked how the past two weeks had gone, Stacey told her that her mother, who lived in another state, was ill, and that Stacey wished she could have done more to support her step-father. The therapist replied empathetically and asked a few questions about Stacey's parents' health. Stacey shared some strategies to help her parents that Rob and she came up with and thanked the therapist for her support.

Next, when the therapist inquired what had happened around feeding since the last meeting, Stacey started talking in the first person: "I decided to serve salmon at dinner, and the kids loved it!" The therapist congratulated Stacey for this achievement and asked if she could explain more about the change. Stacey replied:

> It was not as difficult as I had imagined. I bought fish that is already lightly seasoned, and all you need to do is bake it. And so I did, and it was a success. I felt very proud of myself.

The therapist said, excitedly: "I am also very proud of you, Stacey. Great job! But I noticed that you are again speaking about feeding decisions in the first person. Isn't this interesting?" Stacey smiled and said:

> Honestly, I am not used to including Rob in this type of decision making. Maybe that's not that good. There is a part of me that would like to avoid sharing with him how truly difficult this is for me. But I understand why this is important.

The therapist replied that she acknowledged how hard it must have been for Stacey to involve Rob more, and added that she believed that in the long run it would make things easier for both of them: "One of the benefits of this program is that it helps both parents join forces as they develop more balanced eating habits in their family." Stacey responded that she was gradually realizing that even though Rob's own eating habits would not change he could become more involved in the kids' eating.

Following this conversation, Stacey decided on her behavioral goal for the following week: discussing with Rob adding another type of dish the family would enjoy at dinner. Stacey added that she was wondering whether her fear that her children would not like nutritious food led her to avoid presenting other types of foods than those she felt comfortable with. The therapist found herself wondering how to balance her empathy for Stacey's dilemmas and struggles with pushing for changes. But given her experience in delivering Parent-Based Prevention, she remembered that incorporating the support of the partner, when one existed, was a mutative point in the intervention, and facilitated greater change. Therefore, the therapist asked if these concerns – about her children eating food that was not nutritive and healthy – were things Stacey might want to share with Rob. Stacey agreed that might be helpful. Finally, the therapist reiterated her appreciation of Stacey's dedication to her parents, and asked her to inform her if there were any changes in her mother's health condition.

In the following week, both Rob and Stacey arrived at session 6. The therapist began the meeting by asking Rob how the past few weeks had been for the family. Rob said there had been considerable progress with feeding and admitted that he had not believed that Stacey would reduce her feeding-related stress in such a short time: "She is doing such a great job, introducing new foods, and is trying hard to avoid commenting on how our kids eat." The therapist responded:

> This is great. Nice work, Stacey! I am very happy that you observe this and can complement Stacey for her efforts. But I was also wondering about the process you've gone through in the past few weeks, Rob. Could you please tell me more about it?

Rob and Stacey both laughed and looked at one another. "Me?" asked Rob. "I know we talked about it when we analyzed the family meal, but I am not sure if I can contribute in any way, and whether my attempts to help will just make things worse." The therapist responded that this was a great topic for discussion, and asked Stacey for her response. Stacey said:

> To be honest, I know it has been super difficult to talk with me about these issues. I know I can benefit from getting more support, but I am freaking out just from thinking about changing how things have been

until now. I know you are busy, Rob, and it may be unfair to ask you to be more involved, but I do need you to be more involved.

Rob listened silently as he patted his wife's back. The therapist asked: "Can the two of you think of domains that are not related with food where you are satisfied with your communication and collaboration?" Both parents said that they were mostly very content with their partnership. "So how do you explain what's going on in the food and eating arena?" asked the therapist. Rob replied:

I was hoping it will pass, or that the kids will put up a fight strong enough and I could blame it all on them. But that's not fair. I feel that I don't really know if I should intervene at all and if so, what to do, what to say, how to say it.

The therapist looked at Stacey, who remained silent. The therapist continued: "I don't want to put words in your mouth, Stacey." Stacey smiled and said: "Please, by all means, go ahead. I'm not sure I have any words now." The therapist felt that it was an opportune time to deliver an impactful message. She felt that Stacey was relatively open about her difficulties and had accepted her clinical observations thus far, and that Stacey was struggling with labeling her concerns and conversing about them with Rob. And so the therapist continued:

I think that the key point here is mostly the 'how to' communicate and provide support around these issues. I'd like to reiterate the Parent-Based Prevention perspective. And then I would like to help us figure out how you can apply it in your family. If you hold a mindset of 'intervening,' Rob, then you are already priming yourself to becoming cautious and avoiding conflict. What about you both approach this as a developmental milestone for your family? With younger children, parents really need to make most of the decisions about anything – bedtime, which daycare they attend, what clothes kids are wearing, and their after-school activities. But as the children become older, the mindset gradually changes to facilitating the kids' capacity for making healthy choices, within the boundaries the parents define. And what I see happening here, and many families face the same situation, is that Stacey's eating disorder history models the how your family is behaving around eating. I see this mostly when it comes to the variety of your family's diet. Stacey's attempts to micro-manage what Emma eats, her annoyance when Aidan becomes bored quickly and wants to get out of his high-chair, and in general the stress around eating. Does this make sense to you?

After both parents nodded, the therapist continued: "So if we think about it this way, which kind of help, Rob, you think Stacey would find most useful?"

The therapist felt that by using circular questioning, she would be able to help Rob and Stacey better communicate their perspectives to each other. The couple suggested a few ways in which they could plan together and collaborate in feeding their children, for the remaining time of the session, while the therapist helped bridge any miscommunications and encouraged the couple to decide on a behavioral goal. For instance, Rob first suggested he would feed Aidan and let Stacey handle Emma. However, in their discussion of this option, both parents decided against this behavioral experiment; they agreed that being more flexible about their roles and responsibilities during mealtime would help each of them become familiar with their children's eating preferences and more skillful in feeding.

Over the next two weeks, Stacey continued meeting with the therapist individually and reported a much-improved atmosphere during family meals, a reduction in Emma's demands for larger quantities and a more diversified menu, and lower anxiety when invited as a family to social events that included food. Stacey also reported that Rob informed his colleagues he would be leaving work early once a week to have dinner with his family. She also said she felt more comfortable sharing with him her concerns and dilemmas about feeding their children. In addition, Stacey's mom recovered from her illness, which further helped reduce her stress levels.

Thanks to the parents' hard work, which spearheaded changes in the family, the therapist was able to discuss with Stacey other issues she had observed during the family meal and those that the parents had mentioned in the first session. Particularly, the therapist thought it was an appropriate time to revisit the meal and snack schedule the parents had described, remembering that in her notes from session 1 she had wondered whether breakfast was provided too late in the day, after the children were awake for a few hours. The therapist asked Stacey: "There is something I wanted to bring up. Is this OK?" As Stacey agreed, the therapist continued: "I was wondering whether Emma and Aidan would benefit from having their first meal or snack earlier each morning." The therapist also explained that notwithstanding Stacey's habits, children Emma and Aidan's age should eat regular meals and snacks throughout the day, with at least an hour's pause between meals but no more than three hours. Further, the therapist explored with Stacey the conversations the parents had with their children on physical activity, wondering whether there was some over-emphasis on this matter. The therapist cited the interaction between Stacey and Emma over whether her play at school involved exercise. When Stacey mentioned that she thought it was a good practice to urge her children to engage in more physical activity, the therapist provided psychoeducation on pressure for physical activity and reiterated that the more children felt they were coerced to exercise, the less chance they would develop an intrinsic motivation to do so in the absence of the parent's control. The therapist mentioned that if Emma and Aidan's pediatrician was not worried about their weight, and if they played enough outside, there should not currently be a reason to worry about their habits and weight. The therapist was impressed by Stacey's attention to these messages, and her motivation to adapt her behaviors and avoid commenting on Emma's behaviors. Since this was the last session of Phase Two, the therapist reviewed her notes in preparation for Phase Three, where both parents would reconvene. The therapist thought that she was fortunate to work with Stacey and Rob, as they appeared accepting of her supportive yet sometimes challenging style. She reflected on her work with the family up until now and felt that the couple allowed her to provide a supportive yet confronting intervention to challenge Stacey's eating and weight concerns as projected onto her children, through psychoeducation, warmth, and cheerleading. The therapist assumed that not all parents had similar motivation and capacity for change, and how important it was to adapt her style to her clients.

At the beginning of Phase Three, the couple arrived at the clinic together. Stacey and Rob reported that they met their goals of incorporating the Division of Responsibility in Feeding model and improved strategies for feeding their children. The parents expressed surprise by how quickly Emma's mealtime frustration reduced, and how dinners became a mostly pleasant experience in such a brief while. The parents also reported that Rob was now fully responsible for two family meals: one on a weekday and one over the weekend – he was choosing the menu, grocery shopping, preparing food, and handling the children's negative responses during dinner, should they occur. Both parents expressed Rob's increasing involvement as a positive experience. However, they did mention that Rob managed to be engaged in the first two weeks after the couple's meeting (i.e., session 6), but that in the past week he had been unable to attend more than one family meal the entire week. The therapist explained how challenging keeping the momentum might be, and asked Rob and Stacey to brainstorm some ideas to maintain Rob's active involvement. They decided Rob would reach out to his boss to discuss his work/life balance.

The therapist commended the parents for their achievements over this time-limited program and oriented them to the goals of the meetings during Phase Three. Stacey disclosed that there was something that had been troubling her that she hoped the therapist might help her think through:

> This may sound silly, but to me it's not. I know we told you that we are often invited to social events. And that is correct. But it does not escape me that our family is lacking social support. Or, you know what, I feel lonely. Rob is probably OK with the fact that it is mostly the four of us every weekend. I can understand that he's surrounded with people at work, but the kids and I do not have a strong social network. I am going to moms' meet-ups but it always feels like all these other women also hang out together separately, while I meet them only on those arranged

meetings. And Emma has never been invited to a playdate, so I'm wondering if we can do anything differently. You may think it's nothing, but last night I thought that if something happens in the middle of the night and Rob or I need to go to the hospital, there is no one we can call but our babysitter to come and watch our kids, and the babysitter lives far away and uses public transport. In fact, Emma's lack of good friends bothers me the most. Is this something we can talk about here?

The therapist replied: "Thank you for sharing this concern, Stacey. Before I respond, I'm interested in your thoughts, Rob." Rob said smilingly:

> I thought I was off the hook on this one. But I guess I shouldn't be. I agree this is not how I imagined I would raise my kids, but I also do not know whether there is anything we can do now to change it. You are probably not going to tell me that just like we added more foods to our meals, we are going to add more friends to our life, right?

The therapist responded:

> That is actually an interesting idea, Rob. I'd like first to learn a bit more about this issue and why it bothers you both. You may remember that when I outlined the Parent-Based Prevention program, I said that in Phase Two we will work on making changes around eating, and in Phase Three we will try and capitalize on what we learned in other spheres of your family's life. I do not know if you remember this principle as we discussed it briefly in the first session, and so many things have happened since.

The parents responded that they remembered vaguely the therapist mentioning something about this process. Then, the therapist continued:

> I observed you both working hard to improve the manner in which you speak about your concerns and dilemmas. So we will try and use the communication and problem-solving skills you guys used so nicely in changing the feeding interactions, and implement these skills in cracking this issue. How does this sound?

The parents nodded and said: "This sounds good. We would like that."

The therapist continued to explore the parents' concerns. Stacey spoke of her lifetime experience that the relationships she created felt unstable and that she was repeatedly doubting whether people were really interested in her company. Stacey connected these feelings to earlier experiences in her life when she believed she had to be the thinnest, smartest, and most successful in order to be loved. She said tearfully:

Being a parent is a much more exposed and vulnerable situation than I have ever imagined. I thought that the kids would buffer my need to please the world, but Emma and Aidan became two more things I feel must be perfect. I want to free Emma from this burden, but I am afraid she is just like me. And that just like me she is having a hard time making her friendships last.

For Rob, it turned out that close relationships were not a high priority. Rob spoke of how energy-consuming his routine had become since his children were born, and that he often fantasized of a quiet weekend at home, only to discover that the kids and Stacey had different needs, and were interested in going out and spending time with friends more than he was. Rob reflected on his experiences growing up – since his parents worked very hard, the family spent most weekends watching TV and hanging out at home, and Rob and his brother were left to their own devices. Rob said:

> It never occurred to me until this very moment that the thing I hated the most about my childhood – those long, boring weekends with me and my brother trying desperately to entertain ourselves – I'm expecting my family to endure now.

Using circular questioning techniques (i.e., an interviewing strategy to ask one family member about the mental state, motivation, and belief system of another family member, as a means of increasing mentalization and empathy), the therapist asked Rob: "And what do you think Stacey is most fearful of regarding Emma?" Rob remained silent for a while, and then replied:

> I believe that Stacey would say that it's not OK that a girl as sweet and kind as Emma is not invited to playdates and that we do not host playdates at our home. And I agree. But the problem is that kids in Emma's age often come to playdates with their parents and the last thing I want on a weekend is entertaining strangers at my home.

The therapist turned to Stacey and inquired what she thought might be challenging for Rob. Stacey said: "It is quite clear, I think. He does not have the same social needs Emma and I do. But this is the problem." The therapist responded:

> I hear you, Rob. Your workdays are so long and busy, and many people experiencing your lifestyle just want to rest over the weekend. I think that I am also hearing two things from Stacey, though. I will outline them and please let me know if I understood you well, OK? First, Stacey, you are concerned that Emma does not have necessary social skills. And second, you feel that your own wellbeing, and maybe even

your wellbeing as a parent, will be improved if you had a stronger social network. Is this right?

Stacey nodded, tearful. Rob said:

> This sounds like something that Stacey and Emma need to work out. I am not sure I can help here. I am happy to support them, but they just need to invite some nice girls from school and hope their moms are nice too. Isn't this how it works?

"And before we ask Stacey to reply," smiled the therapist, "what would you anticipate, Rob, that she might say now?" Rob smiled back and said:

> I won't surprise anyone by saying that I think Stacey can handle this all. But maybe she needs some support from me when things don't work out as planned. Let's say, when they will invite a classmate and her parents say she cannot make it because she has a recital or something.

"That sounds about right, Rob," the therapist continued. "Let's say that this is the case. Before we move on to troubleshooting, I'd like to understand whether this issue comes up with Emma only, or is it something you are worried about with Aidan as well?" Both parents smiled, and Rob responded: "Aidan is so young, and he is still homeschooled. Therefore I haven't started thinking about these things with him. I believe it is not bothering Stacey either. Isn't this right, Stacey?" Stacey nodded, indicating she was not worried about Aidan's social functioning. Next, the therapist went on: "So Rob, how can you support Stacey with Emma?" Stacey interjected:

> You know what? I don't always need your advice; I just need you to be there and tell me that our child is awesome and that the most reasonable thing is that this classmate does have a recital, and not that our daughter is not loved or not popular at school. Because I feel so anxious that I immediately think it's my fault. Once I remember there could be other explanations, I will figure it out.

"What can you do, for example, Stacey?" asked the therapist. Stacey shrugged and said:

> I typically do not reach the point of coping with rejection, since I avoid inviting people. Or I never ask anyone again for a playdate if they refuse the first time, for whatever reason. But you will now probably say it is all in my head, right?

The therapist paused for a few seconds, organizing her thoughts; she was struggling how to respond to Stacey's schemas in a way that would be empathetic, non-judgmental, and validating, and yet challenge her avoidance patterns. The therapist looked at Rob, hoping he would intervene. But Rob stared right back at her, waiting for the therapist's response. Therefore, the therapist continued, using a soft tone and a warm expression:

> I cannot tell you that this is entirely in your head, Stacey. I met Emma and found her to be a very sweet girl. I see no reason why her peers will not like her. But there may be some things about her interactions with specific children, or the girls whose company she seeks, that may not be such a great fit for her. I think we will need to collect more information to understand whether there is a problem. You can observe her in playdates and ask her teachers about it, and then we will have a better grasp of whether Emma needs some support in choosing friends or maintaining friendships. But I definitely think we should give it a try, and that you both should collaborate as you did so nicely around mealtimes. What do you think?

After both parents nodded, the therapist continued: "We talked only about Emma's social needs, and we will soon plan an experiment you can test this week. But I want to echo what I heard from you, Stacey. I think I heard you implying you feel lonely." The couple went on to discuss the gap between their social needs and how they could plan their weekdays and their weekends in a way that was agreeable and fun to all family members.

Over the next few weeks, Rob and Stacey made active efforts to befriend some of the families in Emma's school. Emma had a few playdates – some of them were very enjoyable and some not as much. The family also enjoyed a nice picnic at the park with one family they met at Emma's soccer class. As she reached out to more parents, Stacey was invited to a moms' night out, initiated by some mothers in Emma's class. When Stacey returned home from this outing, Rob said jokingly he might organize a parallel dads' night out soon, and Stacey replied this was a nice idea. The therapist contemplated Aidan disappearing almost completely from all the discussions. When she invited the parents to share concerns and dilemmas about him, they dismissed any present challenges with him, alluding to his young age as the reason for not focusing on him in the intervention. The therapist did state, however, that the parents' enhanced communication patterns would likely be beneficial should any worries arise about Aidan in the future. She also encouraged the parents to help Aidan befriend the younger siblings of Emma's new friends.

In the concluding session of Parent-Based Prevention, the therapist asked the parents to summarize their journey in the program. Both Stacey and Rob noted observing that meals became less conflictual and much more pleasant at their home. "Dinners are much more conversational than I had ever imagined," said Rob. "I actually am looking forward to them. The evening is no longer the battlefield it used to be." Stacey maintained Rob's sentiment:

I was very surprised, but also very relieved, to realize that I don't need to fight my daughter and restrict her so much. Maybe I did not say it before, but I wasn't really buying into these division of responsibility rules and what you had said about commenting less. But since you have seemed to believe so much in the program, Rob and I spoke about it and decided we'd give it a try. And it was worth it.

The parents went on to highlight additional changes that had occurred recently, representing a sense of greater competence in their parenting. Stacey mentioned that she felt less worried about Emma's interpersonal interactions. She added:

But this is something I think I still need to monitor and help her develop more skills in. I learned I need to set the general rules but first let her try to find her own voice, and only later provide feedback. That part was harder than I thought. But I understand now why it is important to let her develop her mastery and learn what's good for her. I still monitor her, but from a greater distance.

Rob added: "We actually were thinking about continuing to see someone for parental counseling every now and then, since this was very helpful. I have not anticipated this program affecting our family so tremendously."

The therapist complemented the parents for their engagement in the program, and for their willingness to work through difficult dilemmas and attitude differences. She also reviewed how they might have to overcome new hurdles as the children continued to grow and develop: Emma's changing body, appetite, and body image as she became older and transitioned into adolescence; reduced parental ability to oversee Emma's behaviors, eating, and interaction with the environment as Emma developed; and the role of positive feedback. She reiterated that related concerns about Aidan could emerge further down the road, and discussed with the parents how they planned to address these concerns, should they arise. Finally, the therapist concluded that she enjoyed working with the couple, and was impressed by how hard they worked in the intervention, and expressed her belief they and their children would have a happy, healthy life together.

18 Parent-Based Prevention in Action
Dave and Gabby

This chapter is a continuation of the complete clinical case demonstration detailed in Chapters 5 and 17. The second half of Chapter 5 delineated the first session with Dave and Gabby, who were interested in receiving Parent-Based Prevention, given Dave's past and present diagnosis of binge-eating disorder. This chapter summarizes the presenting issues the parents wanted to address, and how the therapist guided them throughout the program. This case report should be understood as an example of how the Parent-Based Prevention facilitates desired changes in parents and their children, helping them have healthier, more prosperous lives.

Dave and Gabby (aged 31 and 32 respectively) sought treatment because Dave was worried they were not developing healthy eating habits in their 8-year-old twin boys Liam and Mason. Both parents were concerned about using food for non-nutritional purposes such as using food to soothe and distract their children and, in this way, encouraging unnecessary eating, eating more than was needed for growth and energy, and eating foods with low nutritional value. Dave disclosed a lifetime history of binge-eating and depressive symptoms, and passive suicidal ideation. Speaking with the therapist privately, he revealed a recent deterioration in his binge-eating symptoms, but he was willing to share this relapse with his wife. For her part, Gabby reported significant concerns about her weight and shape, but denied having any other symptoms of an eating disorder. In her individual interview with the therapist, she spoke of her interest in making a career change, but asked him not to share this with Dave at this time.

Prior to session 2, the therapist reviewed his notes from the first meeting. He believed that the family meal would provide important information about whether and how the parental symptoms affected parenting practices in general, and feeding/eating behaviors specifically. He also examined his notes suggesting that although the parents appeared happy in their relationship, they struggled with open communication and preferred avoiding problems. He also reminded himself to remain mindful about possible problems in the children's emotion regulation and use of negative language about eating, food, and weight.

The family arrived at the family meal meeting (session 2), which was scheduled for 6pm, a time when the children typically had dinner. The parents held takeaway boxes and the therapist recognized the name of a Thai food restaurant close by. After introducing to the therapist their children, the family sat around a table the therapist had prepared for them. While Dave and his two sons engaged in small talk with the therapist, Gabby took out plastic plates, forks, and chopsticks and started setting up the boxes. Gabby announced the types of foods that were available and asked each family member what they wanted. The therapist observed that both children did not look interested in the food and did not respond to Gabby, who nonetheless added food to their plates. Dave served some food onto his plate but kept looking at the kids and did not eat. Gabby took out another plastic box that contained a vegetable salad and started eating it while encouraging the kids to eat their meals.

During this time, Mason wanted to get off his chair to get a close look at the therapist's book shelves, but his parents asked him to remain seated at the table. As the parents repeatedly encouraged their children to eat, the atmosphere became more conflictual and tense. Both parents urged their kids to eat, talked about how yummy the noodles were, promised the children they would be able to watch their favorite show on Gabby's smartphone later if they would eat now, and even threatened to cancel tomorrow's playdates should the kids refuse to eat. Eventually, the boys started eating but still did not look interested in the food and did not appear to be enjoying it.

When the therapist asked whether typical meals looked like this, Gabby replied:

> Well, yes and no. Sometimes we prepare or order food that I find delicious, but I am always unsure whether they would want to eat or not. To be honest, I picked up the kids today from school and took them to their swim class. Since they were very hungry, I gave each of them a small snack.

As she was talking, Liam interjected: "You gave each of us a whole bag of chips, Mommy!" Gabby smiled, looking uncomfortable, and replied: "Well, these are the only snacks I keep in the car. And they were baked potato chips, not the deep-fried ones. But I did not know they would ruin your appetite for dinner." Dave added: "Since the kids have swim class today right after school, I packed them a bigger lunch than usual, and also added more snacks to eat immediately after their swim class." The therapist turned to the children and asked, "Did you feel hungry when you sat at the table a few minutes ago?" Both Mason and Liam shrugged. The therapist continued using a soft tone so that his words would not be perceived as judgmental:

It sounds like you guys had a very busy day today. You had school, then a swim class, and then came here. All these things require a lot of energy and would make anyone very hungry throughout the day. It's not always easy planning when you'd eat when you exercise, right?

When the parents did not respond, the therapist thought he might use self-disclosure as a strategy to normalize their experience, as this strategy had been effective for reducing shame and guilt in other clients he had worked with: "When I swim, I am super famished immediately after and find it hard waiting for dinner." Gabby responded: "Thank you for saying it like that. I feel less guilty for not thinking this through." As she started packing the food, she added: "I guess I will be having some Thai food tomorrow at work!" The family engaged in friendly conversation with one another and with the therapist, during which he noted to himself that the boys and their parents looked much happier, closer, and relaxed than throughout the meal.

In the following session, Dave and Gabby arrived together for the planned joint meeting, in line with the plan. The therapist suggested he and the parents review the family meal, and asked them whether they had any thoughts about that session. Both parents responded that they did not remember anything that stood out about that meal. It looked like a typical dinner at their home: "We plan a wonderful dinner and they refuse eating it for various reasons," said Dave. "These are exactly the unhealthy eating habits that have become ingrained. You had a chance to see exactly why we came here."

The therapist continued: "I had some observations that I would like to share with you. If I understand correctly, you feel that last week's session was representative." As the parents nodded, the therapist asked: "Was there anything about it that was not typical?" Gabby replied: "No, what you saw was very similar to our experience at home."

The therapist thought that he should help the parents differentiate between their children's behaviors during mealtimes and in other interactions. Therefore, he continued:

First off, I found your sons to be very nice, outgoing, and fun boys. It was a joy seeing the four of you interacting in the second half of the meeting after you finished eating. It may come as no surprise, but while you had the family meal I was wondering whether the children or even the two of you guys were really hungry. When you all sat down at the table, I looked at Liam and Mason and neither of them looked interested in the food. Later, when you shared the events preceding our meeting, it made more sense – they had a bigger-than-usual lunch, then snacks before and after swim class. Most kids, and adults, are less likely to feel hungry and do not fancy eating in such conditions.

Gabby replied: "Oh, I have never thought about it like this. I have not thought about these issues at all. So you are saying that we should not give them any snacks in the afternoon?" The therapist replied:

> I am not saying that at all. But I suggest we take some time to re-evaluate your routine and the meal/snack schedule. Children – very much like adults – typically need three meals a day, and between two to three snacks per day. It is better that there is a gap of at least an hour between these meals and snacks, but also that not too much time passes, probably not more than three hours. This timeline allows for healthy digestion, normalized insulin levels, and gradual development of hunger cues. Ultimately, we would like to help your children eat when they identify hunger cues in their bodies, and not eat when they are full or satiated. But when there is a pattern of snacking throughout the day – that is, eating little amounts of foods many times throughout the day – people may become vulnerable to eating when food is offered and not in response to what their bodies signal. Does this make sense?

Dave replied: "So are you saying that when we decide that 6pm is the time to eat, we are hurting our children? And that we should wait until they declare they are hungry?" The therapist responded:

> Thank you for asking this, as it helps me clarify my point. I think it is great that you, the parents, set the routine, including mealtimes, bedtimes, after-school activities, playdates, and so on. But it is worth figuring out how the meal and snack schedule maps onto your plans. As you work out the right timing to feed your children, you can think when and how you decide which foods and how much you provide them before and after each meal. How does this sound to you?

Gabby replied: "Sure," and Dave said: "Yes, this makes sense." The therapist continued:

> I want to highlight that this schedule could be flexible at times. We are not interested in developing a very rigid plan. But it would be good to think of general times in the day when the kids eat to make sure there is a greater likelihood they arrive at these meals ready to eat, not too hungry and not full.

Gabby asked: "So what do you recommend I do when I pick them up from school and they act like they are famished?" The therapist turned to Dave and said: "Before I reply, do you have any thoughts, Dave?" Dave hesitated before replying:

You know, I sometimes ask myself if they are really that hungry. I am not sure at all. They want to chat and tell me about their day, or they fight in the back seat and whatnot. But typically when I pick them up I am still thinking about work and feel I need to give them something so that they let me have a few more minutes of silence before arriving to the next stop, may it be home, their piano class or swim class, or a friend's house.

The therapist replied:

This is a very common experience for parents: feeling that you have not had enough time to process everything that has happened in your day until meeting the kids, not having time to recompose between leaving work and pick-up. Therefore, I understand why you find yourself using food to soothe the kids and keep them busy so that you buy yourself more time. Is changing this pattern something you would like to mark as a goal in this intervention?

Both parents responded: "Yes, absolutely!"

Next, the therapist asked: "Another thing I was wondering about was how you decided what to serve for the family meal. How did you guys decide it?" The parents looked at one another and then Gabby responded: "I just texted Dave, 'I will bring takeaway food for dinner.'" The therapist said: "I noticed you, Gabby, ate salad, and you, Dave, barely touched the food. Is this how meals look typically?" Dave replied:

I guess that Gabby is on a diet and tries to eat more nutritious meals and I was not hungry. I stopped by a fast food store after work before arriving here last week and was not feeling super hungry at that time. I feel uncomfortable eating in front of my own kids, because I don't want to expose my family to my habits.

Gabby added:

Liam asks me every so often why I eat different things, and why Daddy does not eat with us. I do not know what to tell him. I would like to have these family meals, but I feel like we are too set in our ways and cannot change our patterns. Do you have any suggestions?

The therapist responded:

I have a few suggestions. But before we discuss them, I want to summarize the issues we have mentioned, OK? I think we marked a few things we may want to target in this program. The first is how to reduce a certain kind of snacking or grazing, and second, trying to have more family meals. Does this describe well what we have talked about?

As the parents nodded in agreement, the therapist resumed: "The next issue I wanted to discuss provides a context for making many of the changes. Are you familiar with the Division of Responsibility model?" Both parents answered that they were not. The therapist went on:

> This model describes how parents and children should share the task of eating. Parents are responsible for what is being served, when, and where, and the children are responsible for whether they decide to eat or not, and if they eat, how much they eat. Therefore, for your family meals, this model suggests you put the food on the table in central plates, and each child chooses what he would eat from all available foods. Children often need to be presented with new foods a few times, sometimes even more than a dozen times, in order to be willing to try them. That is fine. The more they see the both of you eating varied, balanced meals, the more they are likely to eat healthier food. How does this sound?

Gabby replied:

> It sounds fantastic, but I am not sure how it applies for our family. You see, none of the kids are interested in the food that I eat, and Dave – I am not quite sure what he even eats, or when his mealtimes are. It is very hard getting a clear picture from him, and he was so resentful last time I had asked him, so I just decided to let it go and manage dinners myself.

The therapist turned to Dave, using a gentle tone: "Is this something you feel comfortable talking about, Dave?" Dave remained quiet for a while, then replied, fighting tears:

> My eating is something I am so ashamed of, that I was relieved when Gabby stopped asking about it. I try to avoid sitting with the kids when they are eating, since I feel like I cannot participate in this healthfully. I feel like a good dad in anything but being a role model for a healthy lifestyle. I have not told you this, Gabby, but I assume you knew – I am bingeing at least once a day, and therefore not really hungry at dinner. Things at work have been stressful, and . . . Anyhow, I think this division of responsibility makes a lot of sense and is not too difficult for us to implement. But I am not sure how I could be involved in a productive way.

Dave turned to the therapist, asking: "What should I do then?" The therapist replied, "I have some ideas, but I am first interested in your thoughts, Gabby." Gabby responded:

> I do not know if it is a good thing they do not see you eating with us. They need to have this experience of regular meals, family-style. I also have been thinking about the kids seeing me eat mostly salad. I was wondering if this is a problem.

The therapist replied: "You have probably realized by now that I am interested in helping you guys communicate about these topics. Therefore, let's hear you first, Dave." Dave responded:

> I agree we should eat together, and that we decide what they eat and when they eat it. But since changing our habits is a huge effort for us, I want to understand what are the implications of maintaining things the way they currently are and not changing anything. Could you explain?

The therapist answered:

> That's a great question. There have been many studies on developing healthy lifestyle in families, and I can tell you what the literature says. Much of what children learn from adults occurs through modeling. Children develop their understandings of the world by observing how we talk, act, respond to problems, and so on. When Liam and Mason see you, Gabby, eating only salad, they might think that other types of food are bad for them, and they should avoid them altogether. Or they would feel guilty for eating other foods. And when you, Dave, are not taking part in any of the meals, it may also make them wonder as for the reasons why you do not eat with them. Children develop their own theories for things they do not understand. For example, they may think that it is better to skip meals, or that food creates negative emotions in you, or that it is not important for you to eat healthfully or with your family.

"So you are saying that family meals will be a good opportunity to teach the kids healthy eating habits," said Dave. Gabby replied: "I think that he is saying we should model something else, with more foods on the table, clearer mealtimes, and more healthy options."

> This makes sense, theoretically. But if I am being honest, I am afraid that some foods, once put on the table, will make me eat uncontrollably. When you put a baguette on the table, mac and cheese, or other high-carb food, my brain is like "Let the celebrations begin!" I understand that this is important for the kids but providing more varied foods could hurt my wellbeing. Is it OK if we do exclude some foods from our family's diet?

Although Dave looked at the therapist, Gabby responded: "I am sure we can find enough nutritious foods to serve that will not make you binge. Just tell me what triggers you, and I will make sure it is not on the table, OK?" The conversation continued with both parents planning a different approach for family meals, with the support of the therapist who facilitated communication and problem-solving strategies. Finally, the parents committed to trying to maintain a planned routine of three meals and three snacks per day, and two family meals in the following week. The therapist encouraged the parents to treat this new routine as an experiment, saying that there was no guarantee what would work and what would not; the parents should try out a change in their present attitudes or behaviors, and if it did not lead to the anticipated results in their children's eating, it would prepare the parents better for the next behavioral experiment.

The therapist concluded the meeting by commending Gabby and Dave for their engagement with the program. The therapist also oriented the parents to the structure of meetings during Phase Two, when he would meet mostly with Dave. When the parents left his office, the therapist documented in his notes that session 3 went well, and that the parents appeared motivated to make changes. He also wondered how inclined Dave would be to meet without Gabby and more explicitly disclose his challenges, given his declared reluctance to try any form of intervention for his enduring eating and depressive symptoms.

After two weeks in which he cancelled the meetings a few days before each one, Dave arrived at the clinic alone for session 4, which marked the beginning of Phase Two. The therapist knew the scheduling might be challenging for many parents receiving Parent-Based Prevention. However, he decided to explore with Dave whether his work and family commitments inhibited him from attending the sessions, or whether there were additional barriers. As Dave entered the therapist's office, he started talking quickly, as if he wanted to get something off his chest:

> I wanted to tell you that something very weird is going on. I have been feeling very bad lately. I have been stopping at the burger shop every day before I get home. I order a couple of burgers and eat them very, very fast. I do not even like how they taste. And then I scold myself for bingeing, and I feel so disgusting.

The therapist replied, empathetically: "Oh, this sounds very hard. Thank you for sharing it with me. Why do you think this is happening?" Dave responded:

> The guys at work have started joking around with me lately about me gaining weight. I gained around 10 pounds since I started working there a few months ago. It is one of these workplaces that have treats freely available all the time, and I feel bad, I feel ashamed of how I eat.

The therapist asked: "Is this something that has been going on before you reached out to me to start the Parent-Based Prevention program?" Dave answered: "I was wondering about this myself. And yes, I can hardly stop thinking about food since we met you for the first time."

The therapist believed that Dave felt that his binge-eating and depressive symptoms as well as his negative mood intolerance were much-engrained patterns, and that for Dave thinking about possibly changing these patterns was anxiety-provoking. Therefore, the therapist decided that he should provide support and validate Dave's difficulties; similarly to his use of self-disclosure in the discussion of his own hunger level after swimming, the therapist elected an approach that was not confrontational, but rather more encouraging and handholding. For that reason, he said, softly:

> This happens to some parents doing this program. The conversations over food and eating could be stressful and trigger their eating disorder again, and consequently parents might feel more worried, agitated, anxious about the forthcoming changes. Many people unintentionally respond to this stress by doing things that have reduced their stress levels in the past, which – for many parents doing this Parent-Based Prevention program – is binge eating. Therefore, I am not completely surprised at what has been happening to you recently. But what I have also seen is that when parents see that this program works for their family, they feel less stressed, and these eating disorder behaviors reduce. So by all means what's been going on for you recently is not unanticipated. We should do everything in our power to improve your wellbeing, not only what is efficacious in your role as a parent. Let's figure out what other things you could try out, that have worked for you in stressful situations, but that do not involve food.

After brainstorming a few ideas for more adaptive coping skills, Dave went on talking about additional concerns he has been struggling with: "I want to be a completely different dad than the one I am presently. But I do not know how to make this change." The therapist thought that in order for Parent-Based Prevention to be effective, Dave needed encouragement and a constant reminder of his strengths and achievements before he could implement any change. The therapist also wondered whether Dave was even aware of how special and heart-warming was his devotion to his family. Then, he replied:

> I am not sure you need to be a completely different dad, Dave. I saw you interact with Mason and Liam in my office and you were very caring, affectionate, and fun. I was impressed by the close relationships I observed between the four of you. Maybe there are aspects in your parenting that are affected by your eating disorder or by other problems, like your mood, but this program is intended to help you work on them.

Dave looked relieved and said: "Thank you for saying this. It actually makes me feel a bit better. My family is my greatest pride and joy, and the thought I am not the best dad possible terrifies me." Dave continued describing how Gabby was the parent mostly responsible for implementing the changes discussed in the last session. He said the family was able to follow the feeding routine the parents had planned, and had two family meals which went well. The children were hungry enough to try new foods and the parents felt they ate sufficient amounts and that the between-meal snacking reduced substantially.

The therapist next asked Dave how he had experienced these changes. Dave replied:

> I am not sure where I am in all of this. I want to be involved and I want to eat more healthfully myself, but I don't think I know how to do it myself. Thereby as far as it involves feeding the kids, I leave it to my wife.

The therapist responded:

> Do you remember I mentioned on the last meeting a specific type of mindset that helps parents make changes? I think I called it an "experimental mindset." This is a state of mind where you test out a certain change, and assess whether it leads to the desired change in your children's eating habits. If it does not work out as planned, we figure out which modifications are needed to prompt the desired outcome. So why don't we test out some modifications to your practices and see how they evolve. If we see the changes do not result in the anticipated outcomes, we adjust our plans. That is the reason I suggest we test in the next few weeks several ways for you to engage in feeding your children and learn different strategies for you to have more balanced eating experiences with your family. In case one course of action does not work out as planned, we will revisit our plan.

In the following session, Dave reported he had been able to become more involved in food preparation, serving, and eating with his family. He reported feeling better and experiencing fewer binge-eating episodes. He reported feeling satisfied and proud of himself for making these changes, but shared with the therapist that they indeed had taken a toll on his wellbeing; particularly, he was unable to sleep well.

The therapist started considering whether he should refer Dave for treatment for his eating disorder and/or his depressive symptoms. He was not sure how Dave – who refused to seek treatment despite Gabby's requests to do so – would receive this suggestion from the therapist. Would a referral hurt the trust and the therapeutic alliance, or would Dave understand how much the therapist cared about him and his wellbeing? Undecided, the therapist decided to first explore with Dave the background of his eating habits, in the hope that this conversation would shed more light on Dave's schemas about eating, and perhaps advance future discussion of treatment for him.

Dave described early eating experiences growing up; treats and candy were very much restricted, and "eating healthy" was synonymous for him with eating things that tasted bland and unappealing. As an adolescent, Dave's binge eating was mostly triggered by foods his family deemed as "not good for you," and much of his diet relied on these foods. Using cognitive restructuring strategy, the therapist noted how complicated the idea of "eating healthily" must be for Dave given his past experiences. But the therapist also urged Dave to explore foods that could be healthy, accepted by children, and appetizing. Dave suggested that home-made pizza could be something he might enjoy preparing and eating with his kids, and the therapist encouraged him to discuss this idea with Gabby.

Gabby and Dave arrived together at session 6, which is the conjoint meeting during Phase Two. The couple were meeting their goals from earlier sessions, such as preventing food consumption during the non-food situations, and maintaining the behavioral changes they had set in motion. Dave and Gabby felt that their efforts resulted in reduced anxiety around feeding, improved family interactions during meals, and even a few meals everyone thought were delicious.

The parents expressed some concerns about Mason's overeating at meals and perceived weight gain. Gabby mentioned that Mason had experienced noticeable weight change, and that his clothes had become tighter. When the therapist inquired more, he discovered that the boys would have a pediatrician appointment scheduled in two weeks. He encouraged the parents to review Mason's growth charts with their doctor, to identify trends and whether concerns about weight gain were justified. Next, the parents collaboratively decided to continue working on addressing parental concerns around their children's eating behavior. Assessment of their concerns revealed that when the children are hungry, they consistently ate a few servings in one sitting, an amount that looked excessive to their parents. However, the parents denied that their children were eating until they were uncomfortably full or sick. The therapist helped the parents identify several areas for improving the family mealtime experience to prevent overeating, e.g., making the meals more conversational, asking children to slow down, and parental modeling of anticipated behaviors. The therapist provided psychoeducation about the benefits of eating more slowly (i.e., allowing the signal from stomach stretch receptors to reach the brain, improving digestion and hydration, and reducing bloating). Then, the therapist urged the parents to set concrete goals to help their children slow down food intake. Dave suggested that Gabby would discuss these issues with their sons first, and that he would provide support during the meals, saying: "I might as well try and reduce the speed of my own eating." As

Gabby agreed to take the lead in this change, the therapist asked the parents to find a way to include Dave in this change. They jointly decided that he would be responsible for providing the children with water between bites and speaking with them about their day. During the next two individual meetings of Phase Two, Dave informed the therapist of continued improvement in the children's eating habits. Mason's visit to the pediatrician indicated that he remained in the same Body Mass Index (BMI) percentile since birth, and the doctor reassured the parents that they need not worry about their son's weight presently.

In Phase Three of the intervention, the intervention focus shifts toward increasing the sense of parental self-efficacy and general wellbeing of all family members. In this phase, the meetings concentrate on assessing the parents' success thus far in reaching the desired changes in their parenting practices and their children's behaviors, and expanding parental attention to and communication of additional risk areas. As both parents and the therapist convened for session 9, Dave and Gabby described considerable improvement in the family's mealtime experiences, including increasing the variety of foods offered and consumed, and having more pleasant family meals. The therapist reiterated the goals of Phase Three, emphasizing that the prospective meetings should focus on additional challenges beyond those related to food and eating, and invited the parents to discuss concerns and dilemmas they might have related to these goals.

Dave opened the discussion:

> The meetings so far were very useful. Gabby and I have been able to communicate better about how the week is going to look, and collaborating like that has been a very good experience overall. There are two things we mentioned on the way here. The first is Liam's approach to life. He does not believe in himself and when you try to encourage him he snaps right back at you. This is very frustrating. The second thing we talked about is the possibility of me considering individual treatment for myself.

He added, smiling: "I hope I can make some changes in my eating and learn some coping skills so that I will not need to go to that burger place on the way home."

The therapist replied:

> These are two great topics for discussion. Dave, I am glad you brought up the issue of treatment for you. I was wondering myself whether you could benefit from individual therapy, and was not sure when to suggest it. I remember that this is something that Gabby encouraged you to do in the past, but it was not the right time for you. I actually think you might find therapy very useful, and I can provide some referrals at the end of our meeting today.

Dave commented: "I probably could have gone earlier, but was dubious treatment would help. Now that we have had eight sessions, I realized it is not as bad as I had anticipated." The therapist smiled, saying: "I am glad you are willing to test this option." Then, the therapist felt he should not over-state his excitement about Dave's consideration of individual therapy, since he assumed that pressing Dave too much about treatment would likely backfire in lower motivation on his end. Therefore, he continued: "Regarding the first issue you mentioned, I am wondering what your thoughts about this are, Gabby." Gabby responded:

Liam just looks sadder than I would expect for a boy his age. It is like the burden of the entire world is on his little shoulders. If anything upsetting happens – let's say a family were supposed to come over but cancelled last minute because someone is sick – the entire day is ruined. He will either cry or get upset, and no matter how much you try to cheer him up, he won't budge.

Dave interjected:

And if he plays any ball game with you and loses, he will say he is stupid, the worst soccer player, the worst basketball player, and whatnot. He crumbles and tears apart his school papers if he is unhappy with what he wrote, he does not like, and so on. It is quite terrible to watch him like that.

The therapist restated Gabby and Dave's concerns: "If I am hearing correctly, you are worried that Liam has challenges coping with difficult emotions, and maybe he experiences some negative beliefs about himself. Does this sound a fair description?" As the parents nodded, the therapist continued: "Do you have any reason to worry about this type of behaviors and attitudes?" Both parents laughed, and Gabby said:

You have probably realized by now that we both are somewhat pessimistic and have this black-and-white thinking. I do not want my child to have the same approach to life, but I feel stuck here, because I am so fixed in my habits.

As she leaned toward her husband, she said: "What do you think, Dave? Do you feel you know how to turn around Liam?"

The therapist responded:

Working on similar issues is the goal of Phase Three of Parent-Based Prevention. We are trying to support healthy long-term adjustment in your children, and to identify any issues that may hinder adaptive development. I think it would be helpful for me to understand your concerns about Liam, if you could describe when you started seeing such responses in him and give me a few more examples of situations when you find yourself worried.

In the following sessions, the parents worked on identifying triggers for Liam's negative, self-defeating, and pessimistic comments, and developed new skills to foster in him more positive schemas and stress-tolerance capacities that were age-appropriate: asking Liam to find corroborating and contradicting evidence to his negative schemas, providing rewards for even the slightest demonstration of coping with anxiety-provoking situations (for instance, ten additional minutes of screen time for any occasion he spoke in class), and channeling him to an after-school activity that fitted his capabilities (playing soccer turned out to be a success). Further, the parents encouraged Mason – who appeared not to share Liam's depressive inclinations – to enlist support for Liam. The parents reported that the twins had become even closer thanks to their parents' efforts, and their greater closeness had a positive impact on both children. In addition, the therapist discussed with the parents the importance of not expressing their own self-criticism, and instead the importance of modeling constructive problem solving and acceptance of undesirable events.

In the final meeting of the program, Dave and Gabby appeared more relieved and happy than when they had begun it. The couple expressed their satisfaction with the progress they had made as parents, and the improved functioning they had observed in their children. By the end of the program, both children ate more diverse foods, a regular meals and snack routine was sustained, and the family had a few family meals each week. The parents also reported that Liam's mood appeared to be more stable, and that they felt more confident in their ability to counter his self-discouraging cognitions and behaviors, should they occur. They also mentioned feeling much less worried about Mason's weight, and feeling less the urge to monitor or restrict his eating. Dave had begun receiving individual treatment, and although it had only recently started, he was feeling hopeful he could get help with his binge eating. On a recent family vacation, Gabby opened up to Dave about her interest in making a career change, and the couple decided that she should explore the option of taking unpaid leave from her current workplace. The parents concluded the final meeting thanking the therapist for his dedication and nonjudgmental approach, saying:

> This program has allowed us to change our daily routines and the way we interact with one another. Our journey for healthier habits is not ending here, but we feel that we have gained sufficient tools to continue it on our own.

Index